W9-CMM-742

n+1

ISSUE 28   SPRING 2017

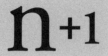

HALF-LIFE

ISSUE 28
SPRING 2017

ESSAYS

REVIEWS

LETTERS

Milquetoast dentists, further left than you

n+1

n+1 is published three times a year by n+1 Foundation, 68 Jay St. #405, Brooklyn, NY 11201. Single issues are available for $14.95; subscriptions for $36; in Canada and other international, $55. Send correspondence to editors@nplusonemag.com. *n+1* is distributed by Ingram and Ubiquity, Disticor in Canada, and Antenne in the UK and Europe. To place an ad write to ads@nplusonemag.com. *n+1*, Number Twenty-Eight © 2017 n+1 Foundation, Inc. ISBN 978-0-9970318-5-0.

EDITORIAL

Editors
NIKIL SAVAL
DAYNA TORTORICI

Senior Editors
ELIZABETH GUMPORT
CHAD HARBACH
CHARLES PETERSEN
NAMARA SMITH

Associate Editors
RICHARD BECK
LAURA CREMER
EMMA JANASKIE
NAUSICAA RENNER

Contributing Editors
KEITH GESSEN
MARK GREIF
MARCO ROTH

Founding Editors
KEITH GESSEN
MARK GREIF
CHAD HARBACH
BENJAMIN KUNKEL
ALLISON LORENTZEN
MARCO ROTH

Special Projects
STEPHEN SQUIBB

Senior Writers
KRISTIN DOMBEK
A. S. HAMRAH

ART AND DESIGN

Design
DAN O. WILLIAMS

Art Editors
IAN EPSTEIN
RACHEL OSSIP
SU WU

FOUNDATION

Publisher
MARK KROTOV

Business Manager
COSME DEL ROSARIO-BELL

Subscriptions Manager
EMILY LYVER

Managing Editor
DAYNA TORTORICI

Production Manager
RACHEL OSSIP

Board
RONALD BARUSCH
CARLA BLUMENKRANZ
KEITH GESSEN
JEREMY GLICK
MARK GREIF
CHAD HARBACH
JYNNE MARTIN
CHRIS PARRIS-LAMB
NIKIL SAVAL
DAYNA TORTORICI
ROGER WHITE

WWW.NPLUSONEMAG.COM

THE INTELLECTUAL SITUATION

A Diary

Now Less Than Never

IN THE UNSEASONABLE HEAT OF WINTER, we've been avoiding the news—or trying to regulate our intake. If we don't, it's everything all the time. On Saturday morning, the President thumbs off a string of tweets accusing the former President of tapping his old residence. The internet bursts, the networks roar. Officials and commentators mug for the camera and deny, harangue, shake their heads. "Norms" are said to be "violated," "democracy" is said to be "at stake." Everything is "unprecedented." It has never been like this, it will always be like this. Now and forever, farewell the tranquil mind. On one station, there's a break in the scrum: terrible images from Mosul, people starving in the streets. If only they could feed on hot takes.

We switch on NPR and—damn, another pledge drive! "Now more than ever, the truth matters," they say. Our phone pings. It's an email from Our Revolution: our donation matters "now more than ever." *Ping.* Lena Dunham: our power is in our numbers, "now more than ever." *Ping.* PEN America: free speech matters "now more than ever." We scan our inbox and it's in all the subject lines: from the DCCC, NARAL, the ACLU, the *New York Times*. And they need our money. So now, more than ever . . . *Ping.* There's 37,000 new tweets in our feed. We read them hurriedly, our armpits damp. There's DeRay Mckesson, truth-teller to power! But wait—he's promoting Verizon's new unlimited phone plan, which apparently we need now, more than ever.

Now more than ever. The phrase is everywhere, its most famous use ("Now more than ever seems it rich to die," from "Ode to a Nightingale") blithely forgotten. Forgotten, too, is Nixon's campaign slogan from 1972. He was funneling money from the Committee to Re-Elect the President (CREEP) to burglars, who were bugging offices, faking correspondence, wrecking the Democratic primaries, and rigging the election. The Justice Department, FBI, the CIA (the "Deep State"!)—everyone was involved. How much did we need it? "Our environment, our cities, our economy, our dealings with other nations—there is much to be done, to be changed," warned the smoke-ragged white-man voice in his political ad. "That is why we need President Nixon, now more than ever."

Sweaty, dirty, grizzled Nixon: now there was another President who got in people's heads every day. But he saved his best, sickest material for the tapes. With Trump, there's no smoking gun to subpoena. He gets there first, spraying you in the face with a buckshot shell of tweets.

To perceive "now" as being "more than ever," one has to be in a period of crisis and disjuncture—or at least feel like one is. And "now more than ever" has always been used to sell things in moments of crisis. Like ASAP, it's an efficiently grandiose way to convey a false sense of urgency.

Google Ngram shows pervasive use of the phrase in the 19th century—mostly, it seems, in missionary tracts, where it conveyed evangelical fervor. It fell out of favor in the early 20th century, then spiked again during the world wars. "During the war," the *Economist* wrote in 1949, "advertisers, in an effort to sell goods totally unrelated to the seriousness of the time, found the value of sentences beginning 'Now more than ever . . .', which helped them to sell tennis racquets and bathing suits with the argument that keeping fit was now more than ever vital." "Now more than ever" went through a steady decline over the course of the postwar era, despite the Nixon plug, as the cold war resolved in favor of capitalism.

But during this apparent decline, the production of nowness grew more pervasive and sophisticated. Radio broadcasts and evening editions gave way to twenty-four-hour TV news and the infinite scroll of social media feeds. To keep up, we made ourselves constantly but abstractedly alert, ready for moments of outrage or disappointment, because there would always be a reason, now more than ever, to feel them. It was how the world made money, too. Producing the feeling of "now more than ever" could get you clicks, views, ratings.

Adding urgency to it all is the growing recognition—still hardly profound enough—of catastrophic climate change. A millennial eschatology has returned, taking the place of false positivism and pseudorational prognoses. We once again imagine the end of days: it is inevitable, and unpredictable. The restrainer—the *katechon*—has been removed, the redeemer will not be kept from the Earth. It's only a matter of when. Fear, now more than ever, the heat of the sun.

For eight years we lived in what felt like a stopgap: the Obama era, with its theater of deliberation. His administration was ineffably calm, a Poussin tableau of studied composure; the awestruck media reported its every move in a kind of trance. The President spoke haltingly and sometimes inscrutably because he was, we were told, careful. Even the murder of innocents was not reckless but part of a plan. He would not order a drone strike until he'd repaired to his chambers to consult Augustine and Niebuhr. Only then, like Antony with his list of the proscribed, would he prick the offending name. The economy languished, buffeted by waves of state-level austerity and federal sequestration. But the market was high: quantitative easing kept things liquid, and loose labor markets kept wages down and inflation in check. So spellbindingly mediocre was this time that it seemed like it could go on forever, punctuated by the occasional, distant annihilation of an Afghan or Yemeni wedding party, conspicuously underreported.

But beneath it all was a growing rage. Obama himself had christened the moment when he exclaimed, during the 2008 Democratic primaries, "*We* are the ones we have been waiting for." He was right, only more than he'd hoped. New movements disrupted the calm: squares were occupied, police impunity met with resistance. We watched it all in real time. As "now" became filled with "more," everything looked like disjuncture, and continuities became harder to see. The war on terror—itself part of a decades-long war for the greater Middle East—receded from view, even as Obama added to its victims in several more countries. The scandal over police killings of unarmed black men and women in the US was—or should have been—a long-standing one, along with mass incarceration, to which it was tied. Still, the "more" became a symbol of unending difference, of moving from one era to another after another.

The feeling of crisis was best exploited by reactionaries. Outlets like Breitbart evoked the vertiginous feeling of a planet unhinged, careening out of orbit, about to smash, like in the final scene of Lars von Trier's *Melancholia*. In the infamous "Flight 93 Election" article in the *Claremont Review of Books*, the anonymous author (later outed as former Bush speechwriter Michael Anton) compared the country to a plane hijacked by terrorists. The only way to save it was to hand the cockpit to Donald Trump—who might, Anton conceded, still kill everyone.

On November 8, the growing din became a ceaseless alarm bell. And there is much to be alarmed about: bans on travel and immigration from majority-Muslim countries, increased deportations, swift rollbacks of regulations on the environment and the police. This is only a month or so into the Trump regime, and the midterm elections are still in the bronze distance. Weekend plans are protests; meetings, to plan more protests, take up the evenings. Now more than ever, we wonder if it's worth thinking or reading anything that doesn't aid our political imagination. But exhaustion attends alertness, and each day closes with the mind spent. What better time to binge on prestige television? But then—*ping*—more breaking news.

If Obama understood the value of deliberation, Trump understands only frenzy. He is the President of "now more than ever." The phrase brings with it an aesthetic of suddenness, of what Carl Schmitt called "decisionism." It matters little that this or that order fails in the corrupt courts or is denounced by seething mobs; what matters is the spectacle of activity, of things taking place. The bureaucracy is demoralized and bewildered—but after all, who needs bureaucracy? Leaks become a flood; the thirsty are no sooner sated than they are parched. Four

thousand new analyses appear at once, trailing a penumbra of several million tweets. Protests assemble in an instant, the biggest ever. Chaos is a sign of consequence.

Now more than ever, we must endure the claim that everything is now more than ever. The past recedes, weak precedent to what is supposedly unprecedented. Equanimity is a crime. A smooth forehead suggests a hard heart.

Party Foul

WHAT ABOUT THE DEMOCRATS? CAN THEY stop this? We call them more than our own families, imploring them to save our health care, to save our civil liberties—not to screw this up again. But we don't have much faith. Trump, an idiot and a buffoon, should have been an easy man to beat. Watching the Democrats lose was like watching a smug tennis player lose a thousand set points on double faults. Since November, the Democratic Party has spent its energy searching for someone to blame. Comey, the Russians, Cambridge Analytica—anyone, it seems, but itself.

Ah, the Democrats. We know their problems like our own faces. They're the closest thing we have to a party. Yes, they represent a panoply of powerful business interests who write the bills. Yes, they are almost as captive to lobbyists as the Republicans. Yes, they've managed to pass legislation that previous Republican administrations could only dream of: welfare "reform," the Commodity Futures Modernization Act, the repeal of Glass-Steagall. Yes, a majority of Democratic senators voted to invade Iraq, later indulging in bathetic recantations as they transferred their animus to Russia. Yes, they are the party—or they're not *not* the party—of testing and charter schools, health-insurance conglomerates and pharmaceutical lobby-ists, university privatization and sham meri-tocracy, deindustrialization and the inter-ests of the professional elite. Yes, they seem incapable of propping up a sturdy sentence without allowing an idiot wind of circumlo-cutions to blow it down. Yes, they seem to have a teeth-grinding fondness for the rhe-torical figure of chiasmus ("We can build on the strength of our diversity, and the diver-sity of our strengths"). Yes, yes—yes. *But . . .*

Is now, more than ever, our moment to yank the Democrats back from decades of rightward drift? It's an old, even farci-cal question for the left. Keith Ellison's lead for DNC chair gave us momentary hope: when Elizabeth Warren, Chuck Schumer, and much of organized labor endorsed him, it seemed as though the Democrats were finally coming around. But then Obama deputized labor secretary Tom Perez to stop the Ellison wave—a signal to cool our hopes. Republican hegemony leaves us with little choice but to work with the Democrats, at least for the moment, and even bring them closer to us. The question is how.

TWO VIEWS OF the Democratic Party suggest two paths.

The first sees it as the prodigal party of the people: the onetime champion of the New Deal that went astray in the 1970s, when a young generation of post-Watergate liberals began to move the party to the right on eco-nomic policy—undoing antitrust protec-tions and encouraging big business—even as it moved left on social issues like femi-nism and civil rights. This rightward drift culminated in the figure of Bill Clinton and, later, his wife, who came under fire during her campaign for giving well-compensated speeches to Goldman Sachs. In 2016, many Democrats who had voted for Obama voted against Hillary, in part to put an end to the Clinton era. So they went for Trump, the candidate who spoke to their downward mobility and insecurity (and perhaps in the case of many, their misogyny and racial resentment).

In this view, the Democrats' grave error was to neglect the working class, the par-ty's natural base. The people wanted popu-lism, and so they turned to the populism on offer. With the party on the rocks, now is the left's moment to take it back. Centrists do not know how to build a left populism to counter the right's phobic, racist popu-lism, let alone mobilize voters around it. But the left does. To win in 2018 and beyond, the Democrats must remake themselves as the party of good jobs, universal health care, paid leave, affordable child care, affordable housing, and free public education for all. In this account, the left understands the Dem-ocratic Party better than Democrats do; it can save the party from itself. The way to do so is to win elections with left-wing Demo-crats, eventually pushing the party back to its home on the liberal left.

The second view is less misty-eyed. Rather than a good party gone bad, the Democrats were never a party of the people, even during the heyday of the New Deal. This is because party ideology isn't deter-mined by the shifting views and needs of voters, but by "investors": lobbies, corpo-rations, businesses, interest groups, and unions who spend time, money, and energy to shape the direction of the party in hopes of seeing a return. This view allows that a party could shift to the right, and also indi-cates why there might be a hard limit on shifting a party—particularly the modern Democratic Party—to the left.

The "investment theory of party competi-tion," advanced by political scientist Thomas Ferguson, holds that investors exert influ-ence through monetary contributions but also through organizations. "Investment," here, is a metaphor: it encompasses activism and money, recognizing that the two are often connected. The Christian Right "invests" in the Republican Party through dogged political work at many levels of civil society. Labor unions have invested in Democrats in the same way. But they also spend lots of money, and money means power. In a capitalist society, the most powerful investor blocs invariably consist of large corporations and industries. "Efforts to control the state, by voters or anyone else, cost heavily in time and money," Ferguson writes in his book *Right Turn* (1986), coauthored with the political scientist Joel Rogers. For all the talk of super PACs and "money in politics," this truism is rarely acknowledged in postelection analyses, where outcomes are mostly figured in terms of voters' shifting views.

Ferguson offers a pleasantly sober account of American party systems. His explanation of the New Deal in *Golden Rule* (1995) dispenses with rosy tales of Franklin D. Roosevelt's immeasurable wisdom and the power of working people. The strength of the New Deal, he argues, came from the alliance between labor and the bloc of "capital-intensive industries, investment banks, and internationally oriented commercial banks" that had emerged in the early 20th century. Because these businesses were less labor-intensive than their predecessors, and their profit margins thus less affected by rises in wages, they could "afford" to have a coalition with organized labor as long as they could still advance their goals on trade. This isn't to say that labor didn't have a role to play—but wealthy investors played an equal if not bigger role, helping convert FDR and the Democrats to internationalism and free trade. What made the New Deal coalition viable for a time was the uneasy harmony of this bloc.

Ferguson also explains how this bloc dissolved. Conventional arguments tend to point to the failure of organized labor to incorporate "new social movements" into its ranks, or to argue that those social movements were responsible for pushing the party toward "identity politics," leaving economic justice by the wayside. Centrist Democrats' preferred explanation for the realignment of the party holds that Americans simply became more conservative during the Carter years, as the working classes fractured over issues like busing and welfare. But this doesn't stand up to scrutiny. According to polling data, from the time and since, most Americans haven't moved right at all: for the most part, they supported (and still support) the types of programs advanced by the New Deal.

Investors, however, did not. By the early 1970s, military spending on the Vietnam War had strained the budget, leading to inflation, while growing competition from other strong economies, like Germany and Japan, was putting pressure on American manufacturing. The American economic picture was already profoundly uncertain before the decade's oil crises struck. The 1973–75 recession—at the time, the worst since the Depression—prompted business leaders to temper wage increases (which meant attacking organized labor) and oppose any tax increases to pay for existing social programs (which would mean reduced spending power for already cash-strapped consumers). The Republican Party was historically the party of balanced budgets, and it was divided on issues of trade. With the rise of Ronald Reagan, however, the party gradually moved toward the magical solution of low taxes and drastically expanded military spending, combined with greater internationalism on trade—this latter move helping to siphon off the free trade bloc that had backed the New

Deal. The 1980 Reagan campaign, Ferguson and Rogers write, thus "opened the way for virtually all of American business to mass behind its candidate."

The Democrats panicked, and left their constituents behind. Over the next decade, they would decide again and again that the only response to the business friendliness of Reaganism was more business friendliness. The new party chair, Charles Manatt, created the Democratic Business Council, whose members included executives of Arco, Chevron, and Boeing. They were invited to participate in taskforces to help create party policies, and to attend, in the language of the DBC, "quarterly meetings of a substantive nature held in Washington" where members could "share their respective business, professional, and political interests with the political leadership of America." By the mid-'80s, Democrats had already begun to pull parts of business away from the Reagan bloc. Central to Walter Mondale's successful campaign for the Democratic nomination in 1984 were executives and board members from Xerox, DuPont, Bechtel, and Lehman Brothers. The influence of this bloc converted Mondale to a program of deficit reduction—an uninspiring proposal that could not compete with "Morning in America"—and he lost catastrophically. But the argument that deficits are bad for business became dogma within the rising neoliberal wing of the party. Democrats had, for the first time, become the party of balanced budgets.

The Democrats would eventually find a secure bloc based in information technology. Michael Dukakis, governor of Massachusetts, symbolized this transformation: he envisioned tech as the central element of the future economy. During the busing crisis of the 1970s, Boston had seemed like the center of the liberal crack-up, but the city and its suburbs had found a source of vitality in the tech industry. A coalition of professionals in and around tech began to "invest" in the party. Dukakis's bid for the presidency failed powerfully in 1988; Ferguson notes that in many areas of the country, turnout fell to lows unknown since the 1820s, when property requirements still restricted suffrage. But Bill "Don't Stop Thinking About Tomorrow" Clinton secured victory in 1992.

Clintonism reflected almost perfectly the importance of new investors in the Democratic Party. After passing NAFTA, he presided over the collapse of the Democratic Congress in 1994, which left Republicans in control of the House for the first time since the 1930s. After passing welfare reform, he won reelection in one of the lowest-turnout races in American history. He then proceeded to balance the budget, partly on the savings secured through the destruction of welfare. His success, such as it was, rested on the notion that the Democrats had a better handle on the future of business—and especially the booming tech industry—than the Republicans, and could therefore be better stewards of the economy.

By 2008, the process of business takeover was complete. A new President rose spectacularly on a message of change while the power elite promised more of the same. To take one example: in an email published by WikiLeaks, Michael Froman, a senior executive from Citigroup, appears to dictate Obama's first-term cabinet appointments. Froman was then appointed to the post of US trade representative, from which he advocated for the Trans-Pacific Partnership, a trade accord negotiated in secret with big business and written in large part by pharmaceutical companies. According to Ferguson's analysis of the 2012 congressional elections, there was a direct, linear correlation between money spent and elections won. Money dominated both presidential campaigns: 59 percent of contributions to Obama's campaign came from the "1 percent" while 79 percent to Romney's did. Where Romney received the lion's share of funding from the shadow-banking sector, Obama's support was concentrated in electronics, computing, and internet companies.

Investment blocs shape party ideologies; they don't necessarily produce wins. A win helps cement the broader ideology of an era, as Reagan's victories helped convince Democrats that they needed to get closer to business. But the strong influence of wealthy investors can also depress turnout, since voters often recognize when a candidate is more in the pocket of donors than of ordinary supporters.

The surprise results of 2016—both Bernie Sanders's unexpectedly strong showing and Trump's final victory—represented, for Ferguson and others, a belated crisis of this system. From 2012 to 2014, Ferguson points out (in an essay coauthored with Walter Dean Burnham), there was a huge drop in voter turnout: 24 percentage points, the second-largest plunge in US history. Americans are "sick to death of both parties," Ferguson and Burnham wrote, and the result "likely heralds a new stage in the disintegration of the American political order." What appeared to be happening was the rejection—through broad abstentionism—of the investment-driven American system. Sanders and Trump made inroads by defying the system: the former through relying chiefly on small donations and eschewing super PACs, the latter by loudly professing to use his own store of money.

TRUMP'S CLAIMS to independence based on his private stash of billions were, of course, fatuous. And Sanders, far from running a campaign on a shoestring, raised quite a bit of money, which he spent on TV ads like any other candidate. But because of that money's provenance, he appeared as a figure of integrity, and correspondingly attracted an army of volunteers—"ordinary" investors. Strategically, then, the investor theory suggests that organizing people (and money) on a more egalitarian basis can change what kinds of candidates make it through the system.

But it's not clear that it can change Democratic Party ideology. As long as the party caters to its tech-led investment bloc, it will not throw its weight behind candidates who challenge those investors' interests. One could take Ellison's near victory as a cautionary tale: Tom Perez is no monster, but he does have, as Matt Stoller wrote on the Intercept, "an established record of not taking on the banks, both at the Department of Justice and the Department of Labor." His belated entry into the race, and ultimate victory, could have been a flash flare to investors not to worry: their interests would still be the Democrats' interests. In the same election that brought Perez to the chairmanship, the DNC members reaffirmed their commitment to party ideology by permanently voting down an initiative that would have ended corporate lobbying of candidates.

So what do we do? Run candidates, yes, and establish a pattern for getting more left populist leaders on the ballot. But we also need to organize outside the party. In an elucidating recent interview with John Judis at Talking Points Memo, the scholar and veteran of social movements Marshall Ganz suggested that the DNC is not and should not be the main avenue for the left. "For one thing, the rise of the conservative movement didn't happen through the RNC," Ganz said:

> Conservatives successfully created a more or less coherent network of organizations linked

to local, state and national politics, which is a traditional form of effective political organization in the US. . . . You look in vain for something like that on the progressive side. There is such a proliferation of groups, all kinds of groups, some of which take up space without filling it.

The Democrats are hostile to the left, but the left, for its part, is too weak to influence the Democrats. Historic moments of electoral and movement breakthrough—such as Jesse Jackson's Rainbow Coalition—haven't always presaged leftward turns in the party, partly because they failed to create an institutional culture of the left outside the party.

At home, the name "Democrat" itself carries less weight every day. Sanders himself failed to increase voter participation in the primary: at 14.4 percent, the turnout for one of the most exciting contests in generations proved lower even than that for the primary in 1984. There may be little hope in building enthusiasm for the Democrats directly, but it might be possible to channel enthusiasm through an outside bloc that can raise money and mobilize people external to any party.

And there are people: millions of people who are disengaged, electorally nonparticipating, unattached to either party. Most of them are among the most vulnerable populations in society. *This* is the working class the media and political organizations should be concerned about, a group that may be more interested in movement building around issues like police and schools and workplaces than questions of party. The Democratic Party evinces little interest in representing or mobilizing them, but they remain a vital constituency for a left still finding its feet. +

OUT NOW

SALTLAND
A Common Truth

THOSE WHO WALK AWAY
The Infected Mass

AVEC LE SOLEIL SORTANT DE SA BOUCHE
Pas pire pop, I Love You So Much

AUTOMATISME   **OFF WORLD**   **JASON SHARP**
Momentform Accumulations   1   A Boat Upon Its Blood

OUT MAY 2017

JESSICA MOSS   **DO MAKE SAY THINK**   **JONI VOID**
Pools Of Light   Stubborn Persistent Illusions   Selfless

ALL TITLES ON DELUXE 180gLP, COMPACT DISC, DIGITAL
CONSTELLATION   CSTRECORDS.COM

ALI KAAF, *RAS RAS*. 2011, BURNING ON SLIDE AND CIBACHROME PRINT ON DIBOND. 20.9" × 31.9". COURTESY OF THE ARTIST.

POLITICS

Memoranda

RICHARD BECK
The Syria Catastrophe

THE SYRIAN WAR IS AT ONCE INCOMPREHEN-
sibly byzantine and very simple. It is complex in the number of countries involved, in
the shifting and fragile internal alliances and
resentments of the groups constituting the
rebellion, in the threads of national interest that circle back and consume themselves
like a snake eating its own tail. To take just
one example: after a decade of friendly relations with Syria, Turkey turned on Syrian
president Bashar al-Assad and decided to
work toward his downfall, and Turkish president Recep Tayyip Erdoğan vowed that his
country would "support the Syrian people
in every way until they get rid of the bloody
dictator and his gang." Since then, Turkey has served as a staging ground for the
rebel Free Syrian Army (FSA), but it has also
been repeatedly accused of funneling funds
and arms to ISIS, which regularly attacks
FSA bases and beheads the soldiers it cap-
tures. Turkey has provided military aid to
the effort to combat ISIS, but it also devotes
energy and resources to fighting Kurdish
nationalists, who have been more effective
in fighting ISIS than any other group to date.
In November 2016, Erdoğan reiterated his
determination to unseat Assad, saying Turkish forces had entered Syria in August 2016
for no other reason than to remove Assad
from power. One day later, he retracted his
statement and claimed Turkey's military
campaign in Syria had been designed solely
to defeat ISIS, the terrorist group whose
operations Turkey had at least tacitly and
perhaps actively supported. Turkey is now
working closely with Russia, which has done
more than any other country to prevent
Erdoğan from realizing his goal of bringing
down Assad. Turkey is just one of at least
nine countries involved in the conflict.

The simple part of the war is that it is a
human, social, and environmental disaster that equals some of the 20th century's
worst conflicts. Around half a million have
died, with another two million wounded,
in a country whose prewar population
amounted to just more than twenty million. Since the conflict's beginning, in 2011,
Syrian life expectancy has dropped by more
than twenty years, from roughly 79 to 56.
More than half of the country's population has been forced to leave their homes,
including some six million internally displaced and nearly five million refugees.
Their movements have in turn contributed
to political upheaval across Europe and
North America, with right-wing nationalists campaigning against the supposedly
dangerous influx of refugees. The use of
torture against political enemies and captured soldiers has been widespread, especially on the part of the Assad regime. Many
refugees cite their female family members'
dramatically increased risk of being raped
as a major reason for leaving. In addition, a
country with a strong national identity and

a tradition of religious tolerance—including for a dozen Christian denominations and esoteric sects like the Druze—has been transformed into a place of bitter sectarian violence. Much of Aleppo, one of the oldest continuously inhabited cities on Earth and one of the region's architectural and cultural jewels, has been reduced to rubble. As regime forces, backed by Russian air strikes and Iranian ground troops, made their final, decisive assault on the rebellion's dwindling territory there in December 2016, many residents found themselves trapped and began to tweet out their good-byes. In one such video, an old man rocked back and forth in the middle of a bombed-out street, pushing his hands away from his face as he called out, "We are starving. There is nothing."

The war's complexity makes it difficult to see a viable path forward, but there is a sense in which it would be foolish to think of the conflict as one big Rubik's cube in need of solving, because the complexity itself is part of the problem—the best thing to do with the Rubik's cube would be to throw it against a wall. Again and again, countries across and outside the Middle East have decided that escalating the war by military means is justified by whatever little sliver of national interest they feel is at stake. The US, Russia, Iran, Saudi Arabia, Turkey, Qatar, China, France, and Britain have all pumped military resources into the conflict, increasing not only the war's capacity for destructive violence but also its duration. To the extent that it needed to take place at all, it should have been a civil war fought by two sides with limited military resources. Instead, it has turned into a series of extravagantly funded proxy wars across two or three separate axes, none of which have any organic connection to the questions of regime tolerance for political assembly and speech that prompted the conflict in the first place. While it would not be

useful to ask nations to stop pursuing their national interests, the ease with which these countries have turned to military means in the pursuit of those interests is shameful. The response required at this late, desperate stage is neither anti-Assad nor anti-ISIS nor even anti-imperialist—it is antiwar.

THE FIRST PERSON to make the mistake of military escalation was Bashar al-Assad himself. In his book *Syria Burning* (2016), the journalist Charles Glass recounts an old joke:

> A dog in Lebanon . . . was so hungry, mangy and tired of civil war that he escaped to Syria. To the surprise of the other dogs, he returned a few months later. Seeing him better groomed and fatter than before, they asked whether the Syrians had been good to him. "Very good." "Did they feed and wash you?" "Yes." "Then why did you come back?" "I want to bark."

The protests that sparked the conflict in 2011 were not originally calls for Assad's fall. They were instead demonstrations demanding reforms: the end of emergency law (justified by a permanent "state of war" with Israel), the release of political prisoners, the removal of a regional governor who allegedly allowed the torture of teenagers by police, an end to the bribes and harassment and other daily humiliations of life under authoritarian rule.

Syria initially seemed to have avoided the wave of Arab Spring unrest that swept across much of the Middle East beginning in late 2010, but beneath its surface stability and continuity lay several of the same factors that destabilized Tunisia, Egypt, Yemen, Bahrain, and other countries. Political power was concentrated among a tiny elite of technocrats and Assad flunkies. The Mukhabarat, a set of brutal intelligence agencies originally trained by the Stasi, snuffed out the faintest flicker of opposition. The introduction of neoliberal economic policies also unsettled Syrian society—Assad had attempted a halfhearted marketization of the economy that produced the worst of both worlds, destroying the country's economic safety net without actually producing more jobs. Farmers who had relied on now-diminished government fuel subsidies could no longer afford to keep their machines running. In the cities, millions of educated young people found there was nothing for them to do with their educations.

The protests that made the world aware of these grievances were expressions of a desire to bark, and they were carried out peacefully. Assad's security forces responded with beatings, water cannons, and live ammunition, killing protesters and then killing mourners at those protesters' funerals. By the time Assad released the teenagers and removed the regional governor (his cousin Faisal Kalthum), it was too late, and the protesters' demands had changed. Assad's now very likely victory in the war should not obscure the fact that his 2011 response to the protests was a disaster—six years later, he remains the leader of what is no longer a functioning state.

The opposition's decision to militarize was a mistake, too, although it's true that Assad's crackdown left few other options. Even after Assad's security forces had made a habit of shooting up funerals, the pro-democracy protesters of 2011 did not reach for their rifles en masse. Instead, they were gradually overtaken and displaced by more than three thousand militias, defectors from the military who established the Free Syrian Army, and the al-Nusra Front, an al Qaeda–affiliated group of Sunni fundamentalists that saw in the escalating chaos an opportunity to topple Assad's Alawite regime (al-Nusra

changed its name to Jabhat Fateh al-Sham before joining up with other rebel groups to form Hayat Tahrir al-Sham, or the Liberation of the Levant Committee, in January). The shift from peaceful protest to military engagement turned a reformist project into a revolutionary one. Yet the revolutionaries had no single vision for what a post-Assad Syria would be. Rather, they had competing visions that were inherently incompatible with one another, ranging from secular democracy to an authoritarian theocratic state under Sunni rule. The revolution as a whole lacked a constructive political project, and so it was doomed from the beginning. One Syrian journalist reporting on the Battle of Aleppo said there was a moment in 2012 during which the FSA, had it been able to muster a unified force of a few hundred, could have seized city hall and "proclaimed Aleppo a liberated city." It didn't.

These fissures in the Syrian rebellion were apparent from an early stage, and external countries should have seen them as a reason to stay away and allow the conflict to exhaust itself. Instead, they saw the rebellion's weaknesses as an opportunity to use it for their own various ends. Within the Middle East, Syria became a flash point in the regional conflicts that had been escalating since the US invasion of Iraq in 2003. Saudi Arabia, the world's only remaining theocracy ruled by an absolute monarch, had been alarmed by the Arab Spring protests in Egypt and Tunisia. It saw in the Syrian conflict an opportunity to spark a counterrevolution, as well as a chance to weaken Iran, its primary opponent and Assad's most important supporter in the Middle East. For its part, Iran saw Syria as a key arm of its regional influence, which has increased enormously ever since the US deposed its primary regional rival, Iraq. When US officials began to criticize Assad's brutal tactics in 2011, supporting his regime also became a useful way for Iran to resist the Middle East's great Western antagonist. Meanwhile, the diplomatically insignificant but very wealthy country of Qatar bet on the rebels in hopes of winning increased regional influence after Assad's fall, a tactic it had previously pursued by supporting opposition forces, particularly Islamists, in other Arab Spring uprisings. The country pumped nearly $3 billion into the rebellion during the first two years of the conflict.

Other countries in that area of the world have used the war to deepen their involvement in the Middle East. Following its unenthusiastic and unsuccessful pursuit of EU membership, Turkey decided to direct its geopolitical muscle to the east instead, and the Syrian rebellion provided what looked like an ideal opportunity to flex. The country hosted Syrian army defectors who eventually formed the core of the FSA; helped to organize Group of Friends of the Syrian People, an international coalition modeled on the coalition that brought about Gaddafi's fall in Libya; and served as by far the most important point of entry for arms and other supplies used by the rebellion.

Then, most famously, there is Russia, without which Assad may well have fallen. In addition to vetoing UN Security Council resolutions calling for Assad's resignation, Russia has lavished the Assad regime with military and economic aid. Russian air strikes have turned the military tide against the rebels in recent months, and in an earlier stage of the war, when Syria's economy was on the brink of collapse, Moscow delivered some thirty tons of new banknotes to Damascus, ensuring that the government could continue to function.

Farther afield, Britain and France decided that toppling Assad would help to stymie Iran. Still pumped from its Libyan escapade in 2011, France demanded Assad's departure and has since provided rebels with arms and communications equipment, as well as conducted a few air strikes of its own. And while the UK's parliament initially decided against overt military involvement in the country, the successes of ISIS and the al-Nusra Front changed its mind. The Royal Air Force carried out air strikes in Syria in 2015, and British Special Forces were operating within Syria by summer 2016.

For the US, the Syrian war has been a long and painful lesson on the consequences of squandering one's status as world hegemon on military adventures in Iraq and Afghanistan. When protests first broke out, the US was slow and reluctant to respond for two main reasons. The first is that, after its experience in Libya, in which toppling the dictator had not produced a flourishing of peace and representative democracy, the Obama Administration was reluctant to involve the US too deeply in another regional conflagration. The second is that the US had not been particularly focused on Syria, and the State Department's resources were already stretched to the limit by everything else happening in the Middle East, a phenomenon referred to by diplomats as the "bandwidth" problem. There are only so many crises any government, even the US, can address at once. Even as Obama and Secretary of State Hillary Clinton began to speak out against Assad's crackdowns, the tone was very much wait-and-see, condemning the violence while also making it clear that Assad would be welcome to remain in power should he implement reforms.

In 2012, as the conflict was maturing into a full-fledged civil war, Obama told the White House press corps that any use of chemical or biological weapons by Assad would be a "red line for us," the implication being that direct military intervention would follow. He used the "red line" phrase twice, saying, "That would change my calculus. That would change my equation." But one year later, when chemical weapons were launched at rebel-held positions in Ghouta, it turned out that Obama's calculus would stay the same, and the expected air strikes never came. While this may have been a wise decision on its own, it could not compensate for the recklessness of having made the "red line" remarks in the first place. Opposition forces had spent a year digging in and escalating the military conflict in the expectation that the American cavalry would soon arrive, and its failure to do so left the FSA in the lurch. ISIS soon seized the initiative that the FSA could no longer hold. Three years later, American diplomacy finds itself marginalized. When Russia, Iran, and Turkey organized a December meeting in Moscow to pursue a political solution to the conflict, the US was not invited.

None of which is to say that America hasn't been involved. Over the past fifteen years, debates over Iraq, Afghanistan, and Libya have steadily moved the discursive goalposts, such that "non-interventionist" now means "anything short of a full-scale occupation." That's the only sense in which one can say the US hasn't carried out military intervention in the Syrian war. In 2011, Hillary Clinton objected to and undermined peace talks that didn't include Assad's removal as a condition. The CIA has assisted rebels with training, arms, ammunition, and supply routes along the Turkish border. The US has also helped train the much-praised "moderate rebels" in Jordan and in 2014 provided anti-tank weapons to the Supreme Military Council, which includes members of the most prominent rebel groups. Kurds were resupplied in 2015, and when it became clear that the $500 million rebel-training program had failed, that money was used

to buy arms, which were then sent to the rebel groups already on the ground, trained or otherwise. Special operations forces have also carried out missions in Syria.

Surprisingly, the US has managed to ratchet up its involvement in the Syrian war without concurrently ratcheting up its anti-regime rhetoric. Assad has not been made into a villain on anything like the Saddam Hussein model. The reason has been the rise of the Islamic State—variously referred to as IS, ISIL, or ISIS. This group is a direct consequence of the Iraq war. It emerged out of the post-Saddam chaos in 2006, just barely survived the US "surge" in 2007, and returned to the scene in 2010. With its kidnappings, videos of hostage beheadings, destruction of ancient temples and other archaeological treasures, and eventual capture of the Iraqi city of Mosul in 2014, ISIS has assumed al Qaeda's former place as America's preeminent terrorist bogeyman, all without ever carrying out a major terrorist attack in the United States itself. It was probably the beheading videos, with their combination of medieval violence and PR savvy, that clinched it. But it could also have been the group's habit of claiming credit for terrorist attacks in Paris, Brussels, San Bernardino, and Orlando, whether it played an actual role in organizing those attacks or not. The group's brutality and destructiveness are by no means unprecedented among either extremist groups or some of the region's authoritarian regimes, but its eagerness and ability to portray itself as brutal and destructive probably are. Assad may have torture chambers of his own, and other groups may carry out massacres, too, but only ISIS is widely thought of as a "death cult," something outside the realm of rational human calculation. ISIS's successes have provided the US with a progressively freer military hand in the Middle East over the past two years, perhaps a freer hand than it has had at any point since the golden days of bin Laden and al Qaeda. In Syria, the group captured the city of Raqqa in 2013 and has subsequently battled the Kurds for control of the country's northeastern region, which shares borders with Turkey and Iraq and holds valuable oil fields. As long as ISIS remains a force in Syria, there is little reason to expect much domestic opposition to America's involvement there.

What benefits have accrued to the states that have invested so heavily in the war? According to Christopher Phillips, author of *The Battle for Syria* (2016), none at all. Assad's likely survival means that Turkey's ambitions of regional leadership are done, at least for the moment. Turkey also faces an increase in domestic terrorism committed by Islamists operating in Syria who have decided to cross back over the border. Qatar's international reputation has been damaged by its alleged connections to al Qaeda. Saudi Arabia is stuck spending huge sums on military operations around the region during a time when oil prices are low, portending an ominous future for the kingdom's economy. Iran protected its ally, but at the cost of its influence everywhere in the Middle East aside from Shia-dominated states. Even Russia shouldn't get too excited. The country dramatically increased its geopolitical prominence at relatively low cost, but it now finds itself responsible for a failed state with no functioning economy and a government regarded by its own citizens and much of the world as illegitimate. Putin's position today may turn out to be similar to that of George W. Bush in May 2003, when he stood on the deck of the USS *Abraham Lincoln* in a flight suit and announced that "major combat operations in Iraq have ended."

o o o

THE SYRIAN CONFLICT is what military scholars call a total war, one in which the lines between combatants and civilians blur, societies devote all their resources to the war effort, and tactics gain acceptance regardless of their brutality. Total war manifests in many ways, from the aerial bombardment of city centers all the way down to what happens between a couple of guards and a prisoner in a locked cell. On the latter end of that spectrum, torture stands out as a favored retaliatory technique on both sides and a central component of Assad's plans for keeping power (as opposed to an ugly by-product of those plans). Summary arrests have regularly occurred since protests broke out in 2011, and except in cases where those detained are prominent figures or members of important families, it is safe to assume that arrests are followed by torture. The war reporter Janine di Giovanni, in her book *The Morning They Came for Us* (2016), interviewed a man called Hussein, a 24-year-old student of human rights law who helped organize protests in the prewar days. Hussein was captured in Homs and then taken to a hospital the government used as a prison for dissidents. There, he was beaten with sticks, electrocuted, burned, and cut. He suffered a collapsed lung, and at night, unable to walk, he was kept in a room with corpses piled on the floor. One night, his captors laid Hussein on top of a body that turned out to be that of his brother. He only escaped, he says, because a doctor assigned to monitor the torture sessions eventually decided he could not bear to watch anymore. He declared Hussein dead and had him smuggled out of the hospital. This story is representative. In the *New Yorker*, Ben Taub has reported on torture conducted at a military hospital located near the presidential palace in Damascus. One detainee, having already been tortured for nearly a year, was taken to this hospital when he began to urinate blood. When he arrived, according to Taub, "a nurse asked him about his symptoms, then beat him with a stick."

Torture is not an inevitable element of war. Its use was not universal in ancient societies, and it was banned in nearly all of Western Europe during the 18th and 19th centuries. These bans did not function perfectly, any more than universal bans on murder function perfectly today, but they constituted a stable and functioning societal taboo. This taboo broke down over the course of the 20th century. By the mid-1980s, nearly three decades after the United Nations' adoption of the Universal Declaration of Human Rights, the regular use of torture was documented in one-third of UN member states. In the past five years, Amnesty International has documented torture in 141 countries, or three-quarters of the world. Torture is accepted by the Syrian regime because it is currently accepted by most regimes, usually in practice and sometimes in theory, too. The Republican Party in the United States is currently one of those regimes.

When one person brings up some wrong committed by a non-US country, and then a second person responds by pointing out that the US has committed the same wrong, the second person is sometimes accused of "whataboutism," a rhetorical technique that seeks to blunt criticism by painting it as hypocritical. There are instances in which whataboutism does serve this propaganda function, but the debate on torture is not one of them, because a taboo is like herd immunity: it only works if almost everyone is immune. Despite its recent difficulties as world hegemon, the United States remains more powerful and influential than any other single country, and there can be no hope for preventing horrors like those

committed by Assad's security forces, or for punishing those responsible for them, so long as the US accepts torture.

The death penalty is not the central problem of America's incarceration complex, and neither is torture the central problem of modern militarism. But as the death penalty stands as a metonym for the prison system's general willingness to effectively, if not literally, end the life of someone who commits even a minor crime, so does torture stand as an emblem of the modern world's acceptance of total war. A world that accepts and practices torture, that is willing to inflict unlimited suffering on a person in order to obtain a confession, is a world that also accepts the destruction of entire states and societies in the pursuit of military victory. During the past fifteen years, the war on terror and the many other civil wars and extremist rebellions that have emerged in its wake have seen the mainstreaming of torture and total war alike. The same editorial pages that lay out a ticking-time-bomb scenario as a justification for waterboarding will also publish pieces arguing that civilian casualties are "inevitable" (meaning "acceptable") when extremist groups so cleverly blend in among the civilian inhabitants of densely populated urban areas. It will be hard, not to say hypocritical, for the United States to call for Assad's arrest and prosecution when the CIA has rendered terrorism suspects to Syria specifically so they could be tortured there. Rebuilding the international community's taboo on torture would require at the very least that the US close Guantánamo, that it pay reparations to those who have been held there, and that it agree to be subject to the decisions of the International Criminal Court, even if that court were to decide to prosecute George W. Bush, Dick Cheney, Donald Rumsfeld, or another architect of the country's rendition and torture programs. For now, Bush Jr. remains a welcome guest at presidential inaugurations and a celebrated early-career painter.

If none of this seems likely to occur in the coming years, that may have to do with how little American debate on the conflict has considered the Syrian war as a moral issue. While the occasional harrowing photograph or chilling testimonial has provoked bouts of public outrage, that outrage has somehow not been channeled back into evaluations of America's extensive involvement in the war. Even absent a full-scale invasion, the extent to which the US and other countries have fueled the bloodshed with arms and other equipment should be a scandal. The arms transfers have increased each side's capacity to kill and wound its enemies, and discouraged the pursuit of diplomatic solutions to the catastrophe. But instead of a clear reckoning with what this has meant for the people of Syria, there is only talk of various US interests: the state of its credibility in the eyes of the world, the terrorist threats allegedly posed by desperate refugees, the exact circumference of America's sphere of influence. It is politically unsophisticated to say so, but none of this matters to a noncombatant resident of Aleppo.

The suppression of war's morality in American public discourse has not only occurred with respect to Syria—it is a general characteristic of foreign-policy discussion. The reason why is pretty simple: America is now involved in so many wars in so many different places, and there exists such an overwhelming bipartisan consensus that involvement in these wars is necessary and to the US advantage, that to confront the morality of our militarism honestly would require an almost total overhaul of America's role in the world. In the years following the revelations of prisoner abuse at Abu Ghraib, the same dynamic could be found in arguments over torture. Instead of recognizing that torture is always wrong, every time, no matter the severity of the threat it is used to address, Democrats and Republicans argued over whether torture produced accurate intelligence, a debate of purely academic interest that should have had no place in the political sphere. Thirteen years after Abu Ghraib, the results of that debate are obvious. "Don't tell me it doesn't work," Donald Trump said at a campaign event in February 2016. "Torture works." He promised to bring back waterboarding and "a hell of a lot worse." Trump very slightly moderated his position after General James Mattis, whose nickname is Mad Dog, told him he'd "never found [torture] to be useful," but there's no reason to think that moderation will outlive Mattis's tenure as a Trump adviser.

Even Barack Obama's guiding principles for weighing the wisdom of military action, so cautious in comparison with those of his neoconservative predecessors, betrayed an eagerness to look away from what war does to those caught in its path. "I don't oppose all wars," he said in a 2002 speech. "What I am opposed to is a dumb war. What I am opposed to is a rash war." He lived up to this self-description, with a few exceptions, during his eight years as President. Except for his "red line" comments, his decisions regarding Syria were thoughtful and deliberate, and none of them have permanently damaged America's international standing. But opposing dumb wars isn't enough. Smart wars should be opposed and avoided too, until the last moment and at all possible costs, *because they are wars.* All military conflict rips apart the social fabric in irreparable ways, and all the US and Russia have done with their careful, self-interested maneuverings is intensify and accelerate the process by which a dictator has reduced his unfree but still stable society to rubble.

How will America's involvement with Syria change now that Trump has assumed office? It is clear that the new President is a racist provocateur who sees Muslims as America's primary antagonists throughout the world. But it remains unclear what kind of foreign policy these racist views will produce, because Trump does not appear to hold foreign-policy views at all (except insofar as foreign countries "steal" American jobs). Though much of the recklessness of his Muslim ban derives from the way it escalated tensions between the US and countries across the Middle East, the executive order was primarily an act of domestic politics meant to shore up and energize his nativist base. He believes terrorism is bad and that the US should be "strong," but he has never indicated how that might translate into a style of diplomacy or a military strategy. Among the many mistakes liberal journalists made during the presidential campaign was their effort to paint Trump as a committed supporter of the Iraq war. This claim was based on a Howard Stern interview in which Trump responded to the question "Are you for invading Iraq?" by saying, "Yeah, I guessss . . . sooo." The obvious conclusion to draw from the hesitant tone of Trump's answer is that he hadn't thought about it all that much and wasn't particularly invested in the outcome, and during the campaign, Trump only brought up Iraq when it could be used as a cudgel to beat Hillary Clinton or some primary opponent. Is Trump an interventionist or an anti-interventionist? The evidence suggests that he doesn't really give a shit.

That's not meant to be reassuring. The importance of presidential diplomacy to America's international relationships makes Trump's erratic personality frightening. In addition, our unprincipled new President is advised by a cabinet and a party stuffed with foreign-policy hawks. Defense Secretary Mattis has refused to rule out the deployment of conventional American ground forces to combat ISIS in Syria, and he has also been careful to not close the door on possible cooperation with the Russian military, which would, by extension, entail cooperation with Assad. On the other hand, ramping up tensions with Assad could go a long way toward antagonizing Iran, a cherished Republican goal. (The party's 2016 platform specified that Republicans "consider the Administration's deal with Iran, to lift international sanctions and make hundreds of billions of dollars available to the Mullahs, a personal agreement between [Obama] and his negotiating partners and non-binding on the next president.") While the specific targets of the Republican Party's foreign-policy aggression under Trump remain to be seen, it is probably safe to assume that American aggression will increase over the next four years, an increase enabled in part by the totally unnecessary $54 billion military-budget increase Trump proposed in February.

Opposing this kind of pervasive, amoral militarism in the US cannot just be a matter of demonizing the executive, however, no matter how repulsive this particular executive may be. American militarism was thriving well before Trump hatched his campaign plans, and will outlast his sad and flailing administration. Even if Trump were to adopt a stance of rigid isolationism, forgoing all direct American military involvement in the conflicts and wars of foreign nations, America would still be one of the single biggest engines of militarism by virtue of its arms trade. US weapons companies were involved in more than half of the world's arms deals in 2015, deals which netted them some $40 billion (France finished in second place with $15 billion). In December 2016 alone, the State Department approved the following sales: a $115 million "Electronic Warfare Range System" to Australia, fighter-jet upgrades to Finland, nearly $700 million worth of infantry carrier vehicles to Peru, $3.5 billion in Chinook helicopters to Saudi Arabia, missiles for Morocco, Apache helicopters for the United Arab Emirates, logistical support services and equipment in Qatar (plus engines and equipment for C-17 Globemaster planes), nearly $2 billion in equipment and support for Kuwait, some planes for Norway, and something called "Sea Giraffe 3D Air Search Radars" for the Philippines. In 2015, the CEO of Lockheed Martin told reporters that she looked at the Middle East and Asia as "growth areas" because of their instability. By approving the sale of arms in such massive quantities, the State Department is helping to ensure Lockheed's profits for years to come.

Drastically reducing the country's arms exports would probably not be in the best interest of the American economy. Weapons manufacturers are conscientious about operating plants within the US, including in politically crucial states like Michigan and Ohio, thus cultivating a broad base of support for arms exports in Congress. Nevertheless, the American arms industry should be an appealing target for protest and anti-war political mobilization. The duration and the brutality of the Syrian war are largely due to nearly a dozen countries deciding again and again that a militarized approach to the conflict was more in keeping with their respective national interests than diplomacy. The political reasons behind those decisions have been as varied as the countries making them, but the availability of every imaginable weapon on the international arms market has been a constant, and no country does as much to maintain that availability as the United States. American activists may not be able to influence Erdoğan's views on

the pros and cons of Assad's continued rule, but they could theoretically influence how many missiles and aircraft the US would be willing to send him.

The anti-imperialist analysis of global conflict, in which America is almost always seen as the primary bad actor, is useful and productive, but the Syrian war has exposed its limits. The political interests involved in the war are so complicated and numerous that even if the US government were persuaded to abandon the pursuit of any of its ambitions in the Middle East, the war would likely continue unabated. Only an international effort to set aside those interests, to remoralize the discussion around war and acknowledge that wars are atrocities by definition, will produce a solution. What's needed is not an anti-imperialist analysis but an antimilitarist one. Fortunately, antimilitarism is an authentically internationalist stance, for the simple reason that war is equally bad for everyone on the receiving end of it. +

THEA RIOFRANCOS
Democracy Without the People

SINCE DONALD TRUMP'S ELECTION TO THE presidency, a steady stream of concern pieces has appeared across the national press: "Is Donald Trump a Threat to Democracy?" "An Erosion of Democratic Norms in America." "Will Democracy Survive Trump's Populism? Latin America May Tell Us." "Trump, Erdoğan, Farage: The attractions of populism for politicians, the dangers for democracy." "How Stable Are Democracies? 'Warning Signs Are Flashing Red.'"

The worry is obvious: *democracy is under threat.* Moving from headline to text, however, one perceives a shift. The basic meaning of *democracy*—the rule of the people, or popular sovereignty—is nowhere to be found. Instead, *democracy* appears to refer to a series of institutions and norms, not all of them obviously democratic.

In the *New York Times*, the political scientists Steven Levitsky and Daniel Ziblatt write that Trump's flagrant rejection of "partisan self-restraint and fair play" poses an existential threat to "our system of constitutional checks and balances." In an interview with the *Atlantic*, the political scientist Brendan Nyhan says he expects Trump to be unconstrained by "bipartisan political norms." Francis Wilkinson at Bloomberg slides from describing democratic institutions as anchored in elite bipartisan bonhomie to equating democracy with deference to the national-security state. "Trump has signaled clearly that he will deal with powerful democratic institutions as he dealt with his Republican rivals," Wilkinson writes. "Look at Trump's approach to US intelligence agencies." Venerating the CIA as exemplary of democracy is symptomatic of a more general tendency—one in which even the most brazenly antidemocratic US political institutions are taken to embody democracy.

Among the confounded political analysts, what followed Trump's victory was an epidemic of self-castigation. "We" had failed to "listen" to "white working-class" voters. Since the inauguration, however, elitism in the guise of centrism is once again on the move. Democracy, they say, is under threat from populism, and only a defense of norms and institutions can exorcise the specter of a reckless citizenry. But what if the truth is the opposite, and populism is not the problem but the solution?

o o o

THE VISION OF DEMOCRACY as an elaborate system of checks and balances—enforced by a combination of constitutional law, informal norms, competing interests, and the distribution of socioeconomic power across a plurality of groups—first crystallized in the 1930s. American political scientists at the time felt the need to define a uniquely "American" model that was distinct from "totalitarianism." This model, referred to as "pluralism" or "liberalism," provided subsequent elaborators with an alternative to democracy in the robust sense of "rule by the people."

In 1956, Robert Dahl's *A Preface to Democratic Theory* coined the term *polyarchy* in contrast with theories of "populistic democracy," which, as Dahl wrote, associated democracy with "political equality, popular sovereignty, and rule by majorities." In *Who Governs?* (1961), an empirical study of polyarchy at work in New Haven, Dahl deployed the concept to argue against the notion that the United States was ruled, as C. Wright Mills and others had it, by a "power elite"—and that the stability of American polyarchy owed in part to the disengagement of American citizens. Dahl's concept accustomed countless students of democracy to what was in fact insipid pluralism, handily justifying existing power relations and institutions. The equation of polyarchy with democracy remains pervasive in comparative studies of democracy and in the measurement of democratic consolidation. Witness the political scientist Jan-Werner Müller, who in his recent essays on populism for the *London Review of Books* and the *Guardian* defines the essence of democracy as "presenting citizens with options." Meanwhile populism is branded as "principled antipluralism."

In the emergent genre of democratic prognostication, political scientists and analysts alike pair this discourse with a pious narrative of the American tradition. As Levitsky and Ziblatt write, "With the possible exception of the Civil War, American democracy has never collapsed; indeed, no democracy as rich or as established as America's ever has. Yet past stability is no guarantee of democracy's future survival." Likewise, the sociologist Carlos de la Torre refers in a *Times* article to the long-standing "foundations of American democracy" and its "tradition of checks and balances to control political power."

But the American political system's stability should not be conflated with its degree of democracy. Painting our overcomplicated Madisonian system as a transcendentally democratic one requires a certain amnesia: to believe it, we must ignore the founders' explicit antidemocratic intentions, the range of exclusions that have structured the boundaries of the demos since, and the more recent impediments to democracy designed and abetted by the very principled "moderates" to whom the authors now appeal for salvation. One might forget, from all these accounts, the Madison of *The Federalist Papers* who denounced any politics that gave vent to "a rage for paper money, for an abolition of debts, for an equal division of property, or for any other improper or wicked project" — the Madison who demanded a "total exclusion of the people in their collective capacity."

The Trump Administration obviously poses serious threats to pluralism and to democracy in the more substantive sense. But Trump's means of threatening democracy are features of the system, not contraventions of it. His executive orders do undermine substantive democracy, but not because they upset a delicate balance of power among branches of government or partisan political forces. The "bipartisan consensus" cast as the moral backbone of democracy has vested in the presidency inordinate war-making and surveillance powers hidden from public scrutiny and unchecked by democratic debate or accountability. From the war on terror to the deportation pipeline, from domestic spying to Wall Street's guaranteed seat at the economic-advising table, Trump inherits a branch of government already well equipped to undermine democracy. The President and his crack squad of billionaires and white nationalists will undoubtedly turn these tools to devastating effect, as they already have. However, our critique of Trump—and our determined political resistance to Trumpism—should not rest on mourning a democracy we have never really achieved.

The bone of contention in all these accounts is "populism." While Trump is seen as an exception to an otherwise democratic American tradition, he is also figured as an expression of populism's transatlantic rise. The authors of antipopulist accounts rhetorically exploit what are obviously alarming right-wing victories to take aim at "populism" tout court, invoking examples that span the ideological spectrum. For the *Globe and Mail*'s editorial board ("Trump, Putin and the threat to liberal democracy"), Trump "is only one expression of a long-incubating virus" that has infected "more and more voters on both the extreme right and extreme left." In regards to Trump's denigration of the media, Levitsky and Ziblatt write that he takes "a page out of the playbook of populist leaders like Silvio Berlusconi in Italy, Hugo Chávez in Venezuela, and Recep Tayyip Erdoğan in Turkey."

In a *New York Times* article, Amanda Taub draws on recent research by political scientists Roberto Stefan Foa and Yascha Mounk, putting Trump in the same category as both right and left "antisystem populist parties in Europe, such as the National Front in France, Syriza in Greece and the Five-Star Movement in Italy." De la Torre suggests that "Americans should take a look at Latin America, where, starting in the 1940s, elected populists undermined democracy"—flattening the distinction between such ideologically opposed presidents as Argentina's Perón and Ecuador's Velasco Ibarra, Venezuela's Chávez and Peru's Fujimori, Bolivia's Morales and Argentina's Menem. The concern over pan-ideological "extremism" recycles post-Brexit commentary as distilled in the tinny voice of the wounded establishment, Tony Blair, who in his op-ed for the *New York Times* ("Brexit's Stunning Coup") warned of a growing "convergence of the far left and far right." Blair sees this "insurgency" in entirely communicational terms: the center's failure to "persuade" voters unmoored from political common sense was due to "polarized and fragmented news coverage" and "the social media revolution."

Seen from the fast-shrinking center, all populism, right or left, is equally suspect, because each represents the unhinged demos that the existing institutional order seeks to moderate, filter, and contain. By this logic, Sanders's invocation of "the 99 percent" must be the same as Trump's celebration of the "deplorables," Occupy Wall Street the correlate response to the Tea Party, and left-wing Latin American populists indistinguishable from their right-wing predecessors. According to these writers, what extremist voters on the left and the right share is an attraction to, as de la Torre phrases it, "politics as a Manichaean confrontation." But in politics that pits "the people" against their adversaries, it still matters *how* the people are fashioned and *who* is identified as their opponent.

Since the rise of "formal" democracy, populism has dogged it like a shadow, dramatizing, as political scientist Laura Grattan argues, a general paradox of democratic politics. "The people" ostensibly govern themselves in a democracy—but who are "the people"? As Rousseau put it, for a people to self-govern, "the effect would have to become the cause"; the people both constitute democratic institutions and are constituted by them. Democracy is in many ways an ongoing political contest to define the people and their powers. By making claims about the identity of the people and how they enact their political power, populist movements and leaders on both the left and the right confront this fundamental problem of democracy. Their answers, however—how they define "the people" and their prescriptions for democratic practice—could not be more opposed.

Populism can shore up exclusionary visions of the people. But it can also do the opposite, fostering unlikely alliances between marginalized groups. The emancipatory potential of populism relies on the political construction of a "social bloc of the oppressed," as philosopher Enrique Dussel has argued, drawing on Gramsci and Laclau. Left-wing populism exposes class antagonisms; right-wing populism obscures them, replacing them with cultural chauvinism, xenophobia, and racism. Where left-wing populism contests inequality, right-wing populism redistributes it—making certain kinds of inequality seem not only acceptable but natural.

What the defense of democracy against populism inevitably amounts to is a defense of political centrism. Democracy is reduced to the separation of powers and the search for bipartisan consensus. In an article for Vox's appropriately titled politics blog, "Polyarchy," political scientists Lee Drutman and Mark Schmitt of the New America Foundation argue that defending "basic democratic norms and maintaining a strong focus on corruption"—as opposed to fighting to preserve social spending—"is the right strategy." Despite the failure of this "strategy" during the Clinton campaign, Drutman and Schmitt assert that "the voters Democrats seem more likely to gain are the more affluent suburbanites who are less susceptible to the politics of resentment and more concerned about basic democratic norms." In his column in *Dissent*, Michael Walzer summoned leftists to defend "the vital center" ("We have to stand in the center and on the left at the same time. That may be complicated, but it is our historical task"). The apotheosis of this defense may be the Clintonite Third Way's $20 million campaign to devise a new strategy for the Democratic Party. As reported in Politico, "Part of the economic message the group is driving—which is in line with its centrist ideology—is to steer the Democratic Party away from being led into a populist lurch to the left by leaders like Sen. Bernie Sanders or Sen. Elizabeth Warren."

AT THE CENTER of critiques of populism is the towering figure of the leader: the demagogue who can channel and summon unruly followers at will. In a piece for *Foreign Policy* summarizing Human Rights Watch's recently published report "The Dangerous Rise of Populism," the group's executive director, Kenneth Roth, equates populism with "demagogues," "strongman rule," and "autocrats." In Jan-Werner Müller's essay for the *LRB*, populism is largely reduced to the unhinged power of tyrants, who "claim that they and they alone speak in the name of what they tend to call the 'real people' or the 'silent majority,'" and who symbolically construct the people in a unilateral, top-down fashion.

This latter point echoes Laclau's analysis in *On Populist Reason*, which emphasizes the role of the leader in unifying disparate demands into a shared identity. But it also misses one of his key insights: that the formation of a shared identity in opposition to the status quo does not begin ex nihilo with a charismatic political genius tapping into latent discontent. The formation of "the people" comes out of a longer process, in which various marginalized groups come to share similar experiences of the state ignoring or rejecting their demands. Prior to the election of a leader, they connect their grievances—a process Laclau calls "equivalential articulation." This pattern of populist self-organization applies to leftist populist parties and to the leftist leaders of insurgent party factions that Müller explicitly excludes ("Bernie Sanders, Jeremy Corbyn, Syriza"). Ultimately, Müller narrows populism to demagoguery and, with the exception of Chávez, the reactionary right. Trump's inaugural address seemed to confirm Müller's vision. As Trump bellowed before an embarrassingly anemic crowd, "January 20, 2017 will be remembered as the day the people became the rulers of this nation again."

But to focus on moments like these is to misread the history of populism and to foreclose the possibility of a grassroots left alternative. "The people" is not an inherently reactionary identity; its boundaries can be disrupted and expanded, its internal hierarchies reinforced or leveled. Its constitutive members are not, by definition, passive spectators to a demagogic variety show, a resentful mob, recipients of clientelistic handouts, or, more generously, victims of a repressed civil society. Rather, for a collective identity like "the people" to crystallize and acquire any political force, it must be enacted in practice, in concert with others, toward some goal.

A cursory glance at the history of left populism in the US and the Americas reveals a wealth of organizational forms, institutional innovations, and modes of social engagement that provided venues for face-to-face interaction and fostered solidarity. Agrarian cooperatives were the lifeblood of the late-19th-century Populist movement. The Colored Farmers' Alliance, excluded by the Farmers' Alliance's whites-only policy until 1889, brought black farmers together in mutual-aid societies and through networks of Baptist and AME churches. The Knights of Labor organized mass boycotts and strikes. More recently and farther south, decades of mobilization against neoliberalism and imperialism in Latin America have been sustained through popular institutions: people's assemblies, indigenous federations, neighborhood associations, rural communes, organizations of the unemployed, water committees, and others. Without them, left-wing leaders would have never come to power across Latin America.

Right-wing populist movements also involve grassroots mobilization. The characterization of the Tea Party as top-down "AstroTurf" neglects the chapter meetings, Constitution-reading circles, and anti-immigrant vigilante groups that supplied the foot soldiers and formed the organizational substrate for this conservative backlash. Left populisms, however, face the specific challenge of mobilizing against entrenched elites, with the aim of reorganizing the distribution of power wholesale.

If populism were always reactionary and never revolutionary, economic elites would not lurch between forceful rejections of populism and calls to "listen" to the aggrieved. At the recent Davos forum, global-elite handwringing was on full display: in between wine tastings and icebreaker activities that included a popular refugee-simulation game, "where Davos attendees crawl on their hands and knees and pretend to flee from advancing armies," attendees encountered a safe space to express their class panic. As reported by Bloomberg, Ray Dalio, founder of the hedge fund Bridgewater Associates, which manages $150 billion in assets, told the crowd at a "middle-class anger" panel, "I want to be loud and clear: populism scares me." (Bridgewater is in the process of creating an algorithm to automate the labor of many of its middle managers. Perhaps they will soon join the ranks of the "angry middle class.")

What is there to fear? A study published in the latest issue of *Latin American Research Review* shows that countries governed by left-populist administrations have witnessed significant increases in the political participation of the poor. The study also demonstrates that redistributive policies cannot undo structural inequality in the political and economic spheres on their own. Without a populist mobilizing strategy—specifically, the "us" (the poor) versus "them" (the rich) framing used by decades of anti-neoliberal social movements—left policies are unsustainable and substantive democracy is impossible.

Political analysts are undermined by their faith in the limited democracy they prize. The center they cling to has been sustained thus far by abysmal voter turnout, mass disenfranchisement, feckless politicians and strategists, and the overwhelming influence of financial elites in politics amid staggering levels of inequality that rival the Gilded Age. A left populism holds the potential to revitalize democracy, and to defend it from the dual threats of technocracy and revanchism. +

YASER SAFI, *CLOWN*. 2014, ACRYLIC ON CANVAS. 51 × 43". COURTESY OF THE ARTIST.

BEAST LEAVE

Trevor Shikaze

IT'S PARM'S IDEA that I should build a beast.

Parm's my best friend. No, we've never had sex. We've been tight since college and there's been times in our friendship when we actually talked on the phone every single day—we're that tight. Parm's totally attractive. I would say she and I are in the same league, attraction-wise, and most people who know us don't believe us when we say we've never done it. *Why not?* they ask. We usually joke that it's because she's brown and I'm white and her folks would *freak*—and you know what? That's pretty much the truth. I mean, Parm's parents love me, don't get me wrong, but it would have been a different thing altogether if we'd started going out at any point. Mom and Pop Dhaliwal are old-school like that.

So I guess racism kept us apart, and in this case I gotta say *Go racism*, 'cause Parm's my best friend and I seriously wouldn't have it any other way. I've never even really fantasized about her—at least, not since she had her first kid, which was almost four years ago, one year after she married a good brown boy. I was at her wedding of course and *that was a weird day*. No disrespect to Vik, but Parm could do way better. I'll be honest, I wasn't on board re: Vik for a long time. But whatever. It's Parm's choice and ultimately I respect that.

So anyway, there I am one day, standing in my kitchen, bitching on the phone to Parm. Bitching about my job. As always.

Parm says, "It's really unpleasant to listen to you talk about work. It's like pure negativity."

Parm can say stuff to me where I'd get super defensive if anyone else said it, but with her I take it in stride.

I go, "I barely ever talk about work."

Parm has this way of pronouncing my name when she's annoyed at me, as if it had four syllables. Wes-uh-*ley*-uh!

Then she's like, *You* always *talk about work*, and I'm like, *No, I don't,* and she's like, *Oh yes, you do. And you're always bitching away. Bitch, bitch, bitchy, bitch, bitch.*

"Do I really complain about work that much?"

She doesn't even answer, which means yes. I can hear her smirk. I swear to God I can hear it, like this tiny moist click. I know exactly what her face is doing right now.

"Take some time off."

"I do take time off."

"Take more time off."

"How can I take more time off? I'm maxed out for vacation."

"So make a beast."

I'm like, really? She's like, yeah.

"I don't know, Parm. Doesn't that seem super self-indulgent? I feel like it's the wrong reason to bring a living thing into the world, just 'cause you want time off work."

"Wesley." I hear the moist click. "That's practically the main reason I had the boys."

Which sounds really horrible, and I tell her that.

Parm says, "Obviously your motivation changes as you go. But I'm saying at first."

I can't tell if she's kidding or not, which usually means she half is and half isn't. She keeps going, saying there's no shame in it, that sometimes you just need a major life change to sort of restart your self-image. Parm can be very convincing when she knows she's right.

So then and there I decide to build a beast.

I GIVE IT A LOT OF THOUGHT before I make the hard decisions. You don't want to rush in, you know? There's all kinds of ways to get a life going—unlike in the old days—so you should really weigh your options and figure out what's right for you. I don't want to hire a consultant. That just seems weird. Some decisions you really should make yourself, I really do believe that. So I spend a lot of time on the internet, learning what's out there, reading testimonials. I find out pretty quickly that a lot of my preconceived notions are just plain wrong. Like, for instance, when is it OK to start telling people? In the old days, you never announced you were making a beast until you got an actual pulse going, but times have changed. Now that so many men go the digital route, the whole mind-set is different. Dudes start posting specs on their Tumblrs *months* before they boot anything up.

The first decision I have to make is bits or brawn, as they say. For me, that one's a no-brainer. I decide right away I don't want to go digital. I guess you could say I'm a traditional sort of guy in that respect. Plus, once I'd made up my mind to build, Parm gave me a copy of this book, *Shop Class as Soulcraft*, and it really got me thinking. I don't want to just download a life. I want to build my man from the guts out, really get my hands bloody.

Once I decide to go with flesh, the first thing I have to do is settle on what kind of heart to use. The heart is the most important part to me. It's symbolic. So I want to get it right. There's these companies online that'll actually grow a heart for you—on like a scaffold thing—and then once it's formed they mail it out. It's so weird. Apparently heart tissue just starts beating and contracting on its own, even without a blood supply or a brain or anything. But for some reason the lab-grown option feels too artificial to me. I've already decided to go with real live tissue—makes sense to try and stay as organic and free-range as possible.

Another option is hearts from dead children, which seemed 100 percent wrong to me at first, but then the more I thought about it and read up on it, the more it really started to make sense. These kids die from natural causes, and there's a whole system in place to make sure the vendors are the actual parents—not just some random child-killer—so I feel like the checks and balances are there. And your payment goes to helping seriously disenfranchised people, so there's even a humanitarian angle. Why kids? Why not old farts who are done with theirs? First of all, when it comes to hearts, the younger the better—it's a wear-and-tear issue. Also, you want to avoid perverse incentives. The beneficiaries of the sale have got to be people who wouldn't want the donor to die, and parents of young children are the only ones you can really trust in that regard. I've given it a lot of thought, and I truly do believe the system's safe and legit. And I was reading this HuffPo article, and the guy's point was like, *It's actually racist to think that Chinese parents would kill their own children just to sell their hearts to rich Westerners*. And I was like, *Yeah! It is!* So I feel pretty comfortable about my decision.

OK, so I order the heart, and then I'm *super* anxious the whole time until it arrives. I've read some reviews on Amazon about spoiled hearts, and it's really just a nightmare. There's all kinds of regulations about sending human tissue in the mail. It's not like some DVD or something. If your heart shows up rotten you can send it back but you don't get a complete refund if you don't follow all the procedures exactly—there's all this paperwork to fill out. I guess it's to discourage illegal trafficking, but man, what a pain in the ass. Needless to say, I want to avoid all that.

When the heart arrives in perfect cryonic stasis, I breathe a sigh of relief. I thaw it and call Parm.

"Is it beating inside the box?"

"Yeah—in its 'nutrient medium.' Here, I'll show you. Hold on."

I hold up my phone and take a video.

"Ew!"

"I know. It's awesome."

"Wes. Barf-land."

So now I've got a pulse, and being the traditional guy I am, I've waited till now to announce. It's crazy how nervous I am. What will people say? I mean, obviously everyone'll be all, *Congratulations, Wes, that's great, Wes, rah, rah, rah.* But what will they really think? It's such a big step. And there's still stigma attached: you know, a single guy going out on his own to make a beast.

But whatever. I've got a big place. I live way out in the sprawl—you'd be crazy not to, if you consider the economics. I could have a shoebox downtown or I could have this. And you know what? Even at the time I bought it I was thinking ahead, thinking about beasting. I was like, let's say someday I want to build a beast. It's seriously wrong to do that in the city, what with the density and everything. I mean, once the rampage starts—assuming a rampage starts—there's way too much collateral damage. Out here in the exurbs, there's tons of empty space. Even if your beast goes totally berserk, the amount of damage it can realistically do before the Squad takes it down is minor. So I really was thinking about that—even back then, it was a factor in my thinking.

Plus the dogs love the big yard. No way I'd get *that* downtown.

o o o

I MAKE THE ANNOUNCEMENT the same way I make all my announcements: I tell my mom, then she goes on Facebook, then everyone knows. It's an OK conversation, when I tell her. Weird but OK. She's supportive, in her way, which for Mom means asking if I need to borrow weapons or if I need money to buy weapons. That's my mom, always looking on the negative side, always thinking about what might go wrong instead of what might go right.

I tell her I don't want to do it that way.

"I thought I'd try it without weapons."

"Oh, that's what all the men say. But then the thing wakes up and at the last minute you're out buying weapons."

"I don't know, Ma—I think I'd rather improvise."

"All I'm saying is it doesn't hurt to have some weapons on hand. If you don't use them you don't use them."

"I just really think I'm saying no."

My conversation with Ron is even weirder, when I go in to talk to him about leave. I assume he'll get mad at me for taking so much time off, but that's not what happens. At first he's all jokey and annoying, as usual, but then he gets serious, reflective, starts talking about how it was different in his day. Back then, you thought of a beast more as an extra set of hands to help out with the yard work. And you never made your beast dangerous, not deliberately.

"I guess the philosophy's different today. I'm not saying that's a bad thing, just different."

He tells me how much pleasure he got from building his beast, and I think of that book, *Shop Class as Soulcraft*. I start trying to explain the ideas to him, but he seems bored, so I stop. I change the subject, ask how it all ended for him and his beast. He tells me the beast finally snapped one Saturday morning while they were out washing his car.

"Had to subdue it with the hose, right there in the driveway." He mimes strangulation. "Then I run it over a few times, for good measure. I won't kid ya. Hardest thing I ever done."

Like I say, it's a weird conversation. But good. I feel closer to Ron. He shakes my hand and wishes me well, tells me not to worry about taking the time off.

"Man's gotta take the time sometime. How far along are you?"

"It's just a heart so far."

"Well, that's how it starts. You gonna use weapons?"

"I was thinking no."

"Good man."

It's the first time I walk away from Ron *not* thinking what an asshole he is.

So yeah, the reactions vary. My sister's like, *What are you doing?* She starts telling me all these horror stories and I'm like, *Yeah, sis, we've all heard the horror stories. But it doesn't have to be that way. I'll be careful.* My brother's like, *Just be sure to complete him.* Otherwise it looks really bad. I know what he means. So many dudes lose control of their monsters when they're only half-built. We've all seen the videos: one-armed beasts totaling convenience stores, partial skeleton beasts on the loose, beasts with no head running around, being all spastic. It's like, really? Couldn't even get the head on? Come on, guys. Try harder.

Which gets me thinking. The head. What should he look like?

I find this company that'll print off a living scan of your face that you can graft on so your beast will look like you. How creepy is that? No way, dudes. I don't even want my guy to necessarily look human. I find this other company that specializes in beast faces, all natural. It's cool—they've got this whole gallery of different kinds of animals they can supply. I click through the most popular faces, the top-ranked ones, which are also the most obvious ones. Tigers, pumas, all the big cats. Mm. Naw. Pass. I'd like something really original. I drag the cursor down to the bottom of the gallery and click way far in, like image seventy, and there it is.

What the fuck *is* that?

It's called a "babirusa," and I guess it's some sort of *pig* or something, but holy shit. That is one mean-looking motherfucker. All tusks and these crazy ferocious eyes. It's like *World of Warcraft*, but real. I click on the price icon and it's actually pretty reasonable. Huh. This just might be my guy.

For the upper body it's straight chimpanzee. Easy to access, and cheap. The drug companies are just grateful there's a market for this sort of industrial waste. It's a nice thought, too, like a second life: these guys sacrificed themselves for medical science, and now they get to live again—or anyway, part of them does. I like the big broad pectorals, the long muscular arms. You can go mechanical for the chest and arms, but I like the look of an organic upper body. I just think it looks better, visually.

I go mechanical for the lower body. You pretty much gotta if you want your guy to walk upright. Sort of half-joking, I wonder if you can't just buy some Chinese kid's legs—then I check into it, and you can. But it looks wrong. Especially if you want to add junk, which of course I do. Oh, man, that's a *whole* 'nother ball of sticky horrible wax. I ask Parm to do the research for me 'cause it feels just a *leeet*-tle bit gay, and she's like, awright! Sign me up! Then she calls me about five minutes later and she's all, I can't do this, it's too disturbing. I have a look at what's on offer and she's right. I mean, bulls, wolves, you name it. These endless dick galleries, all these weird scary shapes. I decide to go prosthetic for the manhood.

THE COMPONENTS TAKE A FEW WEEKS to arrive, but finally they do, and it's time. On my last day at work my associates throw a party. Of course it's Frankenstein-themed. Frankenstein paper plates, green plastic forks and knives, the green guy himself on a cake where the cake people have written in icing, CREATE A MONSTER, WES! And you know what? I have to say I'm actually pissed off about this. When Honario from accounting went on *his* leave, Ron sprang for rubber masks—full-head Frankenstein rubber masks for everyone on staff, and those things are *not* cheap. And we actually did the surprise thing, got to work early and hid behind the furniture and jumped out when Honario came in, the whole nine. He was pretty edgy at the time so his reaction was a bit weird, but the point is that *time and effort were put in.* And money. So, yeah, I'm a little pissed off at my crappy paper plates and this shitty cake. It doesn't even look like Frankenstein. It looks like Arnold Schwarzenegger with green skin and a bowl cut. Were they training someone new? I don't even eat my slice.

We all stand around for a while trying to get along, and suddenly everyone's an expert on beasting. The IT guys come over and try to persuade me to go digital. I'm like, *It's too late dudes, decision's made.* They're like, *No, no, hear us out.* They go on and on about why analog sucks, and I actually have a hard time defending my position, mainly 'cause I can't outright say what I'm really thinking. Which is that they're a bunch of pussies. Dudes, you seriously think a virtual bot could take the place of a real live beast? Y'all spend too much time pounding them keyboards. But I can't outright say that. So instead I talk about how it's more *romantic* to build a physical beast, and they're like, *What do you mean, "romantic"?*

And I'm like, *You know, there's the element of danger.* And they're like, *Danger? Danger? You wanna talk about danger? Need we remind you of the 2009 Great Beast Crash, when practically the entire Eastern Seaboard was out of power for like forty-eight hours? How is that not dangerous?*

Whatever. These dorks. I let them talk themselves out, which they eventually do. From my lack of pushback, I guess they think they've won me over—this guy named Brent gives me his personal email and tells me that if I need someone to walk me through some of the more technical aspects, he'd love to help. Yeah, I bet you would, *Brent.* But forget that. This is *my* time. This is *my* thing. I'm doing this for *me.* Far as I'm concerned, Brent can grow a pair and build his own beast.

The party breaks up and I spend the rest of the day slacking the fuck off. I look at the card that everyone signed. *Good luck! Don't get killed! "Beast" wishes!* Ron comes by for his obligatory long-winded sayonara, and then that's it, I'm free. I walk out of there with the biggest grin on my face, call Parm before I'm even out of the lot. She doesn't pick up so I leave a message.

"I'm free, baby! Six months of freedom! Just me and my beast, doin' our thang."

I'm so stoked. I put on Blink-182 and crank that shit. Six months . . . Now, this is sort of a thing for me—I sort of believe it's discriminatory that men only get six months max to build a beast, whereas a woman can get a year for mat leave, or even more, depending on where she works. But hey, that is one discussion *no man wants to have with the females in his life.* So we take what we can get. Of course, only a tiny handful of dudes ever make it the full six months. Most beasts wake up before then—even if you go as slow as possible, really draw it out. That must be a real bitch, having your beast wake up after only a couple months. Not yet! Go back to sleep! I'm thinking I won't plant the brain until *at least* month four. They say to plant early so the reflexes get a chance to tune up, but once you plant the brain . . . well, once you plant the brain, all bets are off.

I get home.

Now what?

I'm genuinely not sure how to get started. I've got all the components, but something's missing. It just doesn't feel official, you know? I feel like I want to cut a ribbon or smash a bottle of champagne on a ship or something. I can't just *start.* I call Parm.

"Have you started yet?"

"I can't just *start*."

"What are you talking about? Start!"

So I start a blog. I'm not really the blogging type, I have to say, but this whole thing just feels so . . . so . . . so *momentous*. I truly feel the need to document it in depth. It's such a cliché for dudes to blog about their beast-building, but whatevs. I guess I'm a follower, when you get right down to it. So I take a bunch of pictures of all the components, make a little site. Man, setting up the blog takes me a long time. I want everything just right—but I don't even know what I mean by that. I call Parm for help.

"Why are there so many backgrounds to choose from? Which one is good?"

"Wes, it's up to you. Just pick one. No one even looks at the background."

"How about Oriental? I sort of like that."

"*Oriental*? Are you serious?"

"I don't know, Parm!"

In the end we go with something really plain, black on white, sans serif (which Parm says is the hip choice). I do a few posts just talking about my feelings, how I came to all my decisions, where I ordered the components from. My posts get a bunch of likes—of course it's all Parm and Mom and my sister. But this is a good start. This feels right. I think I'm ready to get down to business.

Choosing a room to work in is surprisingly hard. The garage seems like the obvious choice—it's a two-car garage, so plenty of room with just my Mini in there. Plus all the tools are there. Plus it doesn't matter what spills on the ground, and I'll be working with plenty of gross fluids. But the dogs like to hang out in the garage (Lord knows why), and I sort of don't want them around the beast too much. I consider the basement, which I only ever use in the summer. There's a room down there with unfinished floors that I could convert to a workspace pretty easily. But that room feels too isolated. The nice thing about the garage is that it connects right to the kitchen, and it's my understanding that a lot of the materials I'll be using need to be boiled and microwaved, plus it's nice to have the double sink right there. Upstairs is pretty much out, due to carpets—even though there's a whole room I literally never use: the Nothing Room. I guess it's supposed to be a spare bedroom, but I never have guests, and when I do it's just my brother, and he's happier on the foldout couch in the basement where there's a TV and a private bathroom. So I never even bothered to furnish the Nothing Room. It's just an empty room across from my bedroom . . . You know, people think it's weird that I live out here all alone, just me and my dogs, but let me just say for the record that when I bought this place, Kate and I were still sort of seeing each other—I mean, we were on a break, but I was picking up clear signals, I thought, that we'd be getting back together soon. You know what's funny? About buying a house? I think my decision was subconsciously influenced by the Discovery Channel. There was this show I saw once, with these birds, where the male builds this giant elaborate nest and the female comes by and she's either like, *Meh*, or else she's like, *OK, yeah, you got the skills to pay the bills*, and she comes in and lets him mate with her. For some reason that stuck in my head, and I think it factored hugely into my decision to buy. I remember walking into this house with the agent and thinking to myself, *Kate would love this. It has a porch. Kate will want to move into this when she sees it.* So I signed all the papers and the next thing I know I get that text from her.

You remember that guy I work with? James? You met him at the Christmas party when you went that year?

I'm like, *Yeah, I remember James. I thought you two were awful friendly.*

Well yeah about that . . .

It's been five years. Five years, man. Half a decade. Ah, well. The past is the past, right? But the funny thing is, the decisions you made *then* are still the decisions you live with *now*, even if all your circumstances have totally changed. So, yeah. People say it's strange for me to live alone in such a big house, but you know what? I truly do not care what people say. I make good money. I can afford my payments. And the value's just going up. I really bought at the right time—it was fields all around back then. Now there's houses as far as the eye can see, a school, a partly built mall. The dogs like it out here. Sadie and the Dude like a yard to romp around in. And I got *all this space* to build my beast in.

So, yeah. Whatever. The garage it is.

o   o   o

GET AN AMAZON PACKAGE. It's from Parm. A book. I don't recognize the author's name but I look at the cover and apparently this guy's a pretty famous British comedian, and the book's just all his tweets from when he was beasting, collected in one place. Oh, man, it's hilarious. Like laugh-out-loud funny. Some of the British slang I don't get but what I do get is gold. I finish the whole thing in one day.

I sort of feel bad about that, about wasting a day reading, but whatever. I got six months, right? This book is hi-*larious*. I keep putting it down, walking away, coming back, telling myself I'll just read one more page and that's it. Yeah, right. Next thing I know, I'm done. Wow. I don't remember the last time I finished a whole book in one day. Maybe when I was a kid. Maybe *Charlotte's Web.* Anyway, this book's a hit. This British guy is too funny. I decide to blog about it, but when I sit down and look at my earlier posts, I actually get sort of depressed. I can't help but compare myself with the British comedian. Wow—I'm boring. And what's with all the exclamation points? It looks like a teenage girl wrote this. I'm so excited!!!

So I don't bother with a blog post. In fact, I think I'm through with blogging. It's maybe not the right format for me anyhow. Think I'll stick to tweets.

OK. Focus. You got a beast to build.

I call Parm and thank her for the book, tell her I'm probably done with my blog. We say good night. Next morning I take the dogs for a huge long walk. They deserve it. Such good doggies. It's nice that I get to spend real quality time with them now that I'm on beast leave. I make a vow to them: "I will walk you every day. I promise." We go so far that I actually get lost—they've put in a whole new community since the last time I walked out this way. It's confusing. All the street names start with the same letter. Oh, well. More exercise for the dogs, I guess. Where the hell am I?

I finally break down and ask a jogging mom for directions. Man, if looks could kill, my dogs would just keel over right there. Sadie's a rottweiler and the Dude's an American Staffordshire terrier—and they're the gentlest, sweetest animals you could ever imagine. But there is *stigma*. This mom actually recoils. She angles her jogging-mom baby chariot away from the dogs and she won't take her eyes off of them, especially the Dude. Like he's gonna lunge in there and eat her infant. Really? Is that really what you think? *He wears the muzzle because he has social issues with other male dogs if they come sniffing around Sadie.* But he loves kids. I mean, come on, people! Talk about discrimination. Anyway, she tells me where I am and bounces off in her Lululemons . . . Dang. Who designs these Lululemons? Moms have never looked so good.

Anyway, I get home. The dogs do that thing where they flop on their sides and smile. So cute. I head to the garage, where I've assembled all the components. Roll up my sleeves. OK. Let's *do* this.

So I get to it.

I unpack everything and lay it all out, and the bigness of the job hits me. This is a big job. I mean, to create a life. I've set up an old ping-pong table to build my guy on. I spread a plastic drop cloth over it, and suddenly, for the first time, I feel like I'm really doing this thing. I find the cylinder with the spinal column in it. I press a button and the cylinder opens. Wow. I pull out the spine and lay it on the table. The first piece. The first building block. It comes from the factory with all these contact points already attached, like these little plastic sockets. Smells like chilled meat—like uncooked chicken. Should I be wearing gloves? Hm. That's a good question.

I take five and get my tablet, hit the couch, do some googling. There's all kinds of instructional sites on how to build a beast. It's sort of hard to know which one to use. I find this guy with a whole YouTube channel devoted to beasting, and his videos have like 100,000 views, which is pretty good for some random guy with no production values. He's cool. Funny. Not on purpose. He's like super dorky and awkward, but that's what makes him fun to watch. And he's good with his explanations. He has this soft, sort of gurgly, very patient voice. I spend the rest of the day watching.

Well, there goes another day. I get off the couch and head for the garage and boy *am I just in time.* Looks like Sadie's mistaken my beast spine for a chew treat. I freak on her—more than I should, I know. I've never hit either dog but they're well socialized, I can sure put the fear of God in 'em. I'm definitely the alpha around here. Sadie hasn't taken a bite or anything, but she's sniffing around like she intends to, so I pull her away and push her to the ground and bark in her face. Her legs go up in the air and I can see the whites of her eyes. She's limp. This is how you train dogs. They respond to the pack dynamic, and you gotta put 'em in their place. Which is why little dogs are such pricks—no one takes them seriously, so no one ever pins them down and barks in their faces, so they get the idea that they're in charge. With big dogs, you have no option but to discipline. They're too much trouble otherwise. So I enforce a strict pack hierarchy.

The Dude watches from the kitchen steps. He's a smart boy. That spine is a no-no.

I get off Sadie and check the spine. No damage done. I point at the table and growl at the dogs, who bow their heads and slink off to the kitchen. Better close the door to the garage tonight. Usually I leave all the doors open, and the nightly routine goes like this: the dogs lie around wherever I am (usually in the bedroom, watching TV), and when I fall asleep they head to the garage and lie around there. Then at around 6 AM they come upstairs and flop in my bed on either side of me and sigh their dog sighs. Then they stare at me until I get up and feed them.

But tonight we start a new routine. Tonight the door to the garage stays shut.

. . . Which it does, until about three in the morning, when I wake up to the most desperate whining you ever did hear. I go downstairs and Sadie and the Dude are sitting there, staring at the door, and they look over their shoulders with a look that says, *Master, what the fuck?* They stare at me with their puppy-doggest stares, trying to melt my heart. Hey, nice try. But I'm the alpha here. Door stays closed. I growl at them and go back to bed.

Half an hour later and it's whine-central once again. For Christ's sake. Shut up. I go down and growl at them, come back to bed. Fifteen minutes later, same thing. Same reaction from me. I hold out until about four o'clock, when I finally give in and open the door. I lay some plastic over the spine and say *No!* a bunch of times, then I climb back up to bed and try not to look at the clock. Fuck this. I am going to be *so tired* tomorrow. And I get grouchy when I'm tired. I'll take someone's head off. Like that fucking intern. What's his name? Gene? Gene had better watch out tomorrow is all I can say. He'd better not make coffee without putting the filter in again is all I can say. 'Cause if he does—

Oh, hey. Wait a minute. I don't have to work tomorrow. Ha! I don't have to work! Not for *six*—count 'em—six months! I'm on *beast leave*, bitches!

The feeling that floods my brain in the next seconds is truly something to savor. I almost want to cry. It's beautiful. It's so beautiful. I grab my phone and tweet about it, it's that beautiful. Then I nestle into my oh-so-soft pillow and fall blissfully to sleep.

So, DAY FIVE OF BEAST LEAVE and dude sleeps in till two in the afternoon. OK. So? So what? It's a victimless crime.

I get up and check my phone and Parm's sent me about ten zillion texts. I call her but she's not picking up—*probably in a meeting or some fucking thing.* Ha! I see she's retweeted my tweet from 4:16 AM. She's all like, *bff @wezzlicious on #beastleave, just realizes it at 4:16 AM. must be nice.*

I tweet: *just woke up! 2:32 PM. #beastleave rules!*

Then I make pancakes. I tweet about that.

The dogs are slinking around, on affection strike. Yeah, that's right. I'm pissed at you two. No walkies today. I feed them, they eat, then immediately they both go up to the Nothing Room and lie in a corner. Those two, I tell ya. Champion sulkers. Now, how's my spine doing this fine afternoon?

I peek under the plastic. Everything looks OK here. And all those videos I watched yesterday really were helpful. I'm pretty sure I know where to start.

So I start. It's slow going, and, I have to say, pretty frustrating at times. There's all these nerves you gotta connect just right. I attach the organ bundle. The bundle's all artificial and idiot-proof enough, but the heart gives me a hard time. Finally I get it fixed in. I haul out the chimp torso and I'm really disappointed to see that the arms come unattached. I guess it's easier to ship that way, but, like, really? What a pain in the ass. So I pull up the video on how to connect the arms, watch that, and by the time I feel like I've got everything figured out, it's already nine o'clock. The dogs sit at the door, watching me from the kitchen. Oh, decided to get up, did you?

I feed them. I feed myself. I hang around in the kitchen. Call Parm.

"It's going good. I've already got the viscera mostly hooked up to the spine."

"Are there reflexes?"

"Not yet. But I don't think there should be yet."

"Really? Why not? Maybe you're doing something wrong."

"I'm not. I watched a video about it."

"Well, take it slow is all I'm saying. You don't want to rush this part."

"Thank you, Mom. Look, I know what I'm doing."

"Wesley. No one expects you to be an expert right off the bat. You learn as you go."

"Yeah. I know."

"I know you know." I hear her smirk. "How were the pancakes?"

We say good night and I debate whether or not to close the door to the garage. It probably wouldn't hurt to leave it open. The dogs understand they're not supposed to touch anything, right? But at the same time, I'm the alpha, I set the rules. So I close the door.

Three in the morning, whine-central, I open the door. I will kill you both at dawn.

Next day, I attach the torso. This takes all day. *All day.* And I work straight through, only taking the odd break to eat and feed the dogs, tweet a little, and go to the bathroom. I can't tell you how satisfied I am when I step back and it's attached. I'm getting pretty good at sutures, too. You can actually tell which ones I did in the morning, which ones I did in the afternoon, and which ones I did in the evening—there's that much of a difference in the quality. I'm a quick study, what can I say. I pull out my brand-new vitaMeter and hold it over the torso. A few of the little bars light up faint orange. Hm. Is that normal? I mean, the heart's alive, right? I take the vitaMeter into the yard and wave it over Sadie. The bars light up bright green, all of them. As an experiment, I hold the meter over a dandelion, and the bars light up green for that, too. This dandelion is more alive than my beast torso? Hm. Why are there even dandelions here? Is that weed stuff not working?

I spend some time online and find a lot of long discussion threads about vitaMeter readings, what to expect, what's normal. *Long* threads about when exactly life begins. Some dude is like, *I held the vitaMeter over my spooge and all I got were some weak yellow bars. How can* that *be?* Oh, man, this thread goes *on.* I look at the time and it's past midnight. I send Parm an email about the guy who vitaMetered his spooge, complete with a link, and then turn in.

A MONTH GOES BY. I attach the arms and the neck region. These attachments take time. There's so much matching of blood vessels and nerves, and you have to get the muscles all fastened together right. Parm sends me *The Anatomy Coloring Book*, which seems super cheesy at first, but I swear to God it saves my life. Once the arms are on I discover this cool trick. You poke a finger into the top of the spinal cord and the arms jiggle. That's called reflex, ladies and gentlemen.

"He's got reflexes!"

"Congratulations, Wes!"

"Here, let me show you."

I video myself diddling the spine.

"Omigod, that is so freaky. That is—agh!"

She screams and laughs. Her laugh makes me laugh. Always has.

The war with the dogs continues. They actually let me sleep through the night one night, though the next morning they don't join me in bed like they usually do. I go downstairs and find them piled up by the closed door, looking betrayed. Who's the alpha! Then that night they go at it extra hard, yelping at me until I crack. I open the door and watch them climb down the steps and flop on the concrete floor. Why? Why must you sleep on this cold concrete floor? What's the draw?

More weeks come and go, and I get the mechanical pelvis attached. This mechanical stuff takes a whole new set of skills. Just when I was getting the hang of skin and bone, too. A lot of drilling involved, and a lot of wiring. I get the legs on. He's really taking shape, this guy.

But the vitaMeter still reads orange. Why, why, why?

I go online and soon find the answer, or anyway a bunch of long discussion threads about the question. There's a whole range of opinion, but it all centers around the brain. I knew this would come up. What I take away from the whole discussion is that the brain is key. I do a bit more research—man, there's a lot of opinion. People have literally written books on this topic. So I download one. It's by a brain scientist. I send Parm a text: *Wesley just bought his first book!* But then I find out the author's got a TED talk, and I watch that instead. Five minutes in, I am convinced. And I feel bad about it, to tell you the truth. This scientist guy's like, *We do our beasts a grave disservice if we do not plant the brain in the very early stages of building.* The point is that the body is an integrated system, and the brain is just this crucial component, so to leave it out really stunts your guy's development. Yeah, I hadn't thought of that. Sorry, guy. I haven't attached the skull yet, haven't even peeked at the babirusa face—I wanted to wait until the body was complete before I took a look at him, don't know why, sort of like leaving the biggest

Christmas present till last or something. I've avoided everything above the neck. But now it's time.

So the next day, I attach the brain to the spinal cord. Lots of blood vessels, lots of nerves. The brain's just a bulb at this stage, real small, and I have a heck of a time working at that scale. But I get the thing connected. Brain sourcing is the most controversial aspect of the beast industry, the part where you see the most protests and anger. But it seems to me that if you really want to do justice to the memory of a fetus—like if you really think it's a person and deserving of dignity and all that—then giving its brain a chance to flourish in a beast is much better than just flushing it. People make arguments, saying you should go with the brains of executed prisoners or whatever. Yeah, right. 'Cause that's just what I want to implant in my beast—some serial killer's used brain. No. You want a blank slate. So the fetus is really perfect. Some people will never see eye to eye with me on this, and I respect their right to their opinion, but that's how I see it. End of discussion.

I inject the brain with growth serum. Wipe my hands. I'm sort of shaking as I wave the vitaMeter over my brain-equipped beast. I guess I expect pure green, all the bars. Nope. Just faint orange. To say I'm disappointed would be a huge understatement. I call Parm.

"Maybe I'm doing something wrong!"

"You're probably not. I think this is normal."

"I don't think it is!"

"Well, every beast is different, right? So what does 'normal' even mean? Every beast has its own developmental path."

"I'm just afraid I'm doing something wrong."

"I know. But we both know how careful you are when you put your mind to something. I'm sure it's fine. Just give it some time."

"Paaaaaarm."

"Wesley. Do you want me to come over?"

"Naw. Why, just to watch me mope?"

"The boys are in bed. Vik's here. Why don't I come over?"

"It's OK, Parm. You're right. I gotta give it time, that's all. Gotta give it time."

I'VE JUST UNPACKED THE FACE when life begins.

I'm crouched on the floor, staring for the first time at the frozen pig flesh, when I hear the vitaMeter hum. I'm instantly on my feet. I've left the meter by the body, just carelessly placed by an elbow, and at first I can't find it. Then I see the green. All bars. Bright green.

I cannot resist.

"It's—it's *alive!*"

The dogs come bounding in like I've called them, but they see I'm not wearing my walkies and they slink back off to the yard. I brace myself against the ping-pong table. Between my feet, the horrible babirusa face sleeps under the frosty window of its cryobox.

Look at you down there. My baby.

I kneel and admire the huge tusks, the folds of bristly gray skin, the giant flared nostrils. I lift the cryobox and cradle it in my arms. The body looks the same as it did just a few minutes ago, when I finally got the skull locked in place and told myself that now, at last, after all this time, I'm allowed to peek at the face—it looks the same, but I know it's different. The spark's there. I feel happy, excited, relieved. The spark's there.

I spend the next week attaching the face. It's harder than I thought it would be. There's this gloop they sell in buckets that you paint onto the skull, layer by layer, and it turns into muscle tissue. So I have to do all this research and follow this instructional video that the animal-face company sent me a link to. Oh, man. The musculature takes forever. But they're like, *If you want your guy to snarl realistically and all that, you gotta get the muscles right.* So I get the muscles right. My consolation in all this is waving the vitaMeter over my beast and seeing those green bars light right up. It's been two and a half months. I've worked hard on this thing. And it's coming along as well as I'd hoped it would.

Eventually I get the face on. I've done a good job with the musculature and the face fits snug, all the contact points connect. I spritz it with this special chemical and the skin begins to "innervate." That's a new word that's really become part of my vocabulary this past little while. I've learned lots of new words. Sometimes I'll drop one in a conversation and Parm always seems really impressed. I know she's proud of herself for suggesting that I do this. I think she thinks it's a huge positive step for me, and I'd agree with her on that. She's never been anything but positive and supportive about it. Good ol' Parm.

Now that the face is on, my whole feeling about my beast changes. There's still months of work to do—he's rough around the edges and needs lots of trimming and musculature touch-ups, plus I want to add hair and tattoos and all kinds of detailing—but it really is a dude in

there, lying on that table. Up till now, he's felt sort of abstract . . . I guess
that's why I held off on looking at the face. The face makes him real.
Makes him a man.

Well, except for one thing. There's still the tackle, which I haven't
attached yet. I just didn't want it lying around all exposed like that—I
dunno, man, you can guess why. But now that my guy's fully formed, I
figure it's time to give him a reason for living. I unpack the cylinder with
the manhood in it. Wow. Ha-ha. Whew!

OK, so, yeah, maybe I went overboard on size. This was the one
decision that Parm just *would not let go of*. I mean, she got serious mile-
age out of it, making-fun-of-me-wise. I'll be honest: she got under my
skin. I just didn't want to talk about it—but Parm did. She thought the
whole thing was a gas.

"But why *sixteen*? That's not even *sort of* realistic."

"There's dudes with sixteen inches."

"Wesley. I'm not saying there's not. I'm just saying it's absurd."

"Well, what am I gonna do? Go small?"

But I kept my temper. Now that I've popped this cylinder, all I can
think is, *Parm was right*. This is absurd. Realistic-looking too, veins and
all. Actually pretty gross. I'm gonna have to buy pants for my guy—he
can't be swinging this thing around with every step he takes. Why didn't
I think this through? I should call Parm. Tell her she was right.

Amazingly, just at that second, she calls. Women, right? Sixth sense.

"How's it coming along?"

"It's OK. I just unpacked the manhood."

"Ha! Sorry. That sounded funny. How . . . uh . . . does it look?"

She cracks up. This entire conversation is just a gold mine for Parm.

"I think you were right."

"See?"

"It's gigantic."

We both crack up. I go to the kitchen where the reception's better,
and we have a really good talk. It's so weird, right? Apologizing? Somehow when you apologize to someone that you know really well, it sort
of opens up these emotional floodgates. The apology itself can be about
something stupid—just something minor—but it has this power, just
saying you're sorry. I guess it's like acknowledging that you're imperfect
and that you know it's OK, like it'll be received OK, like you trust the
other person to receive your imperfection OK. That's friendship, man.

So we're just shooting the shit, she's talking about Vik and how he's always so stressed about work, how maybe Vik should make another beast, when the Dude runs by with a trophy in his jaws.

"Oh, shit!"

"You OK?"

"Yeah—no—it's the Dude! The Dude's got the manhood! I gotta go!"

I've left the back door open so the dogs can come and go as they please, and he's out like a flash. And I'm out after him.

"No! Bad Dude! Drop it!"

He runs to the far corner of the yard, turns, faces me, does his growl. Shit, I know where this is going. He whips his head around like crazy and the manhood slaps his ears. Damn. He's in play mode. I usually don't buy a lot of chew toys for the Dude, since he goes through them like crazy. I really can't give him anything that isn't *industrial strength*, 'cause he just chews it up in a few minutes and then gets diarrhea. This schlong's made of—what, silicone? It doesn't stand a chance.

I do my mad voice: "Dude!"

I do my I'm-not-kidding voice: "Duuuuude."

But he puts his butt in the air and looks at me with those play eyes. Oh, God.

I lunge at him and he dodges, zips out of the way, zips back so that I can grab the dick. I tug, he tugs, growling through his clamped teeth. Sadie comes bounding out of nowhere, jumping around, barking. Oh, yeah, really great fun! I yank on the manhood. Now we're doing that thing where I twirl and the Dude levitates. I swing him around for a few minutes, but there's no point. Once the Dude's got his jaws clamped on something, *he will not let go*. You'd have to shoot him in the head, which part of me wants to do, not that I own a gun.

So I let go. Dick's all torn up anyway.

The Dude carries it to a corner and starts chowing down. You know what? Fine. Eat it. A responsible owner would try harder to take it away—maybe bring out the hose—but I decide to let him get diarrhea instead. That will be his punishment. He'll have to sleep in the yard tonight.

I turn around and walk back to the house, but I pause on the deck when I notice my neighbor glaring at me through his window. I shrug. This guy hates me. I don't even know his name. I tried to talk to him once when we were both out hosing off our driveways, and he just ignored me. Like a total prick. So from then on, nada. We just glare at each other sometimes. I don't know what his problem is—I mean, I *know* what it is. He's a dad. And he hates my dogs. Again, *discrimination*. It's not like I didn't *fence in the entire yard* when I got them. And not some shit chain link either. Seven foot tall, wood, dog-impervious. *Costly*. But still. He glares at me from that window. You just know he fantasizes about his daughters running in with their faces mauled. Has he ever come over to pet Sadie? To pet the Dude? I would let his girls come over and play with my dogs, and he would see how gentle and sweet they are, that they love kids. But no. He'd rather be a prick about it. Fine. You know what? Glare away! In fact, I hope one of your precious daughters looks out the window right this second to behold my *killer dog* eating a *giant cock*. That's what I hope.

"He ate it."

"Oh, Wes." She can't help herself. "I'm sorry. I shouldn't laugh."

"It's OK. It's obviously funny."

"What are you going to do?"

"I don't know, man. Maybe nothing. It's sort of weird to attach a dick anyway. Right?"

She doesn't need to answer that, and she doesn't. Good ol' Parm.

So it's just before eleven when the yowling begins. Sorry, my little man, welcome to diarrhea city. Population: one bad little doggy. I turn up the TV. But I can hear him over the TV. I get out of bed, go into the Nothing Room and look out the window. It's a full moon night, and I can see the Dude as clear as anything. He's groaning, scooting around the yard on his ass. Sadie's up too, like on vigil or something. I feel bad—but hey, man, I'm the alpha. I go back to bed.

OK, so now it's past midnight, and they're barking. Well, Sadie's barking—the Dude's producing ungodly werewolf moans. It sort of sounds like Sadie's egging him on, which she does sometimes. I picture my neighbor in his bed, lying there, glaring at the ceiling, thinking about how he's gonna burn my house down tomorrow. I gotta do something. Let them in, I guess. Shit, I should've thought this through. Usually if I know the Dude's eaten something wrong I go out and grab an armful of newspapers and cover the living-room carpet. But now it's too late. I have to drive so far to get newspapers—there's nothing in my community. I have to drive about three communities over, where there's a supermarket, and pick up a stack of those free real-estate-listing things. That is a massive pain in the ass. Hm. Except, hold on. I've got yards of drop cloth in the garage. Hey, perfect!

So I go down there, pat my beast on the forehead, gather up the roll of drop cloth, spread a plastic cover over the entire living room, and open the back door. The dogs come charging in. Sadie runs to the garage but the Dude heads for the living room. He *always* does this. Only time I ever see him in the living room is when he's got diarrhea. I guess it feels good to drag his fiery anus all over the carpet. Well, not tonight buster. 'Cause I've condomized the place.

I go to bed. I actually fall asleep. They're quiet for half an hour, then it's yelp time again. I swear I want to throttle them. But then I think of hernias. I have this irrational fear of my dogs getting hernias, especially the Dude, especially when he's scooting around the living room with diarrhea. I don't really know what a hernia is—I think it's like a hemorrhoid. I don't really know what a hemorrhoid is either, but a hernia is ugly and it involves the rear end and apparently it can kill you. I worked with a guy whose dog got a hernia and died. So I'm paranoid. Not that I'd know what to do if the Dude had a hernia or even what one looks like. Anyway, I get out of bed and go downstairs.

Before I can flip the light switch, the Dude slams into me and knocks me to the ground. I mean *slams*—we fly together halfway across the living room. I grab him out of shock and his face is all wet. Only it's not water or slobber. It's a mess, it's gore. Then I realize his whole lower jaw is missing and he's fucking dead.

I scream and push the body away, scramble to my feet. I can see dark smears all over the drop cloth like someone's dragged a big blood-soaked paintbrush around. I hear a snort and I look up and there's a person standing on the kitchen island with a sack under his arm. The guy squeals and I know it's him. It's my guy. Oh, shit. It's alive.

The beast swings out his arms and I see that the sack he's holding is Sadie, and she's obviously dead too. Then he starts spinning, spinning around holding Sadie by the hind legs, using her as a sort of counter-weight. He slams her into the fridge. He slams her into the stove. He spins and spins, spinning Sadie over his head, takes out the spice rack and the spider plant Parm gave me and the shelf of Jamie Oliver books Parm also gave me. Then he whacks Sadie against the counter a few times, squeals again, and charges upstairs. He drags Sadie along like a kid with a blankie.

Holy shit. I listen to his footsteps. Holy fuck. *The beast is in the bedroom.* I run to the garage and slam the door.

OK. Holy fuck. OK. I tell myself to calm down. *Calm down.* What do you do? Shit—where's my phone? It's in the bedroom! Oh, fuck, I should be *tweeting this shit out.* Wonder how dangerous he is. He killed the dogs. Shit, he killed the dogs. Poor good dogs.

I need a weapon. I consider the power drill, which would be good for close range, but I know how long my guy's arms are. By the time I got close enough to drill him, we'd be practically hugging. Plus he'd have to sit still for it, which I'm thinking he's not gonna want to do. How about the shovel? That's a good weapon. You can use it as a bludgeon, and then if you turn it edge-on, it's an ax. Wish I had a real ax. But this was how I wanted to do it, no weapons. Improv only. Shit. I'm not ready. Like, psychologically. I thought I'd have more time. It's only been a couple months. I wish this hadn't happened this way. Why did it have to happen this way?

OK—stop. It happened, so deal. Your beast awoke prematurely. It's not the end of the world. Make the best of a bad situation. You can still salvage this. You can still come out on top. Shovel will do.

OK.

Here's the plan: get upstairs, get into the bedroom, subdue the beast if you can. If you can't, grab the phone and run to the Nothing Room, barricade yourself in, and tweet this shit out. That's good TV. The civilian is trapped in an upstairs room, beast is in the next room over. We can't go in guns blazing, as we might injure or kill our civilian. We'll have to be precise. Surgical. Maybe bring in a helicopter.

Dude, that's good TV.

So I crack the door and peek out. No beast. I creep around the island, get to the stairs. Shit. This staircase. You can't see what's coming. It's stairs halfway up, then a landing where you turn, then stairs in the opposite direction. When I round the corner at the landing, he might be right there. I should've put a mirror in the landing. Should've beast-proofed this place. Hey, that's actually a great business idea. Beast-proof your home! I could do consulting. If I survive.

I creep up the first half of the stairs, shovel raised over my head. I round the corner swinging. No beast. I creep up the second half of the stairs. Now I'm on the second floor, in the open area between the bedroom and the Nothing Room. There's a skylight in the open area.

That's good. They can dangle a guy from a helicopter and crash through the skylight. That's *good*.

I creep to the bedroom door. Oh, man, I can hear him snuffling around. Didn't get a great look at him in the kitchen, what with the lights off, but the bedroom light is on. Moment of truth, man. Face-to-face. OK. Let's do this thing. Stop thinking about it. Just do it.

I round the corner and there he is, on the ground, on all fours, like a giant spider. He's facing away—he hears me come in, looks over his shoulder. Aw, shit! Holy shit!

I'm outta there. I run to the Nothing Room and slam the door. Omigod. Omigod. I've created a monster. I try to stop panting, hold my breath, listen. I lie on the carpet and try to see under the door . . . shit! He's right there. I can see his feet. The tip of his slimy nose pushes under. He's sniffing me out. He sniffs around for a bit, then sneezes. I haven't breathed. I'm pressed against the wall, my shovel raised. The tip disappears and I hear him stomp off. Oh. My. God. This is insane.

I look around the Nothing Room. No furniture to even improvise with. Maybe I could rip up the carpet and roll him up in it, smother him. Yeah, right. I swear I almost crapped my pants when he looked at me. Holy Christ. That is one *ugly* mother. Those *tusks*, man. And what's with the eyes? They're like pure white except for this one black dot. Christ.

I lie on my back. I'm safe enough, for the moment. I'll hear him coming. I don't think he wants to kill me. I *made* him, after all. OK, I gotta just try to calm down, regroup . . . Huh. Haven't really looked at the Nothing Room in years. Maybe I should rent it out. But then I'd have a total stranger sleeping right across from me. Maybe I should move. Why the hell *do* I live all alone out here? It's the rising property value, right? This house is an investment. Five years, man. Half a decade. Ever since Kate. How many girlfriends has it been? Five. One per year. There was Anjali, and what's-her-face, and Aliya, and Faiza, and then Kareena. Oh, Kareena. That long black hair. What's wrong with me? I should sell this place. Don't need a yard anymore—the dogs are dead. The dogs! My poor little dogs! Wish I had my phone. Wish I could call Parm. She'd want to hear all about this, be with me through it. I remember when Vik made a beast. That was before they married, when she wasn't sure yet. You know, they say men come to resemble their beasts. Vik's was this spindly daddy-longlegs thing—Vik isn't spindly, but I thought the beast looked like him anyway. It came alive while Parm was over and Vik beat it to death with a Cuisinart. That sealed it for Parm. He risked his life. I thought it was pretty brave too—until now. Really? A Cuisinart? My beast would eat that shit for breakfast. I saw what he did to the Dude. That is some serious fucked-up shit.

OK, shut up. Focus. Stop it. The phone. Gotta get the phone.

OK, here's the plan. Open the window. OK. That's a long drop. If I aim for the bush, though, I should be fine. So. Go back into the bedroom. Use the shovel if you have to, but *get that phone*. It's right there on the bedside table. If the beast chases you, run and jump out the window. If not, get back in here, close the door, call Parm, then tweet this shit out until the Containment Squad arrives. So it was premature? It's not the end of the world. There's still good TV in this.

OK.

So I open the door. The beast has retreated to the bedroom—I can just see a sliver of him. He's bent over something. Sadie, I guess. Is he *eating*? This is awful. I creep to the bedroom door. There's the phone, right on the bedside table. Just a few feet away. Oh, shit, he heard me.

Beast gets up slow, looks me right in the eye. Oh, crap. He comes toward me. I take a step back but he's advancing fast—OK, that's too close, buddy. I swing. He slaps the shovel. I swing again—he's *slapping the shovel*, like it *does not hurt*, like he *does not feel it*. Didn't I wire up the nerves properly? I'm using all my strength and he's just slapping the blows away. For fuck's sake! I raise the shovel over my head and bring it down as hard as I can right between his eyes. And you know what happens? Shovel splinters. The top part breaks right off. On dude's forehead. He doesn't bat an eyelash. I don't know if babirusas have eyelashes, but what I'm saying is, dude is UNFAZED. Oh—except that now he's pissed. He opens his mouth and shrieks this bloodcurdling, ear-raping shriek, and I scream too, and then *I am out of there*.

I run for the window. I can hear him galloping behind me. Oh, no. No, no. Please, God, not like this. I dive—right through the frame. Midway down I realize what's about to happen, and I turn a somersault, trying to not land on my head, and the pain when my feet touch down is out of control. My shins break off and ram into my kneecaps, which explode. Oh. My. God. I now have a new standard that all sensations will get judged against. My body goes sort of quiet for a second, and I hope what they say is true, about how when you're grievously wounded your brain sort of shuts off the pain response, fills your body with happy chemicals. Yeah, that happens. For about five seconds. Then the pain comes back like Terminator.

Just before it does, I have the presence of mind to look up and get a read on the situation. My guy's leaning out the window, looking down at me. He snuffs, snorts, and goes back in. I fully expect him to charge downstairs and run out here to finish me off, but he doesn't. Instead, I hear him smashing shit. Great. There goes the house. The pain returns and now it's just me and the pain and the lawn and the moonlight. I gotta get safe. Gotta get outta here. Gotta call the Containment Squad. No one even knows this is happening! I didn't get a single tweet out!

It takes me literally ten minutes to crawl the twenty feet to the gate. I heave myself up, flip the latch, and butt the gate open. This is the worst thing that has ever happened to me. I'm so alone. Apparently no one has heard my screams of terror or my howls of agony. I almost give up right there in the gravel—the thought of having to crawl across my neighbor's lawn, up his back steps, up to his door, knock on his door, somehow wake him up, somehow persuade him to take pity on me . . . it's almost too much. But then I tell myself, don't give up. I think of Parm and that's all I think of, and that's what keeps me going. Believe it or not.

I pull myself through the gate and around the fence, crawl across my neighbor's property line. I hear a window slide open. And there's my bullshit neighbor. Standing at his window, all lit by the moon.

He says, "I called 9-1-1 half an hour ago. I don't know why they're not here yet."

I'm like, really? Thanks for running out to help, you *fucking prick*. But I don't say it out loud. Because I can't speak. I just flop forward and puke and pass out.

N EXT THING I KNOW, it's flashing red lights. The ambulance is parked and there's a medic working on my legs. The Containment Squad car pulls up and the Containment guys get out. Their camera crew tapes the arrival. I try to look heroic, toughing out the pain, but let's be real. Look at me. Yep. I'm *that* guy. Beast woke up prematurely and I guess both my legs are broken. It's someone else's problem now. Hi, Mom!

The Squad goes in, followed by the cameras. More vehicles arrive: cop cars and a fire truck. The medic guys lift me onto a stretcher. I fight hard not to cry.

"No, don't take me away. I can't leave yet. I can't leave until it's over."

Before I'm even done speaking, there's this pop. Like a firecracker.

One of the medic guys says, "It's over," and they lift me into the ambulance.

"Wait! My phone!"

The medics seem pissed off. There's this cop standing nearby.

Cop goes, "Do you know where it is?"

"Yeah. It's in the bedroom. Upstairs. On the bedside table. Please, I need it."

Cop looks at a medic, who says, "He's stable."

"OK. The beast is neutralized. We'll send someone in."

I try to thank them but my voice is gone. I get very sleepy, then that's it. It's over.

I WAKE UP IN A HOSPITAL BED, all walled off with curtains. My legs are locked in weird machinery—I look like a Transformer. I hear people around me, other patients and their loved ones. After a while an attendant comes in, checks my vitals, seems annoyed. Then a doctor comes in and seems annoyed. He leaves and the attendant comes back with a bunch of pills and a glass of water. Apparently I've been in surgery for an ungodly number of hours. The hospital's notified my parents, who didn't get the message until this morning, but who are on their way, and who I'm guessing have notified my sister, who'll also be on her way once she gets the kids to school. I wouldn't be surprised if my brother flies in too, if he can carve out some time. Oh, man, I do not want to see them. Not in this condition.

I ask about my phone and the attendant points to this little shelf.

"But you're not allowed to make cell phone calls in here. There's a pay phone in the lobby."

The attendant leaves. I call Parm, tell her what happened.

"I'm not supposed to use my phone, so if I have to hang up that's why."

"I'm just so glad you're OK. How are you feeling?"

"I don't know. Pretty disappointed."

"I'm sorry. I know you were hoping for something different."

"Yeah. I probably won't even make it onto *Containment Squad*."

"You might."

"Not a whole episode, though."

"Maybe during the credits. They always do a bunch of clips."

"Maybe."

"Oh, my poor baby, though. How are your legs? *Both* broken?"

"It's ugly, Parm."

"Will you walk again?"

"Yeah, yeah. You'd be amazed—they've got all this bionic stuff. The doctor says I'll be just fine."

"How long will it take to recover?"

"Well, the bones have to heal and your nervous system has to mesh with the interface. Doctor says nine months."

"Nine months?"

"Yeah. At least."

I hear that moist click. Parm's smirking.

She says, "But that means . . ."

"*Disability, baby!*"

She giggles.

"Omigod, Wes, I'm so sorry. I'm so sorry. I shouldn't be laughing about"—she cracks up—"your tragedy—"

But I'm laughing too, we're both laughing, we can't help ourselves. And that's how it ends. Not how I'd wanted it to, but hey, what does, right? At least we have a good laugh over it, me and Parm.

Yep. That's friendship, man. That's friendship. +

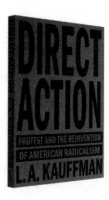

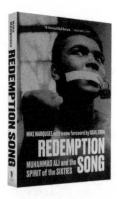

Direct Action
Protest and the Reinvention of American Radicalism
by L.A. Kauffman

A groundbreaking history of protest

"A must-read for those who have committed themselves to the life of the mind and of struggle."
—Rev. Osagyefo Uluru Sekou

Modernism in the Streets
A Life and Times in Essays
by Marshall Berman
Edited by David Marcus and Shellie Sclan

Essays tracing the intellectual life of a quintessential New York City writer and thinker

Redemption Song
Muhammad Ali and the Spirit of the Sixties
by Mike Marqusee
Foreword by Dave Zirin

"A thrilling book about a true and enduring hero ... Mike Marqusee has done him, and us, proud." —John Pilger

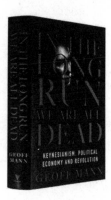

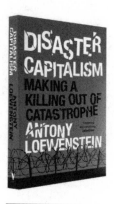

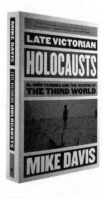

In the Long Run We Are All Dead
Keynesianism, Political Economy, and Revolution
by Geoff Mann

"Urgent and lucid ... A bravura inquiry into the intellectual history of the present and the ambiguous vitality of Keynes's *General Theory*."
—Alberto Toscano, author of *Fanaticism*

Disaster Capitalism
Making a Killing Out of Catastrophe
by Antony Loewenstein

"Chilling study, based on careful and courageous reporting, and illuminated with perceptive analysis, helps us understand all too well the saying that man is a wolf to man." —Noam Chomsky

Late Victorian Holocausts
El Niño Famines and the Making of the Third World
by Mike Davis
Foreword by Dave Zirin

"Davis has given us a book of substantial contemporary relevance as well as great historical interest." —Amartya Sen, *New York Times*

@versobooks

Available now at versobooks.com or wherever books are sold.

VERSO

CD WU, *UNTITLED*. 2016, ACRYLIC GESSO, PENCIL, AND NEON ON CANVAS. 48 × 120". PHOTO BY EVAN JENKINS.
COURTESY OF SHANE CAMPBELL GALLERY, CHICAGO.

WHY WERE THEY THROWING BRICKS?

Jenny Zhang

" **I** LOST HEARING IN THIS EAR when a horse jumped over a fence and collided against the side of my face," my grandmother told me when she arrived at JFK. I was 9 and hadn't seen her in four years. "In Shanghai you slept with me every single night. Every week we took you to your other grandmother's house. She called incessantly, asking for you. 'Can't I see my own granddaughter?' I said, 'Sure you can.' But—let's not spare any feelings—you didn't want to see her. Whenever you were at your *waipo*'s house you cried and called my name and woke up the neighbors. You hated her face because it was round like the moon, and you thought mine was perfectly oval like an egg. You loved our house. It was your real home—and still is. Your waipo would frantically call a few minutes after I dropped you off asking me to come back, and I would sprint all the way there. Yes, my precious heart, your 68-year-old grand-mother ran through the streets for you. How could I let you suffer for even a second? You wouldn't stop crying until I arrived, and the minute I pulled you into my arms, you slept the deep happy sleep of a child who has come home to her true family."

"I sleep by myself now. I have my own bed with stickers on it," I told her in Chinese, without knowing the word for stickers. I hugged my body against my mother, who was telling my father he would have to make two trips to the car because my grandmother had somehow persuaded the airline to let her bring three pieces of checked luggage *and* two carry-on items without any additional charges.

"And did you see that poor man dragging her suitcases off the plane for her? How does she always do that?" my mother said. She shrugged me away and mouthed in English to me, "Talk. To. Grandma."

My father threw his hands up. "You know exactly how," he said, and went off with the first two bags.

"You remember how uncanny it was," my grandmother continued, tweaking her hearing aid until it made a small shrill sound and then a shriller sound and then another even shriller sound. "They called me a miracle worker and I said, 'No, no, I'm just her *nainai*,' but everyone said, 'You're a miracle worker. You're the only one who can make that child stop crying.' They said there was no need for me to be modest. 'This child prefers her grandmother to even her own mother and father! Why sugarcoat the truth?' I had to stop myself from stopping other people from saying it after a while. Was I supposed to keep insulting everyone's intelligence? Protesting endlessly? Your nainai isn't that type of person. And the truth is, people don't make things up out of nothing. There's truth in every widely believed saying, and that's just true."

"What?" I said. "I don't understand Chinese that good."

"I knew you wouldn't forget a moment of your real life, your real home—the place you come from. Have you learned English yet?"

"That's all I speak. It's America."

"Your nainai is so proud of you. One day your English will catch up. It's such a gift to be here now with you. You don't know how many lonely nights I've spent dropping tears for you. It was wrong of me to let you go. Remember how you called for me when you let go of my hand and boarded the airplane with your mother? Remember how you howled that you wanted to take me with you? Four years ago, your father wrote to me, 'You can't keep my own wife and child away from me any longer. I'm sending for them immediately.' I wanted to know if he ever considered maybe you and your mother simply didn't want to go to America? In those days, you would've rather eaten a basement full of rats than be separated from your nainai. Your father's also stubborn, but I'm not the type to insult the spoonful of food nourishing me. You see what I mean? I won't say any more. I'm living in his house now and even though he has only made fatally wrong choices, we still have to listen to him. But remember how at the airport you cried and said, 'Nainai, I love you the most of everyone. I want to stay with you. I don't want to go to America.'"

"I don't remember that," I said to my grandmother. "Sorry."

"You remember everything, don't you? But it hurts too much to dredge up bad memories." Her hearing aid buzzed again and she twisted its tiny hidden knob with her thumb and index finger. "This thing works for a moment and then it goes dead for days. Your father said he would get me a proper hearing aid so I can hear your beautiful voice. You speak up now and let your grandmother look at you. She's only missed you every minute of every hour of every second of every single iota of a time unit that's elapsed since you last slept with your nainai every night, refusing to even close your eyes unless I was in the bed with you. You know what everyone's favorite joke was? 'Who's the mom? You?' Oh, I laughed."

"That's not a joke."

"That's right. It was the plain truth," she continued. "They all asked me, 'Doesn't your granddaughter ever want to sleep with her mother and father?' And I had to tell them—not in a bragging way, just in an inform-ing way—'No. Her father is in America learning how to build computers and her mother works late at the factory and even if her mother didn't come home from work so late, my granddaughter has made it clear she can only sleep with me. I know it's not proper while her mother sleeps alone in another room under the same roof, but when a child wants something, how can you look her in the eye and deny her?'"

My grandmother lived with us in America for a year. She taught me how to knit, and after school I watched her make dinner and do dishes and sew curtains. At first I wouldn't let her sleep with me in my bed. She cried and came every night to my bedroom and sat at the edge of the bed saying nothing. She had small red eyes and no teeth at night, except for four on the bottom row and a couple in the back. She ate daily bulbs of garlic so she'd live to be 117 and see me grow for another forty-five years, and the first few times she brought it up, I imagined myself running away from home just to get a few years to myself. But after a month, the smell was comforting, and I needed it near me before I could close my eyes, and just when I started to call for her more than she called for me, my parents announced that she had to move back to China to be with her dying hus-band. "Your grandfather," my grandmother said with disgust, "says the only proper way for a man to leave this world is in his own home with his wife by his side. Have you ever heard anything so spineless?"

My grandfather had been begging her to come back for six months. He had been diagnosed with lesions in his throat and he didn't want to die without her. For a year, I had slept in her bed, pressed up against her like she was my bedroom wall, and after she left, I stayed in her bed for two weeks, refusing to return to my own bed even after my mother threatened to push me off if I didn't get out.

"This room reeks," she said. "It smells like several people have died. You still want to sleep in here?"

I nodded.

"On sheets that haven't been washed for weeks?"

I nodded. "She said she's coming back after Grandpa dies."

"She also said you'd learn English in middle school. She said she learned to drive in her dreams and that's how she'll pass the driving test and take you to Mount Rushmore for your birthday. You believe everything she says? Have you gone back in time and lost all sense?"

I shook my head. Finally, she and my father dragged me out, my arms wrapped around the cheap white lacquered bed frame as my father held my legs and my mother pried my fingers free.

"You're going to sleep on your own," my mother said. "Like you did before she came around."

"You hear your mother?" my father said, wiping the tears from my face and blowing softly on my hot red cheeks. "Just a day at a time."

"Don't indulge this," my mother said.

"You want to beat the sadness out of her?" my father said. "Because that's what your mother wants. For us to be the bad guys and her to be the hero when she comes back."

"I'm not inviting her back," my mother said.

M Y GRANDMOTHER CAME BACK two years later. I was in middle school, and my pathetic puberty struck like a flash of lightning in the middle of the night—I suddenly saw all my surroundings for what they were: hideous and threatening. I had no friends, social life, interests, talents, breasts, straight teeth, likability, normal clothes, or charm, and every day I came home weighed down with dread. I started to fake illnesses so I could stay home with my 2-year-old brother. I followed him around everywhere, crawling when he crawled and walking on my knees when he learned to walk so that we were the same height.

When my grandmother moved in for the second time, she told us that this time she wasn't leaving. She was going to apply for a green card and raise my brother until he was old enough to be on his own—18, maybe 19.

"We'll see about that," my father said in Chinese, and then to me and my mother in English, "Let Grandma believe what she wants to believe. My gut says we'll be back at the travel agency in March, or my name is not Daddy, problem solver of this house."

I laughed at him. "But that isn't your name."

I made a point of telling my grandmother that I'd been sleeping by myself this whole time. "I also know how to cut my own toenails and braid my hair and make my own snacks." My mom was looking at me without pleasure. "Hi Grandma. I missed you," I added.

Then she was babbling, hugging me up and down and side to side, "*Nainai xiang ni le,*" she said. "Grandma missed you, oh, Grandma missed you, oh, Grandma missed you—"

"Kay, got it," I said.

She stepped back and took my hand. "*Baobei,* you can sleep with your nainai if you want, but your brother will, too. I don't know if three will fit, but I'm very happy to try. Does anything make your nainai happier than having her two grandchildren by her side? Your brother will sleep with me until he's old enough to sleep in his own bed. Most people say 13 is the age when a child learns to sleep on their own but most people are selfish and looking out only for themselves. Not me. I say 16. I say 17. I say 18. And if he needs me to, I'll gladly sleep with your brother until he's 21!"

I laughed. "Allen's not going to do that. It's different here. We wrote you about this."

My grandmother pulled me in so close I faked choking noises to make my point known. "Oh, baobei, I missed you. My hearing has gotten worse. In China doctors are crooks and charlatans. They take your money and make everything worse, or if you're lucky, exactly the same. I lost my hearing in this ear running away from boys who were throwing bricks. Why were they throwing bricks? Who knows. There was a violence back then no one can understand now. And where did those boys get the bricks? That's the real question. In those days no one had brick houses. Everyone lived like animals. You wouldn't have been able to tell your nainai had skin as white as a porcelain doll because she was covered in dirt. These rotten boys chased me until I tripped over a fence and a sharp spike of wood pierced my eardrum. I lay there for a night until the shepherd's daughter found me, curled up like a child."

"I thought you lost your hearing when a horse ran over a fence and trampled you."

"They took me to the village doctor and he grafted skin from my knee to my ear. I was bleeding so much I thought I would die. That was the worst I've ever experienced, and I've experienced awful things. Your nainai has lived through two wars and saw her own mother gunned down by Japanese soldiers. No child should see their mother die. But do you know what was worse than lying there in the mud with blood in my ears? Worse than seeing my own brother come back from war with only half a leg and no right arm? It was living in China with your grandfather, who didn't have the decency to die like he said he would, and being thousands of miles apart from you and your brother. I was hurting for your brother so much I told your lowlife grandfather that unless he died right this instant, he would have to learn to leave this world just as he came into it—without me. What could he do? Stop me from going to America? I said to him, 'Come with me if you need me around so badly.' 'But no,' he says. 'I'm comfortable here. This is our home. You should want to live in it with me. These are our golden years.' Blah blah blah. My home is where you and your brother are. Oh, I've missed him like I miss the skin from my knee."

"You just met him today."

"Speak louder, my heart, so your nainai can hear you."

"My mom says I can only call my grandmother on my dad's side nainai, and you're actually my waipo."

"Your father said he's going to replace this hearing aid. I might as well have kept that spike of wood in here. They wouldn't know technology from the inside of their asses in China. And it's filthy over there. Can you imagine some illiterate doctor with dirty hands touching your nainai's ear? This is why I couldn't stay in China. I missed your brother's birth because your grandfather said he was dying, and then I go back and guess who isn't dying? Guess who's walking around the garden and smoking? Every day he goes to the *lao ganbu huodongshi* to gamble. Does that seem like a man on his deathbed to you, my sweetheart, my baobei? Do you think your grandmother will forgive your grandfather for making her miss the birth of her one and only grandson? Will your grandmother fall for his bluff again? Not ever. I'll be here until I pass to another realm, my baobei."

"I'm not going to call you nainai."

"All of my grandchildren call me nainai because nainai is the dearest, closest name you could call a person in your family. You refused to call me waipo when you were little. You said to me, 'You're not my waipo, my waipo is that strange lady over there who feeds me food I don't like and who has a cold bed.' Remember how you said that? Where's your brother now? I missed him so much. I pray hummingbirds peck my eyes and leave their droppings in my pecked-out sockets before I have to experience this heartbreak again. But I'm healing already. When I see your brother's precious face, I'll never know sadness again. My heart will be overrun with joy until my last dying breath. Where's your brother, baobei?"

THE THIRD TIME MY GRANDMOTHER came to live with us, I was 15 and my brother was 5. "Please don't let her get to you again like last time," I said to him. "You were obsessed with her."

"No, Stacey. Was not."

But soon he was sleeping in her bed again and talking back to my parents and getting mad when I wouldn't let him have the last Rice Krispies Treat. Whenever he was upset with me, he ran to my grand-mother, and she would come into my room and pretend to spank me in front of him, when really she was just clapping her hands near my ass.

"Your sister is crying so hard from my spanking," my grandmother said to my brother. "See? Nainai is punishing your sister for taking what's rightfully yours. You hear how hard I'm spanking her? Her tears are everywhere."

"I'm not crying," I said over my grandmother's clapping. "I'm not crying," I repeated until I was so frustrated that I actually did start crying.

My brother cried on the weekends when my grandmother went to work at a factory where she folded dumplings for five cents apiece. Most of the other workers could do only fifty an hour, and when the owner noticed my grandmother typically clocked in at a hundred and was teaching her trade secrets to the other ladies during their fifteen-minute lunch break, he instituted "quality control" rules, mandating a certain amount of flour on each dumpling and folds at the edge between 0.4 and 0.6 centimeters. My grandmother pointed out that he was arbi-trarily docking pay for "unfit dumplings" without any real inspection, and all the dumplings she folded, including the unacceptable ones, were thrown into the same freezer bags, and that was exploitative. She per-suaded the other workers to collectively demand back pay for all the rejected dumplings, and even organized a walkout one morning for higher wages. "Six cents a dumpling!" they chanted. The owner caved, and that day my grandmother came home pumping her fists like she was at a pep rally. Listening to her recount the day's victory, even I had to admit that she'd done a great thing.

"Don't you worry," she said, "you'll grow up to be just like your nai-nai one day."

"See, Grandma's a hero," Allen said. "She can do anything."

"Ugh," I said. "She just did it to get paid more. What's so great about that?"

I tried to save my brother, but my grandmother was too cunning. When we walked around the neighborhood at night, he hid inside her big, long nightgown. If I tried to ignore them, my grandmother would tap me on the shoulder until I turned around and then she would ask, "Where did your brother go?" and I'd begin to say, "Oh God, no, please no," but it was always too late—by then, my grandmother had already flipped her dress up to expose my brother, tumbling out from under her and onto the grass.

"I'm alive," he shouted. "I'm born. I'm born. I'm zero years old. I'm born. I'm suddenly born."

"That's how you were born," my grandmother cried out. "It was beautiful and majestic and everyone cried, and I cried the most. When you fell out of me, you awakened the gods and made them turn this world from an evil, corrupt world into one that is good and beneficent, eliminating poverty and hunger and violent death."

"You have to stop doing this with her," I said to him. "That's not how you were born and you know it."

"Grandma says it is."

"She's wrong," I said.

"And when your brother was little," my grandmother shouted with her hands in the air as if waiting to receive something promised to her, "he suckled on my breast because your mother's milk dried up, but my breasts have always produced milk whenever my grandchildren were born. Your cousin drank from my nipple too, but no one drank as hungrily as your brother. He drank until it was all dried up. And when it hurt for me to produce any more, he would cry out in anguish for it. I had to pray to the gods for more milk so your brother could go on."

"This is disgusting. This never happened," I said, but as usual no one was listening, not the trees that bent away from me; not the road ahead that sloped up and curved into a C; not my grandmother, who only heard what she wanted to hear; not my brother, who was being slowly poisoned by her; not my parents, who didn't listen when I said they'd lose my brother if they didn't start spending more time with us. What time? my father demanded. Yes, what time? my mother asked. Should we stop working and paying our mortgage and saving for your college fund? Should we go back to sleeping ten people to a room where someone's kid was screaming all night about needing to scratch her legs? Should we stop eating and stop owning clothes and a car for this "time" you speak so highly of?

But I knew what I knew. One day, he'd be 16 and still cowering underneath our grandmother's dress, clinging to her before she woke him up, waiting for her to make lunch or clear away dinner, curled up around her like a twisted vine in the living room. Don't you want more than this? I would ask him. Don't you want to make friends and kiss someone you aren't related to? And he would say, No, I just want nainai, and then I'd see her next to him, with her toothless nighttime smile and small, satisfied eyes, and the outrageous lies she inserted into our lives until they became strange trivia in our family history, and there was nothing any of us could do to stop it from being that way.

ONE AFTERNOON I CAME HOME to an empty house. An hour later, I saw my brother and my grandmother walking down the street, hand in hand. He was sweating even though it was still winter.

"Why are you sweating like that?"

"I was jumping."

"Jumping?"

"Grandma did it too."

"She was jumping with you?"

"Yeah. On that bouncing thing."

"What bouncing thing?"

"There's a purple bouncing thing and Grandma said it was OK to play on it."

"You mean a trampoline?"

"What's a trampoline?"

I drew him a picture of our grandmother in her nightgown suspended over a trampoline and, in the distance, five cops with their guns raised and pointed at her. Over their heads, I drew a collective dialogue bubble: *Kill her! It's the LAW!!!!!*

"Oh yeah, that's the bounce thing," he said, ripping the police officers out of the picture. "It was at the purple house."

"Let me get this straight. There's a purple trampoline in that purple house down the street where no one lives?"

"Not *in* the house. In the backyard. Grandma said I could jump on it. She did first."

"She jumped on the trampoline?"

"Like thirty times."

"Did you tell her to?"

"No, she just did it on her own. Then she was like, 'Allen, come jump on the trampoline with nainai.'"

"My God. You two are criminals. How many times did you do it?"

"Jump on the thing?"

"How many times did Grandma take you there?"

"I don't know. Every day."

"Jesus," I said. "Didn't you see my picture? You're breaking the law."

"No, we're not."

"Yes, you are, and you're going to go to jail if someone finds out. I could call the police right now," I said, walking toward the kitchen phone.

"Stacey, don't. Please don't put Grandma in jail."

"Who cares if she goes to jail?"

"I don't want her to. Please, Stacey."

"Who would you rather go to jail, then? Someone has to go. Mom or Grandma?"

"Mom."

"I can't believe you just said that."

"I don't know."

"This is stupid," I said.

"Don't call the police, Stacey. Grandma didn't do anything."

"Grandma didn't do anything," I said, imitating him.

o   o   o

S HE LEFT THAT YEAR after a neighbor's dog knocked her down against the asphalt. She split her head open and had to get stitches, several CAT scans that turned up inconclusive, and an MRI. She had overstayed her visa and we didn't have insurance for her, so the hospital bills ended up burning through several months of my parents' savings. They were never able to diagnose her with anything, but she complained of frequent headaches and started sleepwalking. Once, our neighbor down the street, a retired judge who'd fought in Vietnam and walked on crutches, returned her to us. "She knocked on my door. Now I'm knocking on yours."

"We have to send her home or we'll have to sell our home just to keep her alive," my father said to my mother, later.

"I know," she said. "She won't go. But I know."

Things reached peak crisis mode when one night my grandmother sleepwalked her way to the main road and stepped out into oncoming traffic, causing a four-car pileup and several police to show up at our door.

"I won't send her back in a body bag," I overheard my mother say to my father.

"We'll have to tell her that she either leaves on her own accord or INS will have her deported and banned from ever coming back."

"I'm not going to lie to her."

"Do you think she agonizes like you do every time she tells a lie? Look, I know you want to be fair to her, but this isn't the time to be virtuous."

The night my grandmother left, I told my brother she was never coming back and he tried to hit himself in the face with closed fists.

"You have to get used to this," I said, holding his hands together. "I know how you feel. I felt this way once, too. I thought I was going to die without her. But it's not so bad. You think it is now, but it's nothing. You just have to get used to it. Every day you'll miss her less. And then one day, you won't even think about her at all. I promise. And you can always talk to me if you feel sad."

He wasn't listening. His face was red all over like someone had slapped every part of it. The only time I had ever heard someone cry so violently was in a documentary about the Vietnam War. This village woman had jumped into her dead husband's freshly dug grave. She wanted to be buried with him. The sight and sound of her crying, seized-up body being dragged out of her husband's grave haunted me for days.

"This is a good thing, Allen. It's not even the worst thing you'll ever experience. Honestly, I'm happy. I'm happy she's gone, and you know what? I won't let you ruin this moment for me," I said, my voice cracking a little.

T HE FOURTH AND FINAL TIME my grandmother came to live with us, I was 17. My brother had forgotten her in the two years that had elapsed. He and I were close again. He slept on my floor or in my bed whenever I let him and played computer games with headphones on while I did my homework. He asked me to sit with him when he practiced the violin, which he was terrible at, though it wounded him if I laughed. When my friends came over, he lurked in the corner pretending to check the doorframe for bugs. I told him he couldn't always attach himself to someone, even though I liked it. I liked his small body leaning on mine in restaurant booths, and the way he pulled his chair up close to mine at home and sat with half his body on my chair, and how he often said he wished I didn't have homework or friends so I could spend all my time with him.

My grandmother tried to get him to sleep with her at night again, but he only wanted to sleep in my room. He taunted her sometimes, like when she asked if he would get under her dress like old times, and he did, but then punched her between her legs and scurried out and into my room. That was one of many days when she came and sat on the edge of my bed, waiting for my brother to apologize and tell her that he loved her and never meant to hurt her, but he never did.

This time around she was deafer than ever and wore hearing aids in both ears. They were a new model my father had purchased at Costco but worked just as poorly because she'd only use five-year-old batteries. Sometimes I saw her in her bedroom taking old batteries out and putting new old batteries in. She'd developed new interests and was teaching herself calligraphy and the history of American Indians. "America belongs to the Chinese," she said. "We were the first to settle North America."

"I thought the Native Americans were first."

"The Indians are the Chinese. Christopher Columbus saw Chinese faces and called them Indians. We invented spices and gum and paper, block painting on wood and then movable type for paper, paper money, gunpowder, fireworks, tea, silk spinning, alchemy, which later became modern chemistry, navigational tools for maritime exploration, weapons for war and machines for peace. That is why China sits in the center of the map."

"Not in American classrooms."

"This is why you should be proud to be Chinese."

"Nainai, the Chinese aren't Indians."

"The first Africans were Chinese. The first South Americans were Chinese. No one lived in Australia for a long time. The civilization there was and is backward. Just think—all of North and South America, all of Africa, and most of Eastern Europe, all of Russia, Siberia—all first settled by the Chinese."

All of her was laid bare now—I saw her. She was just an old woman, raised in the country without education, who'd been told as a girl that women had been put on this earth to give birth and rear children and not be a burden in any way but to live as servants lived, productively, without fatigue or requirements of their own, yet had been resourceful and clever enough to come up through the feminist movement that Mao had devised to get women out of the house and into fields and factories, who had been given more power than any of the women in her lineage, who alluded to all the people she "saved" but never the people she turned in during the Cultural Revolution, whose hearing loss fed her fears of becoming useless, and who to counter those fears adopted a confidence that was embarrassing to witness, an opinion of herself so excessively high that it bordered on delusional. She tried to make her children believe they would perish without her, and when they learned better she tried the same with her grandchildren. But we were learning better, too, and it would be years before we had our own children, and by then she would be dead. My grandmother's unwillingness to be a victim was both pathetic and impressive, and she deserved compassion. But fuck, why did she have to be so greedy for it? It repulsed me that she wanted my brother and me to love her more than we loved our own parents, more than we loved each other, more even than we loved ourselves.

So I taunted her. I ignored her. I told her that she spoke Chinese like a farmer, the deepest cut I could make. "Here comes the Trail of Tears," my brother and I would say whenever we heard her whimper and sniffle. We bet on how long she could hold out, sitting on the edge of my bed and being ignored by us, before she went downstairs to practice her calligraphy. She had a third-grade education and was teaching herself characters so that she could write a book about her grandchildren.

"The world needs to know about you two," she said. For a moment, I was moved. But I knew that for either of us to grow up into the kind of people other people would ever want to know about, we had to leave her behind.

"You should write about your own life, nainai," I said. "People should know about you, too."

"You and your brother are my life," she insisted, tracing the strokes of my Chinese name in the air.

A FTER I GRADUATED HIGH SCHOOL, my parents took my brother and me on a cruise to Canada with some other Chinese families. The night before we left, my brother started crying and wouldn't tell my parents why.

"Are you worried Grandma will be alone in the house crying a Trail of Tears?" I asked him when we were alone.

He nodded. "Don't you feel bad for Grandma, Stacey?"

"I mean, it sucks to be alone in the house, but she can handle it. I know she can. That's life. Not everyone can have everything they want."

"But Grandma doesn't have anything she wants."

"That's not true. She got to go to America four separate times and live with us each time. Some people don't get to come even once. Ever think about that?" Allen's lip was trembling again. "Look, why don't we find her something really cool to bring back from the cruise. Wanna?"

The cruise was so much fun we forgot to get her a gift. On the car ride back, I rifled through my backpack and found an empty mini Coke can with a bendy straw stuck in it. We tossed the straw and wrapped the can in a food-stained pamphlet about onboard ship safety.

"We got you a present, nainai," Allen said.

"It's a souvenir we bought from Ontario," I added.

"Sorry we drank it already."

"Oh, my two precious baobei. You have given me a gift fit for kings." She hugged Allen, then hugged me, then hugged both of us in an embrace so tight that all three of us started crying for different reasons.

That summer, my grandfather wrote to tell her that he was about to be diagnosed with lymphatic cancer. It was real this time, he wrote, and she had to go home and be with him.

"He's a liar, you know," she told me and my brother.

"We know, nainai."

"He's jealous that it's my fourth time in America when he's too chickenshit to come even once. Why should I leave my grandchildren and my real home for that worthless sack of bones?"

She returned to Shanghai shortly afterward. At the last minute, as my father was dragging the last of our grandmother's suitcases to the car, I said that I wanted to go to the airport with them.

"There's no room for both of you," my father said.

"Who said I wanted to go?" Allen said.

"Well, you can't stay alone," my mother said. "I suppose Daddy can stay with Allen."

"Forget it," I said. "It's too complicated."

My grandmother was kneeling next to Allen, who was on the couch playing *Super Smash Brothers*. She was trying to turn his body toward her but he kept shrugging her off.

"My own grandson won't even look at me because I've let him down so completely," she said. "I'm so ashamed. I'd rather die by his side than live a long life in China without him."

"He doesn't give a shit," I mumbled in English.

When we finally got my grandmother into the backseat of the car, she reached through the open window and grabbed Allen's arm. My father started the engine.

"I said I don't want to go," Allen said, and started to cry.

"Oh," my grandmother wailed. "And now he's crying for me."

My father nodded at me, and I stepped between them. It took all my strength to pry her fingers off his arm.

"It'll be too sad for him, nainai," I said quickly. "We love you, have a good trip, see you next time." Allen ran back into the house without looking back or waving. I heard my father raise the windows and engage the child-safety locks. My grandmother was trying to open the door, banging on the window with her fists like an animal. My father backed the car out of the driveway and drove up the C-shaped hill out of view. I heard a familiar low whine by my feet and looked down to see one of her hearing aids on the ground.

"It's like you just won't go," I said. I kicked it away from me, then ran to pick it up. I cradled it in my hand and tenderly brushed the sediment away, just like I did when I found my grandmother three years earlier, fallen on the asphalt, bleeding from her head.

T HE NIGHT MY GRANDMOTHER told me she was leaving again for the third time, I felt strange inside. My father reassured me she would have the very best doctors back home, who would figure out what was going on with her headaches and sleepwalking, and once she was healed she could come back again. I wanted her to get better but I didn't necessarily want her to come back. I lay in bed until everyone was asleep and then crept downstairs and out of the house, as I often did back then. I circled the neighborhood under a sliver of moon and imagined being born to a different family. On the walk back, I stopped in front of the purple house and followed the stepping stones to the backyard.

I had a feeling she would be there, and she was, crouched by the chain-link fence, facing the purple trampoline. "Nainai," I called out, even though I knew she could not hear me. I wanted to jump with her. Though I would forget in a few days, though my resistance to her would rise again, I felt her loneliness and it scared me.

She stepped forward and then she was running, so fast that she looked like a young girl, no longer saggy and round in the middle. She was a straight line—something I could understand, something I could relate to. I closed my eyes, afraid she would trip. When I opened them again she was high in the air, her dress flying up. I knew there might come a time in my life when I would want to sleep next to her again, return to her after the uncertain, shapeless part of my life was over, when no one would mistake me for a child except for her. Her children and children's children were children forever—that was how she planned to become God and drag us into her eternity.

I was about to run to her, to reveal myself, when I realized she wasn't awake.

"Mother," she said, as she jumped on the trampoline. "Mother, I didn't want to leave you, but I had to go with Father into the mountains. Mother, you told me to take care of my brother and I let him fight and he lost his legs. Mother, I let you down. Mother, you said you wanted to die in my arms and instead I watched our house burn with you inside as I fled to the mountains. I told Father I wanted to get off the horse and die with you and he gripped me to his chest and would not let me get down. Mother, I would have died with you, but you told me to go. I should not have gone."

I took a step toward her. Her eyes were open but they did not see me. In the dark, I thought I would always remember this night and be profoundly altered by having seen her this way. But it was like one of those dreams where you think to yourself while the dream is happening that you must remember the dream when you wake—that if you remember this dream, it will unlock secrets to your life that will otherwise be permanently closed—but when you wake up, the only thing you can remember is telling yourself to remember it. And after trying to conjure up details and images and coming up blank, you think, *Oh well, it was probably stupid anyway,* and you go on with your life, and you learn nothing, and you don't change at all. +

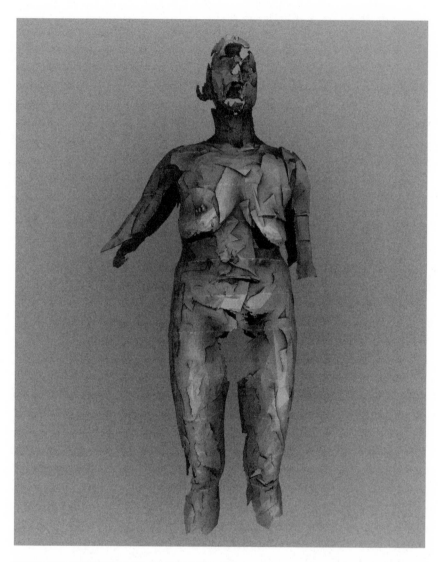

CLAUDIA HART, *SELF SCANNING*. 2014, INKJET PRINT OF A VIRTUAL MODEL ON PAPER. COURTESY OF THE ARTIST.

GHOST IN THE CLOUD

Meghan O'Gieblyn

" **I** DO PLAN TO BRING BACK MY FATHER," Ray Kurzweil says. He is standing in the anemic light of a storage unit, his frame dwarfed by towers of cardboard boxes and oblong plastic bins. He wears tinted eyeglasses. He is in his early sixties, but something about the light or his posture, his paunch protruding over his beltline, makes him seem older. Kurzweil is now a director of engineering at Google, but this documentary was filmed in 2009, back when it was still possible to regard him as a lone visionary with eccentric ideas about the future. The boxes in the storage unit contain the remnants of his father's life: photographs, letters, newspaper clippings, and financial documents. For decades, he has been compiling these artifacts and storing them in this sepulcher he maintains near his house in Newton, Massachusetts. He takes out a notebook filled with his father's handwriting and shows it to the camera. His father passed away in 1970, but Kurzweil believes that, one day, artificial intelligence will be able to use the memorabilia, along with DNA samples, to resurrect him. "People do live on in our memories, and in the creative works they leave behind," he muses, "so we can gather up all those vibrations and bring them back, I believe."

Technology, Kurzweil has conceded, is still a long way from bringing back the dead. His only hope of seeing his father resurrected is to live to see the Singularity—the moment when computing power reaches an "intelligence explosion." At this point, according to transhumanists such as Kurzweil, people who are merged with this technology will undergo a radical transformation. They will become posthuman: immortal, limitless, changed beyond recognition. Kurzweil predicts this will happen by the year 2045. Unlike his father, he, along with those of us who are lucky enough to survive into the middle of this century, will achieve immortality without ever tasting death.

But perhaps the Apostle Paul put it more poetically: "We will not all sleep, but we shall all be changed."

FIRST READ KURZWEIL'S 1999 book, *The Age of Spiritual Machines*, in 2006, a few years after I dropped out of Bible school and stopped believing in God. I was living alone in Chicago's southern industrial sector and working nights as a cocktail waitress. I was not well. Beyond the people I worked with, I spoke to almost no one. I clocked out at three each morning, went to after-hours bars, and came home on the first train of the morning, my head pressed against the window so as to avoid the specter of my reflection appearing and disappearing in the blackened glass. When I was not working, or drinking, time slipped away from me. The hours before my shifts were a wash of benzo breakfasts and listless afternoons spent at the kitchen window, watching seagulls circle the landfill and men hustling dollys up and down the docks of an electrical plant.

At Bible school, I had studied a branch of dispensational theology that divided all of history into successive stages by which God revealed his truth: the Dispensation of Innocence, the Dispensation of Conscience, the Dispensation of Government . . . We were told we were living in the Dispensation of Grace, the penultimate era, which precedes that glorious culmination, the Millennial Kingdom, when the clouds part and Christ returns and life is altered beyond comprehension. But I no longer believed in this future. More than the death of God, I was mourning the dissolution of this teleological narrative, which envisioned all of history as an arc bending assuredly toward a moment of final redemption. It was a loss that had fractured even my subjective experience of time. My hours had become non-hours. Days seemed to unravel and circle back on themselves.

The Kurzweil book belonged to a bartender at the jazz club where I worked. He was a physics student who whistled Steely Dan songs while counting his register and constantly jotted equations on the backs of cocktail napkins. He lent me the book a couple of weeks after I'd seen him reading it and asked—more out of boredom than genuine curiosity—what it was about. ("Computers," he'd replied, after an unnaturally long pause.) I read the first pages on the train home from work, in the gray and spectral hours before dawn. "The twenty-first century will be different," Kurzweil wrote. "The human species, along with the computational technology it created, will be able to solve age-old problems . . . and will be in a position to change the nature of mortality in a postbiological future."

Kurzweil had his own historical narrative. He divided all of evolution into successive epochs: the Epoch of Physics and Chemistry, the Epoch of Biology, the Epoch of Brains. We were living in the fifth epoch, when human intelligence begins to merge with technology. Soon we would reach the Singularity, the point at which we would be transformed into what Kurzweil called Spiritual Machines. We would transfer or "resurrect" our minds onto supercomputers, allowing us to live forever. Our bodies would become incorruptible, immune to disease and decay, and we would acquire knowledge by uploading it to our brains. Nanotechnology would allow us to remake Earth into a terrestrial paradise, and then we would migrate to space, terraforming other planets. Our powers, in short, would be limitless.

It's difficult to account for the totemic power I ascribed to the book. Its cover was made from some kind of metallic material that shimmered with unexpected colors when it caught the light. I carried it with me everywhere, tucked in the recesses of my backpack, though I was paranoid about being seen with it in public. It seemed to me a work of alchemy or a secret gospel. It's strange, in retrospect, that I was not more skeptical of these promises. I'd grown up in the kind of millenarian sect of Christianity where pastors were always throwing out new dates for the Rapture. But Kurzweil's prophecies seemed different because they were bolstered by science. Moore's Law held that computer processing power doubled every two years, meaning that technology was developing at an exponential rate. Thirty years ago, a computer chip contained 3,500 transistors. Today it has more than one billion. By 2045, the technology would be inside our bodies and the arc of progress would curve into a vertical line.

Many transhumanists like Kurzweil contend that they are carrying on the legacy of the Enlightenment—that theirs is a philosophy grounded in reason and empiricism, even if they do lapse occasionally into metaphysical language about "transcendence" and "eternal life." As I read more about the movement, I learned that most transhumanists are atheists who, if they engage at all with monotheistic faith, defer to the familiar antagonisms between science and religion. Many regard Christianity in particular with hostility and argue that Christians are the greatest obstacle to the implementation of their ideas. In his novel, *The Transhumanist Wager* (2013), Zoltan Istvan, the founder of the Transhumanist political party, imagines Christians will be the ones to oppose the coming cybernetic revolution. Few Christians have shown much interest in transhumanism (or even awareness of it), but the religious right's record of opposing stem-cell research and genetic engineering suggests it would resist technological modifications to the body. "The greatest threat to humanity's continuing evolution," writes transhumanist Simon Young, "is theistic opposition to Superbiology in the name of a belief system based on blind faith in the absence of evidence."

T HOUGH FEW TRANSHUMANISTS would likely admit it, their theories about the future are a secular outgrowth of Christian eschatology. The word *transhuman* first appeared not in a work of science or technology but in Henry Francis Carey's 1814 translation of Dante's *Paradiso*, the final book of the *Divine Comedy*. Dante has completed his journey through Paradise and is ascending into the spheres of heaven when his human flesh is suddenly transformed. He is vague about the nature of his new body. In fact, the metamorphosis leaves the poet, who has hardly paused for breath over the span of some sixty cantos, speechless. "Words may not tell of that transhuman change."

Dante, in this passage, is dramatizing the resurrection, the moment when, according to Christian prophecies, the dead will rise from their graves and the living will be granted immortal flesh. There is a common misunderstanding today that the Christian's soul is supposed to fly up to heaven after death, but the resurrection described in the New Testament is a mass, onetime eschatological event. For centuries, Christians believed that everyone who had ever died was being held in their graves in a state of suspended animation, waiting to be resuscitated on the Day of Resurrection. The apostle Paul—who believed he would live to see the day—describes it as the moment when God "will transform our lowly bodies so that they will be like his glorious body." Much later, Augustine meditated on the "universal knowledge" that would be available to resurrected man: "Think how great, how beautiful, how certain, how unerring, how easily acquired this knowledge then will be." According to the prophecies, Earth itself would be "resurrected," returned to its prelapsarian state. The curses of the fall—death and degeneration—would be reversed and all would be permitted to eat from the tree of life, granting immortality.

The vast majority of Christians throughout the ages have believed these prophecies would happen supernaturally. God would bring them about, when the time came. But since the medieval period, there has also persisted a tradition of Christians who believed that humanity could enact the resurrection through material means: namely, through science and technology. The first efforts of this sort were taken up by alchemists. Roger Bacon, a 13th-century friar who is often considered the first Western scientist, tried to develop an elixir of life that would mimic the effects of the resurrection as described in Paul's epistles. The potion would make humans "immortal" and "uncorrupted," granting them the four dowries that would infuse the resurrected body: *claritas* (luminosity), *agilitas* (travel at the speed of thought), *subtilitas* (the ability to pass through physical matter), and *impassibilitas* (strength and freedom from suffering).

The Enlightenment failed to eradicate projects of this sort. If anything, modern science provided more varied and creative ways for Christians to envision these prophecies. In the late 19th century, a Russian Orthodox ascetic named Nikolai Fedorov was inspired by Darwinism to argue that humans could direct their own evolution to bring about the resurrection. Up to this point, natural selection had been a random phenomenon, but now, thanks to technology, humans could intervene in this process. "Our body," as he put it, "will be our business." He suggested that the central task of humanity should be resurrecting everyone who had ever died. Calling on biblical prophecies, he wrote: "This day will be divine, awesome, but not miraculous, for resurrection will be a task not of miracle but of knowledge and common labor." He speculated that technology could be harnessed to return Earth to its Edenic state. Space travel was also necessary, since as Earth became more and more populated by the resurrected dead, we would have to inhabit other planets.

Fedorov had ideas about how science could enact the resurrection, but the details were opaque. The universe, he mused, was full of "dust" that had been left behind by our ancestors, and one day scientists would be able to gather up this dust to reconstruct the departed. Another option he floated was hereditary resurrection: sons and daughters could use their bodies to resurrect their parents, and the parents, once reborn, could bring back their own parents. Despite the archaic wording, it's difficult to ignore the prescience underlying these ideas. Ancestral "dust" anticipates the discovery of DNA. Hereditary resurrection prefigures genetic cloning.

This theory was carried into the 20th century by Pierre Teilhard de Chardin, a French Jesuit priest and paleontologist who, like Fedorov, believed that evolution would lead to the Kingdom of God. In 1949, Teilhard proposed that in the future all machines would be linked to a vast global network that would allow human minds to merge. Over time, this unification of consciousness would lead to an intelligence explosion—the Omega Point—enabling humanity to "break through the material framework of Time and Space" and merge seamlessly with the divine. The Omega Point is an obvious precursor to Kurzweil's Singularity, but in Teilhard's mind, it was how the biblical resurrection would take place. Christ was guiding evolution toward a state of glorification so that humanity could finally merge with God in eternal perfection. By this point, humans would no longer be human. Perhaps the priest had Dante in mind when he described these beings as "some sort of Trans-Human at the ultimate heart of things."

Transhumanists have acknowledged Teilhard and Fedorov as forerunners of their movement, but the religious context of their ideas is rarely mentioned. Most histories of the movement attribute the first use of the term *transhumanism* to Julian Huxley, the British eugenicist and close friend of Teilhard's who, in the 1950s, expanded on many of the priest's ideas in his own writings—with one key exception. Huxley, a secular humanist, believed that Teilhard's visions need not be grounded in any larger religious narrative. In 1951, he gave a lecture that proposed a nonreligious version of the priest's ideas. "Such a broad philosophy," he wrote, "might perhaps be called, not Humanism, because that has certain unsatisfactory connotations, but Transhumanism. It is the idea of humanity attempting to overcome its limitations and to arrive at fuller fruition."

The contemporary iteration of the movement arose in San Francisco in the late 1980s among a band of tech-industry people with a libertarian streak. They initially called themselves Extropians and communicated through newsletters and at annual conferences. Kurzweil was one of the first major thinkers to bring these ideas into the mainstream and legitimize them for a wider audience. His ascent in 2012 to a director of engineering position at Google, heralded, for many, a symbolic merger between transhumanist philosophy and the clout of major technological enterprise. Transhumanists today wield enormous power in Silicon Valley—entrepreneurs such as Elon Musk and Peter Thiel identify as believers—where they have founded think tanks like Singularity University and the Future of Humanity Institute. The ideas proposed by the pioneers of the movement are no longer abstract theoretical musings but are being embedded into emerging technologies at places like Google, Apple, Tesla, and SpaceX.

L OSING FAITH IN GOD in the 21st century is an anachronistic experience. You end up contending with the kinds of things the West dealt with more than a hundred years ago: materialism, the end of history, the death of the soul. During the early years of my faithlessness, I read a lot of existentialist novels, filling their margins with empathetic exclamation points. "It seems to me sometimes that I do not really exist, but I merely imagine I exist," muses the protagonist of André Gide's *The Counterfeiters*. "The thing that I have the greatest difficulty in believing in, is my own reality." When I think back on that period of my life, what I recall most viscerally is an unnamable sense of dread—an anxiety that would appear without warning and expressed itself most frequently on the landscape of my body. There were days I woke in a panic, certain that I'd lost some essential part of myself in the fume of a blackout, and would work my fingers across my nose, my lips, my eyebrows, and my ears until I assured myself that everything was intact. My body had become strange to me; it seemed insubstantial. I went out of my way to avoid subway grates because I believed I could slip through them. One morning, on the train home from work, I became convinced that my flesh was melting into the seat.

At the time, I would have insisted that my rituals of self-abuse—drinking, pills, the impulse to put my body in danger in ways I now know were deliberate—were merely efforts to escape; that I was contending, however clumsily, with the overwhelming despair at the absence of God. But at least one piece of that despair came from the knowledge that my body was no longer a sacred vessel; that it was not a temple of the holy spirit, formed in the image of God and intended to carry me into eternity; that my body was matter, and any harm I did to it was only aiding the unstoppable process of entropy for which it was destined. To confront this reality after believing otherwise is to experience perhaps the deepest sense of loss we are capable of as humans. It's not just about coming to terms with the fact that you will die. It has something to do with suspecting there is no difference between your human flesh and the plastic seat of the train. It has to do with the inability to watch your reflection appear and vanish in a window without coming to believe you are identical with it.

What makes the transhumanist movement so seductive is that it promises to restore, through science, the transcendent hopes that science itself obliterated. Transhumanists do not believe in the existence of a soul, but they are not strict materialists, either. Kurzweil claims he is a "patternist," characterizing consciousness as the result of biological processes, "a pattern of matter and energy that persists over time." These patterns, which contain what we tend to think of as our identity, are currently running on physical hardware—the body—that will one day give out. But they can, at least in theory, be transferred onto nonbiological substrata: supercomputers, robotic surrogates, or human clones. A pattern, transhumanists would insist, is not the same as a soul. But it's not difficult to see how it satisfies the same longing. At the very least, a pattern suggests that there is, embedded in the meat of our bodies, some spark that remains unspoiled even as our body ages; that there is some essential core of our being that will survive and perhaps transcend the inevitable degradation of flesh.

Of course, mind uploading has spurred all kinds of philosophical anxieties. If the pattern of your consciousness is transferred onto a computer, is the pattern "you" or a simulation of your mind? Another camp of transhumanists have argued that Kurzweil's theories are essentially dualistic, and that the mind cannot be separated from the body. You are not "you" without your fingernails and your gut bacteria. Transhumanists of this faction insist that resurrection can happen only if it is *bodily* resurrection. They tend to favor cryonics and bionics, which promise to resurrect the entire body or else supplement the living form with technologies to indefinitely extend life.

It is perhaps not coincidental that an ideology that grew out of Christian eschatology would come to inherit its philosophical problems. The question of whether the resurrection would be corporeal or merely spiritual was an obsessive point of debate among early Christians. One faction, which included the Gnostic sects, argued that only the soul would survive death; another insisted that the resurrection was not a true resurrection unless it revived the body. For these latter believers—whose view would ultimately become orthodox—Christ served as the model. Jesus had been brought back in the flesh, which suggested that the body was a psychosomatic unit. In contrast to Hellenistic philosophy, which believed the afterlife would be purely spiritual, Christians came to believe that the soul was inseparable from the body. In one of the most famous treatises on the resurrection, the theologian Tertullian of Carthage wrote: "If God raises not men entire, He raises not the dead. . . . Thus our flesh shall remain even after the resurrection."

Transhumanists, in their eagerness to preempt charges of dualism, tend to sound an awful lot like these early church fathers. Eric Steinhart, a "digitalist" philosopher at William Paterson University, is among the transhumanists who insist the resurrection must be physical. "Uploading does not aim to leave the flesh behind," he writes; "on the contrary, it aims *at the intensification of the flesh.*" The irony is that transhumanists are arguing these questions as though they were the first to consider them. Their discussions give no indication that these debates belong to a theological tradition that stretches back to the earliest centuries of the Common Era.

W HILE THE EFFECTS OF my deconversion were often felt physically, the root causes were mostly cerebral. My doubts began in earnest during my second year at Bible school, after I read *The Brothers Karamazov* and entertained, for the first time, the implications of the classic theodicies—the problem of hell, how evil could exist in a world created by a benevolent God. In our weekly dormitory prayer groups, my classmates would assure me that all Christians struggled with these questions, but the stakes in my case were higher because I was planning to join the mission field after graduation. I nodded deferentially as my friends supplied the familiar apologetics, but afterward, in the silence of my dorm room, I imagined myself evangelizing a citizen of some remote country and crumbling at the moment she pointed out those theological contradictions I myself could not abide or explain.

Still, mine was a glacial severance from the faith. I knew other people who had left the church, and was amazed at how effortlessly they had seemed to cast off their former beliefs, immersing themselves instead in the pleasures of epicureanism or the rigors of humanitarian work. Perhaps I clung to the faith because, despite my doubts, I found—and still find—the fundamental promises of Christianity beautiful, particularly the notion that human existence ultimately resolves into harmony. What I could not reconcile was the idea that an omnipotent and benevolent God could allow for so much suffering. I agreed with Ivan Karamazov that even the final moment of glorification could never cancel out the pain and anguish it was meant to redeem.

Transhumanism offered a vision of redemption without the thorny problems of divine justice. It was an evolutionary approach to eschatology, one in which humanity took it upon itself to bring about the final glorification of the body and could not be blamed if the path to redemption was messy or inefficient. Within months of encountering Kurzweil, I became totally immersed in transhumanist philosophy. By this point, it was early December and the days had grown dark. The city was besieged by a series of early winter storms, and snow piled up on the windowsills, silencing the noise outside. I increasingly spent my afternoons at the public library, researching things like nanotechnology and brain-computer interfaces.

Once, after following link after link, I came across a paper called "Are You Living in a Computer Simulation?" It was written by the Oxford philosopher and transhumanist Nick Bostrom, who used mathematical probability to argue that it's "likely" that we currently reside in a Matrix-like simulation of the past created by our posthuman descendants. Most of the paper consisted of esoteric calculations, but I became rapt when Bostrom started talking about the potential for an afterlife. If we are essentially software, he noted, then after we die we might be "resurrected" in another simulation. Or we could be "promoted" by the programmers and brought to life in base reality. The theory was totally naturalistic—all of it was possible without any appeals to the supernatural—but it was essentially an argument for intelligent design. "In some ways," Bostrom conceded, "the posthumans running a simulation are like gods in relation to the people inhabiting the simulation."

It began as an abstract theological preoccupation. I didn't think it was likely we were living in a simulation, but I couldn't help musing about how the classic theodicies I'd struggled with in Bible school would play out in a simulated cosmology. I thought I'd put these problems to rest, but that winter they burbled back to the surface. It would happen unexpectedly. One moment I'd be waiting for the bus or doodling on a green guest-check pad during the slow hours of my shift; the next, I'd be rehashing Pascal, Leibniz, and Augustine, inserting into their arguments the term *programmers* instead of *God*. I wondered: Could the programmers be said to be omniscient? Omnipotent? Benevolent? Computers got bugs that eluded even their creators. What if evil was nothing more than a glitch in the Matrix? Christian theology relied on a premise of divine perfection; God himself was said to be perfect, and he was capable, in theory, of creating a perfect universe. But what if our creator was just a guy in a lab running an experiment? The novelist John Barth, I recalled, had once jokingly mused that the universe was a doctoral candidate's dissertation, one that would earn its author a B–.

One afternoon, deep in the bowels of an online forum, I discovered a link to a cache of "simulation theology"—articles written by fans of Bostrom's theory. According to the "Argument for Virtuous Engineers," it was reasonable to assume that our creators were benevolent because the capacity to build sophisticated technologies required "long-term stability" and "rational purposefulness." These qualities could not be cultivated without social harmony, and social harmony could be achieved only by virtuous beings. The articles were written by software engineers, programmers, and the occasional philosopher. Some appeared on personal blogs. Others had been published in obscure, allegedly peer-reviewed journals whose interests lay at the intersection of philosophy, technology, and metaphysics.

I also found articles proposing how one should live in order to maximize the chances of resurrection. Try to be as interesting as possible, one argued. Stay close to celebrities, or become a celebrity yourself. The more fascinating you are, the more likely the programmers will hang on to your software and resurrect it. This was sensible advice, but it presumed the programmer was a kind of deist's God who set the universe in motion and then sat back to watch and be entertained. Was it not just as probable that the programmer had a distinct moral agenda, and that he punished or rewarded his simulated humans based on their adherence to this code? Or that he might even intervene in the simulation? The deeper I got into the articles, the more unhinged my thinking became. One day, it occurred to me: perhaps God *was* the designer and Christ his digital avatar, and the incarnation his way of entering the simulation to share tips about our collective survival as a species. Or maybe the creation of our world was a competition, a kind of video game in which each participating programmer invented one of the world religions, sent down his own prophet-avatar, and received points for every new convert.

By this point I'd passed beyond idle speculation. A new, more pernicious thought had come to dominate my mind: transhumanist ideas were not merely similar to theological concepts but could in fact *be* the events described in the Bible. It was only a short time before my obsession reached its culmination. I got out my old study Bible and began to scan the prophetic literature for signs of the cybernetic revolution. I began to wonder whether I could pray to beings outside the simulation. I had initially been drawn to transhumanism because it was grounded in science. In the end, I became consumed with the kind of referential mania and blind longing that animates all religious belief.

I 'VE SINCE HAD TO DISTANCE MYSELF from prolonged meditation on these topics. People who once believed, I've been told, are prone to recidivism. Over the past decade, as transhumanism has become the premise of Hollywood blockbusters and a passable topic of small talk among people under 40, I've had to excuse myself from conversations, knowing that any mention of simulation theory or the noosphere can send me spiraling down the gullet of that techno-theological rabbit hole.

This is not to say that I have outgrown those elemental desires that drew me to transhumanism—just that they express themselves in more conventional ways. Over the intervening years, I have given up alcohol, drugs, sugar, and bread. On any given week, my Google search history is a compendium of cleanse recipes, HIIT workouts, and the glycemic index of various exotic fruits. I spend my evenings in the concrete and cavernous halls of a university athletic center, rowing across virtual rivers and cycling up virtual hills, guided by the voice of my virtual trainer, Jessica, who came with an app that I bought. It's easy enough to justify these rituals of health optimization as more than mere vanity, especially when we're so frequently told that physical health determines our mental and emotional well-being. But if I'm honest with myself, these pursuits have less to do with achieving a static state of well-being than with the thrill of possibility that lies at the root of all self-improvement: the delusion that you are climbing an endless ladder of upgrades and solutions. The fact that I am aware of this delusion has not weakened its power over me. Even as I understand the futility of the pursuit, I persist in an almost mystical belief that I can, through concerted effort, feel better each year than the last, as though the trajectory of my life led toward not the abyss but some pinnacle of total achievement and solution, at which point I will dissolve into pure energy. Still, maintaining this delusion requires a kind of willful vigilance that can be exhausting.

I was in such a mood last spring when a friend of mine from Bible school, a fellow apostate, sent me an email with the title "robot evangelism." "I seem to recall you being into this stuff," he said. There was a link to an episode of *The Daily Show* that had aired a year ago. The video was a satiric report by the correspondent Jordan Klepper called "Future Christ." The gist was that a Florida pastor, Christopher Benek, believed that in the future AI could be evangelized and brought to salvation just like humans.

"How does a robot become Christian?" Klepper asked.

"We're not talking about a Roomba or your iPhone," Benek replied. "We're talking about something that's exponentially more intelligent than we are." He was young for a pastor—late thirties, maybe even younger. He wore a navy blazer and was sweating liberally beneath the studio lights.

"You're saying that robots, given the ability to have higher thought, they will choose Christianity."

"Yeah," Benek replied. "I think it's a reasoned argument."

The segment ended with Klepper taking a telepresence robot around to different places of worship—a mosque, a synagogue, a Scientology booth—to see which religion it would choose. The interview had been heavily edited, and it wasn't really clear what Benek believed, except that robots might one day be capable of spiritual life, an idea that failed to strike me as intrinsically absurd. Pope Francis had recently declared his willingness to baptize aliens. These were strange times to be a man of the cloth, but at least people were thinking ahead.

I googled Benek. He had an MDiv from Princeton. He described himself in his bio as a "techno-theologian, futurist, ethicist, Christian Transhumanist, public speaker and writer." He also chaired the board of something called the Christian Transhumanism Association. I followed a link to the organization's website, which was professional looking but sparse. It included that peculiar quote from Dante: "Words cannot tell of that transhuman change." All this seemed unlikely. Was it possible there were now Christian Transhumanists? Actual believers who thought the Kingdom of God would come about through the Singularity? All this time I had thought I was alone in drawing these parallels between transhumanism and biblical prophecy, but the convergences seemed to have gained legitimacy from the pulpit. How long would it be before everyone noticed the symmetry of these two ideologies—before Kurzweil began quoting the Gospel of John and Bostrom was read alongside the minor prophets?

I MET WITH BENEK at a café across the street from his church in Fort Lauderdale. In my email to him, I'd presented my curiosity as journalistic, unable to admit—even to myself—what lay behind my desire to meet. My grandparents live not too far from his church, so it was easy to pass it off as a casual excursion while visiting family, rather than the point of the trip itself.

He arrived in the same navy blazer he'd worn in *The Daily Show* interview and appeared just as nervous. Throughout the first half hour of our conversation, he seemed reluctant to divulge the full scope of his ideas, as though he was aware that he'd stumbled into an intellectual obsession that was bad for his career. *The Daily Show* had been a disaster, he told me. He had spoken with them for an hour about the finer points of his theology, but the interview had been cut down to his two-minute spiel on robots—something he insisted he wasn't even interested in, it was just a thought experiment he'd been goaded into. "It's not like I spend my days speculating on how to evangelize robots," he said.

The music in the café was not as loud as I would have liked. Several people nearby were flipping aimlessly at their phones in the manner of eavesdroppers trying to appear inconspicuous. I explained that I wanted to know whether transhumanist ideas were compatible with Christian eschatology. Was it possible that technology would be the avenue by which humanity achieved the resurrection and immortality?

I worried that the question sounded a little deranged, but Benek appeared suddenly energized. It turned out he was writing a dissertation on precisely this subject. The title was "The Eschaton Is Technological."

"Technology has a role in the process of redemption," he said. Christians today assume the prophecies about bodily perfection and eternal life are going to be realized in heaven. But the disciples understood those prophecies as referring to things that were going to take place here on Earth. Jesus had spoken of the Kingdom of God as a terrestrial domain, albeit one in which the imperfections of earthly existence were done away with. This idea, he assured me, was not unorthodox; it was just old.

I asked Benek about humility. Wasn't it all about the fallen nature of the flesh and our tragic limitations as humans?

"Sure," he said. He paused a moment, as though debating whether to say more. Finally, he leaned in and rested his elbows on the table, his demeanor markedly pastoral, and began speaking about the Transfiguration. This event, described in several of the Gospels, portrays Jesus climbing to the top of a mountain with three of his disciples. Suddenly, Moses and Elijah appear out of thin air, their bodies encircled with holy light. Then Jesus's appearance is changed. His disciples notice that he "was transfigured before them; his face shining as the sun, and his garments became white as the light." Theologians have identified this as a moment when the temporal and the eternal overlapped, with Christ standing as the bridge between heaven and Earth.

It was a curious passage, Benek said. "Jesus is human, but he's also something else." Christ, he reminded me, was characterized by the hypostatic union: he was both fully human and fully God. What was interesting, he said, was that science had actually verified the potential for matter to have two distinct natures. Superposition, a principle in quantum theory, suggests that an object can be in two places at one time. A photon could be a particle, and it could also be a wave. It could have two natures. "When Jesus tells us that if we have faith nothing will be impossible for us, I think he means that literally."

By this point, I had stopped taking notes. It was late afternoon, and the café was washed in amber light. Perhaps I was a little dehydrated, but Benek's ideas began to make perfect sense. This was, after all, the promise implicit in the incarnation: that the body could be both human and divine, that the human form could walk on water. "Very truly I tell you," Christ had said to his disciples, "whoever believes in me will do the works I have been doing, and they will do even greater things than these." His earliest followers had taken this promise literally. Perhaps these prophecies had pointed to the future achievements of humanity all along, our ability to harness technology to become transhuman. Christ had spoken mostly in parables—no doubt for good reason. If a superior being had indeed come to Earth to prophesy the future to 1st-century

humans, he would not have wasted time trying to explain modern computing or sketching the trajectory of Moore's Law on a scrap of papyrus.
He would have said, "You will have a new body," and "All things will be
changed beyond recognition," and "On Earth as it is in heaven." Perhaps
only now that technologies were emerging to make such prophecies a
reality could we begin to understand what Christ meant about the fate
of our species.

I could sense my reason becoming loosened by the lure of these
familiar conspiracies. Somewhere, in the pit of my stomach, it was
amassing: the fevered, elemental hope that the tumult of the world was
authored and intentional, that our profound confusion would one day
click into clarity and the broken body would be restored. Part of me was
still helpless against the pull of these ideas.

It was late. The café had emptied and a barista was sweeping near
our table. As we stood to go, I couldn't help feeling that our conversation was unresolved. I suppose I'd been hoping that Benek would hand
me some final hermeneutic, or even offer a portal back to the faith, one
paved by the certitude of modern science. But if anything had become
clear to me, it was my own desperation, my willingness to spring at this
largely speculative ideology that offered a vestige of that first religious
promise. I had disavowed Christianity, and yet I'd spent the past ten
years hopelessly trying to re-create its visions by dreaming about our
postbiological future or fixating on the optimization of my own body—a
modern pantomime of redemption. What else could lie behind these
impulses but the ghost of that first hope?

Outside, the heat of the afternoon had cooled to a balmy warmth.
I decided to walk for an hour along the streets of the shopping district,
a palm-lined neighborhood along the canals of the Intracoastal from
where you could glimpse the masts of the marina and, beyond them, the
deep Prussian blue of the Atlantic. Fort Lauderdale is a hub for spring
breakers, but it was only January and the city was still populated by the
moneyed winter set. Argentineans and Chileans and French Canadians
spent all day at the beach and now, in these temperate hours before dusk,
took to the streets in expensive-looking spandex. People jogged along
the gauntlet of beachside boutiques and unfurled polyethylene mats
beneath banyan canopies for yoga in the park. A flock of speed-bikers
swooped along the shoulder and disappeared, leaving in their wake a
faint gust of sweat.

I was thinking of the scene from *Hannah and Her Sisters* where Woody Allen's character, who spends the course of the film searching for the right religion, is in a morbid mood, walking along the footpaths of Central Park. "Look at all these people jogging," he scoffs, "trying to stave off the inevitable decay of the body." I have often felt this way myself when watching people exercise en masse, as though the specter of all those bodies in motion summed up the futility of the whole human project—or perhaps offered an unflattering reflection of my own pathetic striving. But on this particular evening, in the last light of day, there was something mesmerizing in the dance of all these bodies in space. There were old bodies and young bodies, men and women, their limbs tanned and lambent with perspiration. They were stretching and lunging with arms outstretched in a posture of veneration, all of them animated by the same eternal choreography, driven by the echo of that ancient hope. Perhaps it was, in the end, a hope that was rooted in delusion. But was it more virtuous to concede to the cold realities of materialism—to believe, as Solomon did, that we are sediment blowing aimlessly in the wind, dust that will return to dust?

The joggers swept past me on either side of the sidewalk and wove through the crowd, like particles dispersing in a vacuum. All of them were heading in the same direction, up the bridge that crossed the marina and ended at the spread of the ocean. I watched as they receded into the distance and disappeared, one by one. +

FRANÇOISE GROSSEN, *AHNEN GALERIE*. 1997, DYED MANILA ROPE, BRAIDED, TEN BUNDLES, EACH: 13 × 116 × 9".
RACINE ART MUSEUM, PHOTO BY EDWARD ATMAN. COURTESY OF THE ARTIST AND BROWNGROTTA ARTS.

OLD VERANDA

Vinod Kumar Shukla

Vinod Kumar Shukla was born in Rajnandgaon, a small town in central India, in 1937. He attended local schools and went to college in Jabalpur, where he studied agricultural science. For most of his working life he taught at Indira Gandhi Agricultural University, Raipur, from which he retired as associate professor in 1996. His subject was agricultural extension, which involved traveling to the surrounding villages to acquaint farmers with new agricultural techniques.

His meeting with the Marxist poet Gajanan Madhav Muktibodh (1917–1964) is described in "Old Veranda." The encouragement he received from the older poet, who suggested Shukla send his poems to a magazine whose editor he knew, proved to be decisive. Shukla's first collection was a twenty-page chapbook titled Hail India, Almost *(1971), whose ironic title marked him out as a new voice in Hindi poetry. Some of its poems were later collected in his first full-length book,* That Man Put On a New Woolen Coat and Went Away like a Thought *(1981). "There is nothing of me except what is here," Shukla writes in one poem. Shukla's here is a specific place: Raipur, and before that, Rajnandgaon.*

*The author of several works of fiction, three of which have been translated into English—*The Servant's Shirt *(1999),* A Window Lived in a Wall *(2005), and* Once It Flowers *(2014)—Shukla describes lower-middle-class life and its proprieties in elaborate detail. No gesture or flicker of thought is too mundane.*

—Arvind Krishna Mehrotra

T HE HOUSE IN RAIPUR that we moved into later has verandas that are more like rooms. It's hard to say why they aren't rooms, or what makes them verandas. One of them is called the old veranda. The house was built slowly and all at once. Since one of the verandas was the old veranda, the other became the new one. The old veranda of our house in Rajnandgaon is now in the house in Raipur. The pole star in Raipur is the same pole star that was in Rajnandgaon. Because there is the sky and the pole star, the homeless do not feel that they are homeless but that they live in the same one place under the same sky, which is the same everywhere. Even as a little boy in Rajnandgaon, I would think about the universe. However much you may learn about it afterward, you never forget those early associations.

M Y WIFE ASKS, "Do you know where your brass lota is?"
    "It's on the old veranda," I tell her.
    A friend who is sitting there asks, "Isn't the house new?"
    "It is," I say.
    "If you were building a new house, you should've built a new veranda as well."
    "The whole house is new. There used to be a quarry here. It's still around somewhere."
    "How many years ago was the house built?"
    "About seventeen."
    "When will it become old?"
    "Who's to say. When it's torn down."
    "I thought a house was torn down when it was old. Is the old veranda being torn down?"
    "No, it's not. It's the same as it's always been. I don't remember it ever being any different."
    "I should be going. I've got to buy some wheat."
    "Where are you going to buy it?"
    "Gole Bazaar."
    "You won't get new wheat. That only arrives in March."
    "I'll buy the old wheat. There's not a grain left to eat at home."
    "Do you like rotis?" I asked.
    "Yes. But only fresh rotis."
    "Fresh ones?"
    "Hot and fluffy. Not cold and stale."

"I like fermented leftover rice," I say.

"The rice may be fermented, but the grain it's made from is new," he says.

"That man there carrying a pickax must have had some for breakfast," he says, looking toward the road. Someone from the village is walking by with a pickax.

"So you've got this bag and you're going to buy wheat," I say.

"Yes," he says, "to buy wheat."

Then he leaves.

I F A BOY WANTS TO BECOME OLD, he should first add more years to his life. But what kept happening was that the person who was old was not getting old. The place of birth is where you're born. It's never about dying and being born again.

The old veranda in Rajnandgaon ran along the front of the house and the new one was built at right angles to it. The new veranda remained the new veranda even when the house was in ruins. When the foundation for the new veranda was being dug, they found a lot of worthless cowries, enough to fill several gunnysacks. Adjoining the old veranda was the birthing room, where even during the day it was dark inside. The only light came in from the door when it opened, the light like a sentry to keep the darkness from escaping. The darkness of the night remained in the room. In this way there were, in the room, two darknesses.

Whoever entered the birthing room took just two days to forget that there was anything like sunshine. Only the chirping of birds would have told them that it was morning. Had anyone else said that it was morning they wouldn't have believed it. They wouldn't even have believed Ajiya, though her words carried a lot of authority. Sunset happened only when you thought of sunset. If you thought of sunset at high noon it would be sunset. So much so that if you thought of midnight at midday it would be midnight. The birthing room was not a place where you thought of anything except the child who was about to be born.

If you closed your eyes, walked into the birthing room, and there opened them, for a long time it would seem that you hadn't remembered to do so. You could be deceived into thinking that your eyes had forgotten how to see. We stayed away from it irrespective of whether it was occupied or not, nor did we go anywhere near it when we played hide and seek.

Inside the threshold of the birthing room Amma kept her house-hold gods. When someone went into labor the gods were shifted out, and after a month or so they were reinstated. Since ours was a large family this happened twice a year. Sometimes three times. If during the day the darkness did not emerge from the room even when the door was open, at night it would come out even when the door was shut.

Every birthday Amma would tie the year knot. She did not say birthday but used the colloquial word. She'd take a cotton thread dyed with turmeric and tie a knot in it. In the knot she'd put a blade of new grass. We were three brothers, and for each of us there was a separate thread kept in a rusted tin. In the tin was also a yellow two-anna coin, a blackish one-anna bit, and two small betel nuts kept for prayer rituals. The money, even when it was really needed, was never touched. The tin box was kept inside a metal trunk in the birthing room. No one could go into the room without stubbing their toes on the trunk.

A day came when Amma stopped tying the year knots. It would sometimes happen that my knot would get tied on my older brother's thread or my younger brother's knot would be tied on mine. Going by the knots, my younger brother would become much younger than he was and my age would remain constant for several years. Amma would try and keep the record straight by adding more knots. If there were extra knots, she wouldn't allow them to be untied. If at the age of 10 I had twelve knots in my thread, Amma let them be.

Amma would remember birthdays by associating them with events that happened around the same time. Krishna Talkies was inaugurated on the day I was born. The Talkies was built opposite our house. It was Rajnandgaon's first cinema hall and a big moment for the town. It's entirely possible that when, after five weeks, she came out of the birthing room, someone who was going to see a film took me along.

Krishna Talkies was owned by the Sapre brothers. They were my father's and uncle's friends, and they may all have had some business connections as well. The ushers knew us and we had free run of the place. Krishna Talkies was almost a part of our house. When one of us, to escape from the bath that we were being subjected to in the court-yard, slipped naked through the bars of the gate and ran into the Talkies, members of the family would go in search of the *chowkidar* to have the gate opened. Passersby would stop to see what the fuss was about. The family would be afraid lest the boy reach the balcony, where he would be in danger of falling. A hawker selling *rewri* would arrive. He would put his hand through the bars and tempt the boy to come out and get the sweet, so he might catch hold of him. If you saw our house from Krishna Talkies, the house would have looked like an extension of it.

Women would only go to the cinema with other women, not with men. There was a separate entrance for them. The floor sloped toward the screen. It had rows of chairs followed by benches. There were toilets. The women's section took up the back of the hall, but only half of it. The other half had reserved seats. Urine from the women's toilet would spill out and after passing the first-class and second-class seats reach the front of the hall, where the third-class seats were. People would sit crouched, with their legs up on their seats. Few if any wore shoes. When they had to put their feet down they would first light a match to see whether the floor was wet.

One or two people had flashlights, and they usually sat in the first class or balcony. When the electricity went they would shine the flashlights so as to enable those sitting in the front of the hall to see. They would also shine them toward the screen. It gave people the feeling that the electricity had come back and the film would start soon. No one made a noise when the electricity went.

The viewers knew the names of those who were operating the projectors. They were greatly respected because they were the ones showing the films. They were considered to be particularly fortunate because they could watch films day and night. I was too young to understand what *fortunate* meant, though I was fortunate too. I was old enough to know what sadness and happiness were, though sadness was easier to understand. It happened more often and perhaps that's why it was easier. The moments of happiness were few and far between.

The third class was right up in front, where the stage and the projection screen were. Children would lie down on the stage and watch the film from there. I'd often fall asleep. Phulesar Dai would then come looking for me and carry me home. If you knock on the door of the past, the past will come out. Some of it you'll recognize. It will have its age stamped on it. It's not very remarkable to say that I spent my childhood watching the world and watching cinema. Seen from the cinema's point of view, I was just another cinemagoer.

o　o　o

him. It was evening then too, and to me it seemed that it had turned dark only so that Muktibodh could come out with a lantern and dispel the darkness. He was wearing a pajama and a sleeveless *banian*.

Manav Mandir is where Babuji's house used to be. Babuji was my father's brother, the second oldest. He had moved into it while Grandfather was still alive. The house, he said, was built using a mixture of lime, jaggery, lentil paste, and glue. But he fell on bad times and the house had to be sold. Later it burned down, and Manav Mandir Hotel was built in its place. The hotel did not have a door at the entrance, so it was always open. No one who arrived at the hotel had to go away because they found the entrance closed. If people didn't go there, it was simply because they'd decided to go elsewhere.

Once, Amma had given me some money to buy *jalebis*. Moti's shop was where we bought our sweetmeats and it was to the right of our house, on Bharat Mata Chowk. It had been there for ages. The Manav Mandir Hotel had not yet been built then. A dark-skinned man with shaggy curly hair made the jalebis. The *karahi* in which he was making them looked as if it were made of coal and not iron.

I asked him, "So you didn't scrub the karahi today?"

"I haven't scrubbed it in fifteen years," he said.

When I looked at his tangled curls and his oily perspiring face, I didn't have the heart to ask him, "And what about a bath?"

But he said anyway, "And I haven't bathed in eighteen."

GRANDFATHER HAILED FROM JAGATPUR, a small village in Uttar Pradesh. He had come to Rajnandgaon, which was then a native state, and set up a grocery store opposite Moti's shop. The *diwan* of the state was a man called Kutubuddin who would routinely go around the market area to check if everything was in order. One day he stopped in front of Grandfather's new shop and made a few inquiries. Grandfather answered his questions, but he did not stand up and did not fold his hands in greeting. At least this is the story we heard from one of our uncles before he died. "Do you sell liquor?" the diwan asked him. "There's a lot of construction activity going on here," he said. "Why don't you become a contractor?" That's how Grandfather put some of his money into the new business.

Grandfather's family gradually got dispersed. Some of it settled in Rajnandgaon, the rest in nearby towns. If members of the family accidentally came face-to-face, they did not even need to pretend that they hadn't seen each other to go their separate ways. It was not as if they were parting for the first time. They were not meeting for the first time either. When they separated it was as if the separation had been there from the beginning and it had simply continued.

Krishna Talkies showed silent movies when it opened. I imagine that I'm sitting alone, in one of the five hundred seats in the third class, surrounded by quiet. It's a silent film. I have this distinct experience that I, like the film, think in scenes rather than in language, and that the screen on which the thinking takes place is white. I fall asleep in my seat and wake up when I hear a knock. The knock is not outside. It happens inside my mind. I then get up from my seat, still inside the mind. A man sitting behind me in the reserved section gets up and leaves. I don't know the man. He's wearing a blue shirt. I know blue. I know the blue of cloth. More than the cloth, I know the color. The man's wearing a shirt made of blue. The man is wearing blue.

The sky was a bolt of blue cloth. Dina the tailor would call out our names and take our measurements. Because he stitched shirts from blue cloth, we associated him with the sky. Our uncle too got his clothes stitched by Dina. He always wore trousers made from white mercerized cotton manufactured by Rajnandgaon BNC Mills, where he worked as a manager. Dina was also the tailor to Raja Digvijay Das. One day our uncle called me and I went up using the inside stairs. Dina the tailor used the stairs that were on the outside. A bolt of white mercerized cotton had been rolled out on the clean red cement floor, and he measured me for a pair of trousers. Dina lived five or six houses away from us. He dressed like a man from the village but partnered my uncle in bridge at the club. On the day of the Akti festival, I would bring clay dolls for my sisters from Dina's house. Their clothes would be made from tailoring waste and their shiny eyes, their mouths, and ornaments for their hands and feet from silver foil.

The shirt the man in blue was wearing was made from a piece of sky. The day I wore my trousers made of mercerized cotton, my shirt was made from the sky too. I wore it tucked into my trousers and felt as though I were walking on a street that was high up in the air. I was barefoot as always. I took two steps and was over Gudakhu Line. From there, I was not scared when I saw the yard where condemned prisoners were hanged. The first thing that people see when they arrive in this town and come out of the station is Delhi Gate, built to commemorate Queen Victoria's visit to India. Above it was a door of strong gusts of wind that seemed to have been put there for me. I came out of this door wearing my trousers of mercerized cotton and strolled casually over Sadar and Bharkapara. There were others who were walking on air too. The man in a rickshaw coming from the station was returning to Rajnandgaon after many years.

"Back after a long time?" I asked him.

Traveling through the air at great speed was a bus bound for Rajnandgaon. The passengers and the bus driver were shouting with joy. There were no bars on the windows and the passengers waved their hands. Some were standing on the roof of the bus. A pigeon that had flown into it had gotten trapped inside, till a boy standing at the entrance released it.

It was evening, the time when birds return to their nests. All the birds of Rajnandgaon and all the people of Rajnandgaon were returning home. It was a returning crowd.

Since the road that passes through Delhi Gate was not wide enough, other roads were laid alongside it. The gate itself, built to commemorate Queen Victoria's visit, had largely been forgotten. I looked through memory's window and said to my mother, "Amma, I'm going to school." When I turned right from Manav Mandir and reached Urdu School, I realized that my mother had not heard me. So I went back, running all the way, faster than before. Amma was stoking the *chulha* by blowing through a piece of lead pipe and the kitchen was filled with smoke. I was panting when I said to her, "Amma, I'm going to school." "Run along," she replied, putting the pipe down. I was off again and got into the school compound through the place where the wall was broken. I went past the circular school building and reached the primary section. The morning bell had not rung yet.

O N THE IRON FENCING of the town hall, opposite the state high school, is the Latin saying A SOUND MIND IN A SOUND BODY. The words are repeated along the fence so many times that the mumbling is like a strong fence of its own, protecting the ruined garden and its few trees. Beneath one of them is an old man doing his daily exercises, in which he briefly stands up then sits down. Most of the time he's sitting.

M Y NEPHEW WAS BORN in the birthing room the day Raja Sarves-vardas died. He works in the police. His mother, Bittan Jijji, talks a lot about the day when he was born, but as his retirement drew near he began to wonder if his age was not less than what was given in the official record. He wasn't looking forward to retirement. I suggested that he look in the gazetteer, where the date of Raja Sarvesvardas's death would surely be mentioned. If his actual age turned out to be less, I thought to myself, would it make any difference? Who would accept it?

After asking around, he discovered that the *samadhis* of the rajas were behind the Mata Devalaya temple and Raja Sarvesvardas's bore the date of his death.

He said to Bittan Jijji, "Amma, I have to go to Rajnandgaon to find out the year of my birth."

Bittan Jijji said, "Didn't I tell you you were born on the day that Sarvesvardas died?"

My nephew said, "You've said so many times. Today it'll be confirmed."

Bittan Jijji said, "There was so much confusion that day. The constabulary was all turned out in black."

"Who told you?"

"Well, I knew it. Everyone did," Bittan Jijji said.

"How come?"

"They just did. Wear your uniform when you go."

"Why?"

"For no reason in particular."

I said, "You might also inquire at Krishna Talkies. Maybe you'll find the year of my birth written somewhere. I always forget to ask when I'm there."

"A loyal subordinate, that's what I am," the nephew said suddenly, just before leaving. "Not the raja's, a subordinate of the people," he said again, though no one had asked him.

"I am a viewer," I said, closing my eyes. "But not of the world. Of Krishna Talkies," I added, though no one had asked me.

H E WAS POSTED IN BHILAI. It was hard to get a day off from work, but he got permission to go so long as he returned the same evening. He put on his uniform. Rajnandgaon was an hour away. An advantage of the uniform was that the bus conductor didn't accept the fare from him, nor did the bus stop anywhere to pick up passengers. He met an old acquaintance of his at the Rajnandgaon Bus Stand and bought him a cup of tea.

He immediately took a rickshaw to Mata Devalaya and from a distance paid his obeisance to the goddess. He kept the rickshaw waiting. People were beginning to stare at him, his policeman's clothes attracting their attention. He was in a hurry.

Some of the samadhis were in poor shape. One of them looked as if it had recently been cleaned. He moved to the next one. The writing on it was hidden under moss that had dried and turned black, so he could not read what it said. The grass growing beside the samadhi was dry. He pulled some out and scrubbed off the moss. His date of birth was engraved on the raja's samadhi: September 18, 1940. +

Translated from the Hindi by Arvind Krishna Mehrotra and Sara Rai

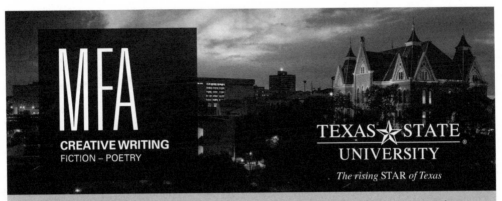

MFA
CREATIVE WRITING
FICTION – POETRY

TEXAS ★ STATE
UNIVERSITY ®
The rising STAR of Texas

Our campus overlooks the scenic Hill Country town of San Marcos, part of the Austin Metropolitan Area. With Austin just 30 miles to the north, Texas State students have abundant opportunities to enjoy music, dining, outdoor recreation, and more.

Tim O'Brien
Professor of Creative Writing
T. Geronimo Johnson
Visiting Professor 2016-17
Karen Russell
Endowed Chair 2017-19

Faculty

Fiction
Doug Dorst
Jennifer duBois
Tom Grimes
Debra Monroe

Poetry
Cyrus Cassells
Roger Jones
Cecily Parks
Kathleen Peirce
Steve Wilson

Visiting Writers*

Elisa Albert
Lydia Davis
Stephen Dunn
Stuart Dybek
Jennifer Egan
Ross Gay
Jorie Graham
Terrance Hayes
Marlon James
Leslie Jamison
Adam Johnson
Ada Limón
Daniel Orozco
Mary Ruefle
Tracy K. Smith

* Recent and upcoming

Adjunct Thesis Faculty

Lee K. Abbott
Gina Apostol
Catherine Barnett
Rick Bass
Kevin Brockmeier
Gabrielle Calvocoressi
Ron Carlson
Victoria Chang
Maxine Chernoff
Eduardo Corral
Charles D'Ambrosio
Natalie Diaz
John Dufresne
Carolyn Forché
James Galvin
Amelia Gray
Saskia Hamilton
Amy Hempel
Bret Anthony Johnston

Li-Young Lee
Karan Mahajan
Nina McConigley
Elizabeth McCracken
Jane Mead
Mihaela Moscaliuc
David Mura
Naomi Shihab Nye
Kirstin Valdez Quade
Spencer Reece
Alberto Ríos
Elissa Schappell
Richard Siken
Gerald Stern
Natalia Sylvester
Justin Torres
Brian Turner
Eleanor Wilner

Now offering courses in creative nonfiction.
Scholarships and teaching assistantships available.
Front Porch, our literary journal: **frontporchjournal.com**

Doug Dorst, MFA Director
Department of English

601 University Drive
San Marcos, TX 78666-4684
512.245.7681

MEMBER **THE TEXAS STATE UNIVERSITY SYSTEM**
Texas State University, to the extent not in conflict with federal or state law prohibits discrimination or harassment on the basis of race, color, national origin, age, sex, religion, disability, veterans' status, sexual orientation, gender identity or expression. Texas State University is a tobacco-free campus. 16-578 6-16

SOPHIA NARRETT, *STILL BURNING*. 2012, EMBROIDERY THREAD AND FABRIC. 33 × 48". COURTESY OF THE ARTIST.

LEAGUE OF MEN

Elizabeth Schambelan

R EREADING THE STORY NOW, the detail I keep returning to is the broken coffee table, the shards of glass. It reminds me of the scene in *Heathers* where Heather No. 1 issues her dying croak—*Corn nuts!*—and then falls, smashing her own glass table. The scene opens with a shot of Heather asleep, not lying down but reclining, in a satin-draped bower. The whole movie has that stylized, magical quality. The same is true of Jackie's story, which is why the article caused such an uproar in the first place. It beggared belief. You read it and thought: *Unbelievable!* And in retrospect, the failures of its naturalism seem so clear. The dark chamber, the silhouetted attackers, gathering close . . . But most of all, it's the table, the crystalline pyrotechnics of its shattering. That's the place where the narrative strains hardest against realism, wanting to move into another register altogether. The shards enchant and wound and scintillate, like the Snow Queen's icy darts. A man's body "barrels into her, tripping her backward." Someone, we're told, is kneeling on her hair. We can picture the strands—"long, dark, wavy"—outspread all around her. I wonder if the model here could be Ophelia as rendered by John Everett Millais: a young woman supine, long tresses floating. Has Jackie ever seen the painting? It's a famous work, and a staple of undergrad art-history classes, which is how I first encountered it. I still have the textbook, one of those volumes in Taschen's Basic Genre series, *Pre-Raphaelites*. I was the type of teenager who liked the Pre-Raphaelites, and *Heathers*. Maybe Jackie has similar tastes. But then what was she doing at a frat party, hanging out with a frat guy?

Speculation is pointless when information is so scant. I've been speculating anyway, intermittently, ever since her story was debunked—speculating about why she told the story in the first place. This has been an exercise in intense frustration. Vague suppositions about her personality and its possible disorders are far from satisfactory. What I'm looking for is something resembling an actual rationale, and this is what has proved elusive. There is no biography, no case history, no leaked documents, nothing at all to go on except the story itself—Jackie's story, as told to Sabrina Erdely, who told it to the world in her now-infamous and now-retracted article. And that is why I keep rereading, not *constantly*, but occasionally, when some random prompt, like a Reddit headline about the civil proceedings against *Rolling Stone*, brings the sorry affair to mind.

But it occurs to me that I've been forgetting one of the basic precepts of my education, which is that a story should not be read as a cryptic map of its author's psychic maladies. The author lies beyond diagnosis, because the author, like Ophelia, is dead. I could read her story the way I was taught to read any story—*as* a story, a work of literature. Such a recalibration opens up other lines of inquiry. For instance, if it's literature, what sort of literature is it? When the specimen is perplexing, begin with the question of kind. What is the category, the Basic Genre?

The story would appear to be a dark pulp-fiction potboiler, melodrama in a gothic vein. But it has no structure to speak of, no real arc, and no suspense, no sense that events are hanging in the balance. To the contrary, a certain inexorability seems to drive the action—people make choices, and yet it feels as if something beyond human volition is at work, some kind of dark enchantment that drives the characters toward their violent rendezvous, which is not a climax in the traditional sense because it's not the culmination of anything. And then there's the question of tone, a particular timbre of weirdness or a specific shade of shadow. These impressions hardly constitute an objective opinion, but my opinion on this matter is admittedly not objective. It's a gut feeling I've attempted to justify with only the slightest effort to correct for my confirmation bias. In my defense, I can only say that taxonomy is an inexact science. My classification of this story as a fairy tale is not necessarily more subjective than any other venture into binomial nomenclature.

The fairy-tale genre has its own internal taxonomy, which is governed by the venerable Aarne-Thompson-Uther system. ATU indexes more than two thousand "tale types" from hundreds of cultures, grouping them under a variety of elaborately nested rubrics (Magic Tales, Stories About a Fool, The Truth Comes to Light, et cetera), and assigning each type a unique code. These designations have long been a lingua franca among researchers, the coordinates in a vast nebula of vernacular narrative.

My first thought on consulting this resource was that Jackie's story should be coded ATU 312, The Bluebeard, a tale type in the Magic category, Supernatural Adversaries subcategory. Angela Carter's retelling is titled "The Bloody Chamber." That's what the frat guy's bedroom is, I thought: the bloody chamber, the site of awful truth, incarnadine. But no—Bluebeard's young wife is on a quest. She's taking risks and she knows she's taking them, defying orders, doing exactly the thing she's been forbidden to do. That's not what happens in Jackie's story. As her tale begins, there is a young woman. She's probably not a virgin, but she's definitely not a wife. A maiden, let's say. She might be looking for sex, romance. Or she might just be trying to get from point A to point B. In any case, she's going about her life, and suddenly this seducer appears.

I T'S SUCH A STRANGE STORY, when you think about it. Not the dark forest, the lurking beast—those elements feel familiar enough. It's the act of impersonation that is so bizarre.

I remember a book from my childhood, the wolf on his hind legs in a dress and apron, with a ruffled lady's cap perched between his ears. It wasn't a scary picture. It was comical and kind of cute. At age 4 or 5, I already understood this was a picture of the past. I knew that the dress and the cap and the whole story were *old-fashioned*, safely cordoned from the present.

But whoever invented the story—ATU 333, another Supernatural Adversaries tale—didn't see it that way, because *old-fashioned* is a modern concept, and the people who invented the story didn't have modernity. They didn't have ruffled caps or gingham aprons or a notion of quaintness to which these garments belonged. And they presumably did not have a concept of the wilderness, not the way we do. We think of the wilderness as bounded and finite. For them, it was the matrix in which everything else took place, the default, always ready to reclaim its territory. What did it feel like to tell this story about a wild beast when the wilderness pressed so close? What did it *look* like, in their heads? If you take away the cozy familiarity of that image—a wolf impersonating a grandmother—what are you looking at?

The story is starkly bifurcated: forest, house. The impersonation happens in part two. Part one is considerably more transparent. Intercepting the girl, the wolf engages, charms, inveigles. In *The Uses of Enchantment*, Bruno Bettelheim puts it flatly: "The wolf... is the seducer." Bettelheim thinks the girl is attracted to the wolf but also frightened of him because she's not yet sexually mature. His influential reading comports with the interpretations of Sigmund Freud, Carl Jung, and Erich Fromm, who all see the beast as a projection of the girl's sexual confusion.

The wolf is a seducer, or he's a rapist whose modus operandi includes a seduction phase. Beyond the psychoanalytic tradition, the latter interpretation predominates. In Carter's brilliant rendition, "The Company of Wolves," the wolf is a handsome if homicidal lycanthrope, and the sex is consensual. But this is a polemical revision, an implicit endorsement of the idea that the canonical tale is "a parable of rape," as Susan Brownmiller argues in *Against Our Will*. Jack Zipes, a leading scholar of fairy tales, agrees. ATU 333 "is about violation or rape," he commented in the London *Telegraph* in 2009.

In view of the foregoing, I feel confident in my classification. The version of the tale that concerns me—Jackie's version—is a loose variation, with additional beasts entering the picture in the second half, and nary a grandmother in sight. But ATU deals in tale *types*: variations, even dramatic ones, are expected. And when you look at her parable's essential lineaments, there really isn't much ambiguity. Interception, flirtation, change of venue, the transformation of seducer into Supernatural Adversary: ATU 333.

FAIRY-TALE EXPERTS are not often quoted in major dailies. Zipes's remarks in the 2009 *Telegraph* article were occasioned by the work of anthropologist Jamie Tehrani, who had used a method called phylogenetics to analyze thirty-five versions of ATU 333. Phylogenetics was developed to evaluate evolutionary relationships among species, but it is also used to study the evolution of cultural phenomena. As the science correspondent Richard Gray reported, Tehrani's genealogical data-crunching indicated that the thirty-five versions of the tale "shared a common ancestor dating back more than 2,600 years." If this finding is accurate, it doesn't necessarily mean that the tale type came into existence around 2,600 years ago; it only means that the recorded versions began to branch, to evolve along separate tracks, at that point. The original story could theoretically be much older.

Last year, in the Royal Society journal *Open Science*, Tehrani and coauthor Sara Graça da Silva published an analysis of some seventy tale types indicating "with a high degree of confidence" that at least thirty-one were rooted in remote antiquity and another nineteen had a "more than 50 percent likelihood" of being similarly aged. Commenting on these findings in another journal, evolutionary biologist Mark Pagel said: "What really interests me is why these cultural forms exist. . . . Why do these things seem to have such longevity?"

Tehrani offered some general but intriguing speculation on that question in a 2013 *PLOS One* article. "The faithful transmission of narratives over many generations and across cultural and linguistic barriers," he wrote,

> is a rich source of evidence about the kinds of information that we find memorable and [are] motivated to pass on to others. Stories like Little Red Riding Hood . . . would seem to embody several features identified in experimental studies as important cognitive attractors in cultural evolution. These include "minimally counterintuitive concepts" (e.g. talking animals) [and] "survival-relevant information" (e.g. the danger presented by predators, both literal and metaphorical).

As defined by anthropologist Pascal Boyer, a minimally counterintuitive concept (MCI) is a concept that meets all but one or two intuitive expectations of a given ontological category. For instance, a wolf that is just like a normal wolf except for the fact that it talks is an MCI. If you keep adding counterintuitive characteristics—the wolf talks, flies, is purple, can turn into water—you will arrive at a maximally counterintuitive concept (MXCI). According to Boyer, an MCI is easier to remember than either a mundane, thoroughly intuitive concept or an MXCI. This memorability is what makes the MCI an important cognitive attractor.

The second type of important cognitive attractor that Tehrani identifies, *survival-relevant information*, needs no explanation. And clearly, ATU 333, aka "Little Red Riding Hood," "Little Red Cap," "Cattarinetta," et cetera, is trying to say something cognitively attractive about predators, literal or metaphoric. The question is what. It tells us to stay away from them, but that is axiomatic where predators are concerned. Other animals don't require a whole cavalcade of concepts to warn them away from creatures that want to eat them (literally or metaphorically), so why should we? There's an issue of economy here, a need to justify the tale's cognitive load. Because human memory is not infinitely capacious, there is a limited amount of space in any oral tradition. If a story, or part of a story, is taking up some of that space, then it's there for a reason.

All the interpreters I've surveyed think ATU 333 works to socialize girls into normative femininity, either by helping them resolve subconscious conflicts (the psychoanalytic model) or by terrorizing them (everybody else's model). Brownmiller argues that the story instills in girls a victim mentality, reinforcing the idea that they are too weak to take risks, and that if they *do* take risks, anything that befalls them is their own fault. By this logic, the moral of the story is not simply *Avoid rapists*; there's an element of preemptive victim blaming as well. Even with this elaboration, however, one detects a mismatch between the simplicity of the message and the convolutions of the plot. *If you stray from the straight and narrow you'll get raped, and your life will be ruined, and we'll all blame you*: there's a short, sharp shock for you, cognitively speaking, especially if you're, like, 5 years old. Threats of violence and draconian sanction tend to stick in the mind all on their own. No need to construct a baroque and bulky narrative edifice.

It's all very murky, like looking at a corroded artifact in a warped, beclouded vitrine. The label says USE UNKNOWN, as museum labels occasionally, hauntingly do. All we can be sure of is that whoever made the thing understood its purpose, and that it *did* have a purpose. At some unknown point in history, ATU 333 made sense—maybe not what we would call sense, rational sense, but sense. Its enchantment had a use, once upon a time.

A BOY IS TRUDGING through the frozen winter steppe. I can picture this vividly. Actually, I don't picture it at all—it's just *there*, a smash cut in a movie in my head. I see it from the point of view of the boy. The icy fur of his hood frames an endless snowscape. The day is very silent, very sunny, very cold. The hood traps a cloud of warmer air, but even within this humid microclimate his face is freezing. His feet crunch through crust then plunge into powder; he sees the crystals of his breath, hears himself breathing, someone else breathing. There's another boy with him, a kid he's known his whole life. Are they best friends? Have they always hated each other? For some reason, my imagination refuses to hazard an opinion on this. Heavy breathing, crunching snow, occasional joking, bickering—two teenage boys, 14, 15—but they're too out of breath to speak much, trudging through the frozen winter steppe. Though they've been psyching themselves up, expressing eagerness to reach their destination, each is secretly consumed by a yearning to turn around and go home.

This is fiction, what I've just written. It might or might not also be history.

I N FEBRUARY 2002, a group of archaeologists working in central France made a startling discovery. Excavating a Gaulish fort known as Gondole, they came upon a grave that contained the skeletons of eight horses and eight men, carefully lined up in two rows. Before burial, the men had been positioned so that each grasped the shoulder of the man in front of him, and the skeletons had stayed that way, perfectly in place. There was no sign of trauma on the bones and no way of knowing how the dead had met their end. But a 2006 report from the archaeological institute Inrap (*Institut national de recherches archéologiques preventives*) hypothesizes that the men committed suicide. The report quotes Julius Caesar, who in *Bellum Gallicum* wrote about Gaulish warriors called *soldurii*. These *soldurii*, he wrote,

> enjoy all the conveniences of life with those to whose friendship they have devoted themselves; if anything calamitous happen to them, either they endure the same destiny together with them, or commit suicide; nor hitherto, in the memory of men, has there been found any [*soldurii*] who, upon his being slain to whose friendship he had devoted himself, refused to die.

Archaeologists Dorcas Brown and David Anthony have linked this grave to a tradition they argue was already ancient when Caesar was leading sorties across the Rhine. They draw the connection in their 2012 article "Midwinter Dog Sacrifices and Warrior Initiations in the Late Bronze Age at Krasnosamarskoe." Krasnosamarskoe is a town in western Russia, not too far north of the Kazakh border. About four thousand years ago, it was the site of a peculiar settlement whose inhabitants killed and ate a great many dogs and a number of wolves, first roasting the animals, then chopping them into tiny pieces and consuming them. All of the animals were slaughtered in winter. (This is known from their teeth, which register seasonal variations in diet.)

The culture associated with the site is known as the Srubnaya. Noting that no evidence of canine feasts has been found at any other Srubnaya settlement, the authors suggest that in this society, "eating dogs and wolves was a transgressive act . . . a taboo-violating behavior of a kind often associated with rites of passage. In this case the passage was a transition to a status symbolized by becoming a dog/wolf through the consumption of its flesh." They conjecture that the site "was a central place for the performance of a winter ritual connected to boys' initiations, a place where boys became warriors." The boys must have "trudged through the frozen winter steppe" from miles around to converge there.

Arguing from evidence too complex to summarize here, the authors assert that the Srubnaya people spoke a language that belonged to the Indo-European family, which also includes Farsi, Sanskrit and its descendants, and almost all European tongues. Proceeding from this premise, Brown and Anthony conduct a rapid survey of Indo-European literature, mythology, and material culture, ranging across millennia to track the persistent association of dog or wolf symbolism with "youthful war-bands that operated on the edges of society, and that stayed together for a number of years and then were disbanded when their members reached a certain age." These war-bands "shared several features":

> they were composed of boys . . . who fought together as an age set or cohort; they were associated with sexual promiscuity (Latin, Vedic, Celtic); they came from the wealthier families (Latin, Vedic); their duties centered on fighting and raiding, but could also include learning poetry (Celtic, Vedic); they lived "in the wild," apart from their families, without possessions (Latin, Vedic, Celtic); and they wore animal skins, appeared as if they were wolves or dogs, and bore names containing the word wolf or dog.

In Vedic texts dating back some three thousand years, the authors find "midwinter dog sacrifices . . . explicitly linked with ritual specialists described as dog-priests." These priests ministered to "youthful dog-like raiders who divided the year between raiding and learning poetry and verses." Brown and Anthony cite a linguist who showed that "the dog priests . . . and their winter sacrifices represented an extremely archaic aspect of Indic ritual," considerably older than the Rigveda.

The authors point to a wealth of suggestive details in European traditions as well. In ancient Greece, noble youth (*ephebes*) trained for war dressed in animal skins, while in the Roman Lupercalia, "the skin of the dog or wolf was carried or worn by the adolescent sons of the aristocrats, who ran around the walls of Rome, symbolically protecting the community." While the etymology of *Lupercalia* isn't conclusively documented, it is widely presumed to derive from *lupus*, in which case it would mean "Wolf-Fest." In the Volsunga saga, Sigmund dresses his nephew in wolf pelts and instructs him in raiding and combat; in Celtic legend, a great hero is called the Dog of Cullan (Cuchullain); and in Germanic myth, the berserker god Odin goes tearing through the forest on winter nights, his dogs baying at his heels.

As for berserking, the Old Norse *Ynglinga saga* describes warriors who "went without shields, and were made as strong as dogs or wolves. . . . And this is what is called the fury [*wut*] of the berserker."

This quote appears in the essay "Homeric *Lyssa*: Wolfish Rage," by Bruce Lincoln, a professor of religious studies at the University of Chicago. Lincoln considers the contested etymology of the Greek word *lyssa*, "martial fury," arguing that it clearly comes from *lykos*, "wolf." In the *Iliad*, *lyssa* is "a state of wild, uncontrolled rage which is possessed by certain highly gifted warriors." While analogues of this concept are found globally, as in Malay *amok*, such frenzied martial rage is "particularly well documented among the various branches of Indo-European." In addition to Germanic *wut*, there is Celtic *ferg* and Iranian *aesma*.

Lincoln emphasizes the historic depth and geographic breadth of this notion of the lupine warrior:

> Of all the powerful or carnivorous animals . . . the wolf seems to have been the most important for the Indo-European warriors. Reflexes of the old word *wlkwo*, "wolf," are found in literally hundreds of proper names, and [in the names of] numerous peoples, such as the Luvians, Lycians, [et cetera]. . . . Stories of lycanthropy are well known among the Greeks, Romans, Germans, Celts, Anatolians, and Iranians, and these would seem to be traceable to these ancient warrior practices.

In Germanic myth and legend, say Brown and Anthony, these feral warbands "are called *Männerbünde* . . . a label often applied [by scholars] to all similar Indo-European institutions." *Männerbünde* means "men-league," league of men.

Toward their conclusion, Brown and Anthony speculate on the psychological benefits of a symbolic transformation into a beast of prey. The wolf warriors, they surmise, "would feel no guilt for breaking the taboos of human society because they had not been humans [at the time]."

Finding some way to deal with guilt must have been crucial, not only for individual members of the leagues but for their societies as a whole. This is because membership in the Männerbünde lasted only for a set period. If you were still alive at the end of that time, you had to integrate yourself back into your old community. In order to perform the roles society now needed you to perform—family man, working stiff—you had to shed your tainted and bloody savage identity.

For some, this would have been impossible, no matter what psychological mechanisms were deployed to help. But many others must have managed the reintegration well enough. The rotation back into normalcy is documented in the Vedic texts: "At the end of four years, there was a final sacrifice to transform the dog-warriors into responsible adult men who were ready to return to civil life. They discarded and destroyed their old clothes and dog skins. They became human once again."

T HE BOYS TRUDGED *through the frozen winter steppe.* That's an evocative phrase, to me. But does it describe something that actually happened? Bruce Lincoln, for his part, is agnostic. In the preface to his 1991 collection of articles, *Death, War, and Sacrifice* (not a beach read), he addresses the then-raging debate over so-called postmodern relativism and stakes out a kind of soft poststructuralist position with which I am in sympathy. "If myths tell stories about the long ago and far away for purposes of the place and moment in which these stories are told," he writes, "the same may be observed regarding other forms of narrative, scholarship included. . . . This is not to say that scholarship differs in no way from myth, or that research produces only fictions. . . . Still, the books and articles which scholars write and the lectures they give are not just descriptive accounts of something that unproblematically 'is.'"

Something that unproblematically is. Another evocative phrase, especially insofar as it implies its opposite: something that problematically is. We are dealing with ontology, with ontological categories (fact, fantasy, history, fiction) and with things that exceed those categories,

pressure them, make them buckle. A supernatural adversary, a werewolf, a psychotic unkillable superwarrior: what is such a creature if not
an ontological affront, a thing that should not exist but insists on existing anyway? That seems as good a definition of a monster as any: a
being that should not be, but is; a counterintuitive concept with a highly
negative valence.

I'm not sure whether one should say that a monster is a minimally
counterintuitive concept or a maximally counterintuitive one. MXCI
is by far the more charismatic abbreviation, but it's only in fiction
that monsters are reliably charismatic. In reality, it really depends on
the monster.

"WHEN THE WIND SETS THE CORN in wave-like motion, the peasants often say, 'The Wolf is going over, or through, the corn,'
'the Rye-wolf is rushing over the field,' 'the Wolf is in the corn.'"

This is Sir James Frazer, writing in *The Golden Bough*. He is using
corn in the older British sense of the word, as a general term for any type
of grain.

The Golden Bough is essentially a real-life version of *The Key to All
Mythologies*, the colossal scholarly enterprise that drives the Reverend
Casaubon to his grave in *Middlemarch*. Most readers know Frazer's
work as a nine-hundred-page book, but this tome, published in 1922,
is in fact an abridgment of a twelve-volume series composed over a
quarter century (1890–1915). We are informed at the book's outset that
Frazer's study grew from his desire to understand a strange Greek ritual
involving a sacred grove, its priest king, and the titular tree branch. In
order to fathom the nuances of this mystery, the author finds it necessary to canvas world folklore in its entirety, paying particular attention
to the relict pagan customs of Europe. As he conducts his tour, Frazer
gradually reveals the *unheimlich* occult logic underpinning such *heim-
lich* festivities as Maypole dancing. (The influence of his studies may
be detected in the inestimable 1973 film *The Wicker Man*, among other
forays into creepy British-bohemian neo-folklore.)

It turns out that a lot of Europe's relict pagan customs involve
wolves. Especially but not only in "France, Germany, and Slavonic countries," the animal is strongly associated with the harvest: the act of cut-
ting the ripe grain is conceptualized as chasing the wolf, or sometimes
the dog, out of the fields. As the harvesters work their way through the

rows, they gradually eradicate the tall, rustling vegetation in which the wolf conceals himself. Danger lurks as long as there is somewhere for the beast to hide. According to old proverbs, "The wolf sits in the corn, and will tear you to pieces." Children are warned not to stray into the fields, or "the Wolf will eat you."

When the last of the crop is harvested, the dog or wolf is symbolically killed—cause for rejoicing. In many communities, this final sheaf ·"is called the Wolf," and may be made into an effigy, often clothed like a person. "This indicates a confusion," Frazer observes, or a conflation. The wolf is simultaneously envisioned "as theriomorphic (in animal form) and as anthropomorphic (in human form)."

Confusion is the rule with the wolf. The relationship to society is tense and conflicted. The wolf shouldn't be where he is, in the fields, and yet his transgression is part of the natural order of things, the annual cycle of ritual and agriculture. Sometimes, instead of being killed or in addition to it, the wolf is feted in procession, given gifts. Near Cologne, "it was formerly the custom to give to the last sheaf the shape of a wolf. It was kept in the barn til the corn was threshed. Then it was brought to the farmer, and he had to sprinkle it with beer or brandy."

While the wolf is killed and/or celebrated in autumn, he sometimes shows up at another time of year. "In midwinter," says Frazer, "the Wolf makes his appearance once more. In Poland a man with a wolf's skin thrown over his head is led about at Christmas; or a stuffed wolf is carried about by persons who collect money. There are facts which point to an old custom of leading about a man enveloped in leaves and called the Wolf, while his conductors collected money." This old custom sounds like blackmail, as if the wolf were running a protection racket.

The wolf-racketeer is enveloped in leaves because, of course, he lives in the woods. The fields he haunts so relentlessly are not his habitat. They are the liminal space between village and forest, the place where the wolf pushes his luck—or plays to the edge, to use the alpha-male metaphor favored by former CIA and NSA chief Michael Hayden. In his memoir, *Playing to the Edge*, Hayden explains that his title refers to "playing so close to the line that you get chalk dust on your cleats." What's interesting is the way this assertion about testing boundaries is in fact an admission of crossing them. Hayden is describing an ethos of maximum risk-taking, of doing whatever you suspect you can get away with as a matter of course and a matter of honor. Hesitance is not for wolves but for animals of a feline persuasion. If you and your teammates are all about getting chalk dust on your cleats, then there is no doubt whatsoever that some of you will cross that chalked boundary, from sheer momentum if nothing else.

IT'S A STORY ABOUT VIOLATION or rape. Let's assume it was always a story about violation or rape, from the beginning, 2,600 years ago or more. But was it always a story about a wolf? Or was it about a boy—a boy, or rather a man, or rather someone on the cusp between the two—in the skin of a wolf?

We are shown a seemingly deliberate contrast. The wolf is in the forest, his proper domain; the story establishes him there. But then he reappears, having infiltrated the human world. We are looking at this old, old story through an incredibly blurry lens, but that much is clear: the wolf is in the forest and then he's in the house. Not just in the house—the figure of the wolf is now merged with a person. And not just *any* person—a little old lady, a grandmother. This is an especially ludicrous confusion of the theriomorphic and anthropomorphic. It suggests that our wolf possesses a deranged sense of homicidal mischief. "The better to see you with, my dear . . ." It's rather a lark, to him, this escapade of stalking, rape, and murder. Of course, his arch locution is a latter-day fillip. But the way he practically teleports from wilderness to house—*ta da!*—suggests to me that his tricksterish nature was always integral to the tale. Like the theriomorphic-anthropomorphic wolf in the grain, the wolf in this story is a liminal figure, an embodiment of some occult state in which binary conditions are impossibly, gruesomely conflated.

I say gruesomely. Let's suppose that we are talking about an actual historical phenomenon: "youthful war-bands . . . that operated on the edges of society, and that stayed together for a number of years and then were disbanded when their members reached a certain age"; cohorts of young men who were educated in poetry and verses and fighting and raiding, who lived apart from their parents, bonded passionately to one another, perhaps less so to everyone else; boys systematically encouraged not just to fight and to vanquish but to depredate, to become wild animals, to wreak maximum chaos on their enemies. Once you make that choice, as a society, to create that institution, how do you keep the chaos at bay? How do you make sure it never turns against *you*? The answer is, you don't. Sometimes chaos redounds, refracts, lurks where it doesn't live, shows up at your door. When it does, if you're lucky, it will simply demand its tribute and be on its way. But sometimes, that's not what happens at all.

Why gruesome? Let's further suppose that this story, ATU 333, originated among people who subscribed to a logic whereby a boy in a wolf's skin is a wolf. This is not an impersonation, not a disguise. It's a deformation of ontological categories achieved through what you might call magic. The boy looks nothing like a wolf—he looks like a boy wearing a wolf pelt—but he *is* a wolf. So, if a boy in a wolf's skin is a wolf, wouldn't a wolf in Grandmother's skin be Grandmother? Yes, yes, I'm being morbid, lurid and morbid, but still, might that be the picture the story initially conjured? A boy who has become a wolf transforms himself into yet another thing, obscenely lampooning the ritual that made him what he is, perhaps to make a point (*You expect me to stop being this monster I've become, to suddenly become something else? How's this for something else?*), perhaps just for the fuck of it. Slaying, flaying, grotesque travesty . . . Is that what ATU 333 is asking us to see? Here is an image of maximum chaos, to be sure, a violent collapsing of binaries that must not collapse if life is to make any sense: male/female, young/old, outside/inside, bestial/human, slaughtering/nurturing, profane/sacred. An MXCI, no doubt about it, but not at all difficult to remember, because it achieves its counterintuitive excess through a single operation, this spectacularly sanguinary rupture of oppositions, this ontological carnage. This image—this vision of total, totally malign misrule—would be a powerful cognitive attractor, would it not?

Our contemporary interpretations of ATU 333 are really so patronizing, so presentist. It may be true that, in recent centuries, the story became a tool for cowing girls into sexual docility, but that was not necessarily its original function. With this in mind, how might we reinterpret the tale?

We might at least entertain the possibility that ATU 333 reflects the values of a society with more mettle and less hypocrisy than our own. Perhaps the story was first told by people who understood how grossly contemptible it is to make decisions, *as* a society, and then assiduously deny the consequences of those decisions—deny those consequences with an intensity that looks very much like hysterical blindness. Maybe this unknown ancient society, however grievous its flaws, at least had the guts to confront its own ugly choices. It could have been a parable of rape, yes, of rape and murder and the most extravagant transgression imaginable. But possibly it was less a warning than a ritualized mnemonic. Maybe its function, or one of them, was to ensure that no one could forget or deny the price they had agreed to pay, the price of maintaining a Männerbünde, an institution of wolfishness.

There is no darkly romantic teleology here, no unbroken chain of historical inheritance linking wolf boys to frat boys, just as there is no primordial wellspring of masculine violence that forces wolf boys to kill or frat boys to rape. There are two institutions, two leagues of young men, one belonging to an archaic and semi-mythic past, the other flourishing here and now. Institutions, by definition, are not natural or primal. They are not what just happens when you let boys be boys. They are created and sustained for a reason. They do work.

In order for the Männerbünde to do its work, it was necessary to turn boys into wolves. We don't even know, we cannot and will not name, what we are creating when we somehow transform boys into people who have lost the moral intuition that a woman's body belongs to the woman—who don't suspect that a woman's body is not like a piece of furniture on the curb, not something that belongs to whoever can lift it. We don't know what this means, this absolute objectification that cannot, logically, be just a vile anomaly in an ethical system otherwise egalitarian and humane. We don't know what these crimes mean, these assaults that could not occur so regularly, so predictably, were it not the case that all the players are playing to the edge, not just the small percentage who actually cross the line and rape. We don't know what work this institution performs—this institution of American alpha-bros, of jocks, frat guys, popular dudes, these tight-knit cliques of privileged and socially dominant young men—and we don't know what bargain we have struck, and strike every day, when we permit this institution to exist in a status quo that appears impervious to growing scrutiny and serial outcries and ever-increasing awareness of "incapacitation rape," this so often bloodless and invisible violence. There is, as yet, nothing and no one to make us know it, nothing to make it public knowledge, knowledge that we all share and that we all *acknowledge* that we share. To create that kind of knowledge, you must have more power than whatever forces are working to maintain oblivion. This, too, was a basic precept of my education. Of course, analogous things could be said about so many regimes of disavowed violence—but I'm concerning myself with the one that Jackie concerned *her*self with.

THIS IS THE STORY I'VE COME UP WITH, about the story Jackie told: she did it out of rage. She had no idea she was enraged, but she was. Something had happened, and she wanted to tell other people, so that they would know what happened and know how she felt. But when she tried to tell it—maybe to somebody else, maybe to herself—the story had no power. It didn't sound, in the telling, anything like what it *felt* like in the living. It sounded ordinary, mundane, eminently forgettable, like a million things that had happened to a million other women—but that wasn't what it felt like to her. What it felt like was lurid and strange and violent and violating. I have no idea what *it* was, whether a crime was involved. There's a perfectly legal thing called hogging, where guys deliberately seek out sex partners they find unattractive so they can laugh about it later with their friends. Maybe it was something like that, or maybe it was much milder, an expression of contempt that was avuncular, unthinking, something that transformed her into a thing without even meaning to. Whatever it was, this proximate cause, she didn't know what to do about it. To figure out how to go on from that moment without dying from rage, you need something she didn't have. You need self-insight, or historical insight, or at the very least a certain amount of critical distance, a wry appreciation of the ironies of it all. She didn't have any of that, and that's why she lied, knowingly or unknowingly—or, most likely, both at once.

So she told the story to Sabrina Erdely, who told it to everyone else. Erdely frames the bloody melodrama against a backdrop of dry reportage, to extraordinarily compelling effect. We know she decided to write about campus rape before she knew *which* campus rape she would focus on. She needed to find the right crime, one both exemplary and outrageous, something to create the shock of defamiliarization, to rivet and enrage. I wonder if any journalist in that situation could have resisted the story she found. Imagine interviewing the young woman who had survived a gang rape, and imagine her telling you that one of the rapists had ordered: "Grab its motherfucking leg." If ever there was a fact that was too good to check, it's this one, this amazing line, with its hideous, show-stopping pronoun. And the haunting thing is that Jackie couldn't have come up with that lotion-in-the-basket locution without knowing something true about the way some guys talk and think. That knowledge really is powerfully, memorably distilled in those four blood-curdling words.

To the extent that Jackie was aware that what she told Sabrina Erdely was not true, it was destructive and wrong, cruel and stupid. If she really was not in command of reality, that would mitigate her culpability, but it wouldn't change the nature of what she did. It was violence. And to me, it was a betrayal—or that's what it felt like. I knew it was irrational to feel that way, but that's how I felt. I want to condemn it, and I *do* condemn it, but I also think I can guess what she was saying, or would have said, which can't be said reasonably. It must be said melodramatically. Something like: Look at this. Don't you fucking dare not look. I'm going to *make* you look. I'm going to *make* you know. You're going to know what we've decided is worth sacrificing, what price we've decided we're willing to pay to maintain this league of men, and this time, you're going to remember. +

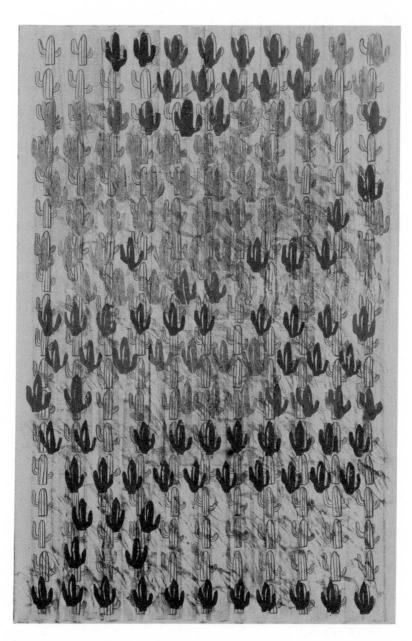

DESPINA STOKOU, *MACHISMO (LIGHT) III*. 2015, CHARCOAL, CHALK, AND COLLAGE ON LINEN. 71.6 × 47.6".
PHOTO BY MAXWELL SCHWARTZ. COURTESY OF GALERIE EIGEN + ART LEIPZIG/BERLIN.

OLDCHELLA

David Samuels

H AS IT COME TO THIS? Songs of youthful longing and rebellion, transformed into the electrified wail of ultramillionaires in their seventies who hang out with other rich people. Onstage, before the inhabitants of the world's largest open-air old-age home, caught in the middle of a desert dust storm, is Pirate King Keef, the original dancing bag of bones, dressed in a billowing shirt of royal purple. The shirt shows more than a comfortable hint of a gut. I can see it from my seat in the fourteenth row at Oldchella, i.e., Coachella for old people.

Desert Trip, as the weekend-long, see-'em-before-they-croak festival is officially known, occupies the space of seven polo fields. With bleachers on either side and a flashing neon Ferris wheel at the very back, there's room for 85,000 people of whatever age. Tickets cost between $250 and $1,000 per night. Wisely, no one smokes.

The surrounding landscape suggests a different planet, like Tatooine in the Star Wars movies, a giant necropolis in shades of sandy-beige monotone. Del Tacos, Starbucks, and Cold Stone Creameries are sprinkled among the specialized hospitals and compounding pharmacies that stand at key intersections between gated communities. Streets with sibilant Spanish names alternate with streets named after Presidents Washington, Jefferson, Adams, and Madison, and some streets identified only by numbers to make retired engineers and accountants feel at home. The cold hand of death touches everyone here, mussing the hair of one and turning it white, squeezing someone else's heart so hard that they can no longer walk without assistance. Here and there you might see someone in their mid- to late fifties, red-faced but still healthy, growing up outside of London, we thought that we discovered the blues. Obviously, we didn't. But it was the music that brought us all together."

"I can't think of anyone who deserves it better," Keith says. "Meanwhile, we got a show to do, right?"

Before the Stones came onstage, Bob opened the evening with "Rainy Day Women #12 & 35," better known as "Everybody Must Get Stoned"—a funny way to acknowledge his Nobel Prize. He followed with "Don't Think Twice, It's All Right," then "Highway 61 Revisited," a song that contains what may be his hippest line: "God said to Abraham, kill me a son / Abe said, 'Man, you must be putting me on.'" But in his stage performance, the choreographed succession of pretty melodies and nasty put-downs delivered in his prewashed, bored monotone was reduced to another grayscale nostalgia trip through the cliches of 20th-century American industrial iconography. Lonesome railway trains, smoke-puffing smokestacks, neon-lit gin joints, black men picking cotton—all these images were in the video, straight-faced, like an ad for Levi's, the American jeans. Not that Dylan cared. "Throw your parties overboard," he hooted into the darkness. "It's dark out there." Or maybe he said "panties." He couldn't care less if his audience had even the slightest inkling of what he was talking about.

"I dated four guys like him, insufferable," my wife texts from the glowing dust-covered screen of my iPhone. Standing behind the piano in a jack-legged stance, Dylan was both there and not there. He'll continue to do whatever he's told to do by the Spirit of Whatever. Tonight that consisted of an odd backward shuffle-dance away from the microphone stand, his Italian bedroom-slipper loafers rasping against the desert sand carpeting the stage, which is perfect for Dylan's soft-shoe nostalgia trip. The band played a cool, nearly unrecognizable orchestration of "Desolation Row" that sounded like Dire Straits. Every third beat, Dylan stiffened and then humped his piano. But my own sarcasm rings hollow here. Yes, it's true that there's something rigid and dogmatic about his art. He's the Socialist Workers Party of self-righteous male egomania, still handing out his mimeographed fliers outside the old cafeteria, which long ago became a Starbucks. So what? Like any great artist, Dylan doesn't care what you think, which makes you the bigger asshole. In his famous Bob Dylan voice, he offered a howling, wounded-animal rendition of "Like a Rolling Stone."

How does it feel to be Bob Dylan? Lonely, I guess. Still, what I'll remember best from the evening is Mick Jagger performing "Sympathy for the Devil" and "Brown Sugar" in a sequined black cutaway evening coat he probably bought at the Siegfried and Roy estate sale, to illustrate his fantasies of copulating with underage slave girls. Who can deny that these fantasies, however racist, misogynist, cartoonish, and deeply rooted in the American psyche, are also Mick's own? To even things out, he invited a multicultural student choir from USC to lead the crowd in "You Can't Always Get What You Want," the anthem of mass resignation that Donald Trump played at his rallies. He followed that with "(I Can't Get No) Satisfaction," which he clearly could have sung all night. I can't get no! Hey hey hey! as fireworks went off over the stage.

L IFE IN A DESERT IS TENUOUS AND FRAGILE. Raise the temperature by five degrees, take away shelter, and you're cooked food for scavengers. Maintaining hospitals and golf courses for hundreds of thousands of people in the middle of a desert is a project that can only be sustained through the marshaling of technological and organizational resources on a quasi-military scale. Human beings were not meant to live in deserts in such numbers, especially not these human beings—pink, overweight, with bodies compromised by sedentary occupations and habits. The fake handmade signs produced for pennies by the poor and sold in local gift shops speak to the aching loneliness behind this Soviet-style resettlement project: GOOD FRIENDS ARE LIKE STARS. YOU DON'T ALWAYS SEE THEM, BUT YOU KNOW THEY ARE THERE.

The view of the golf course from the deck of my borrowed McMansion is calculated to hit the pleasure center of every human brain: a still pool of water framed by an undulating ribbon of greenery. Above the fairway, the desert mountains rise like great heaps of bone and ash that have been welded together by the sun.

The unsustainable consumption of scarce resources undercuts the promise of comfort and ease in a desert oasis. The paucity of context for anything underlines the hurried construction of the buildings, which are in turn reduced to the sourcing and cost of their component parts. Each Florentine mansion looks like it could be disassembled and shipped off somewhere else at any moment. When I ask the acne-faced young guy at the gate of PGA West for directions, he smiles and shakes his head. "I've of "Harvest Moon," with an actual orange moon overhead and a nice swirling smoke effect onstage that I recognize as a sign that the desert dust is getting out of control. In the center of an orange cloud, Neil takes a post-9/11 turn toward darkness, muttering about terrorist suicide hang gliders. "How can I tell if they're bad or good?" he wonders, in the plaintive voice of an abandoned child to whom nothing truly bad or good has happened yet. Even if the horror-show ending seems inevitable, maybe it isn't. Maybe it will all be one big prairie let-down.

Neil Young was also a writer of protest songs, his protest being against the human condition in general. At the same time, he found beauty in the changing of the seasons and the possibility of harmony between man and nature as expressed in the rhythms of cultivation. Nature is big, and man is small. As Neil laid it out in his songs, vulnerability was the path to wisdom. The realization that we are helpless and alone is a form of togetherness. Once that work is done, he takes up his big Gibson, which is a mighty instrument for any guitar-playing John Henry to wield, and plugs in to the ur-rock of Buddy Holly and the Everly Brothers, which he softened into a distinctive, dreamy sound somewhere between a hymn and a dirge.

It's the sound of a stoned young man with an open heart who knows that he lacks direction, more fragile than the sex-and-death blues that Keith Richards endeavored to copy note for note from Howlin' Wolf and Muddy Waters. While the Stones embraced blues and sex, Neil took that energy in a different and—despite the surface misogyny of the Stones' lyrics—more exclusively masculinist direction. Male listeners identify with Neil, while women, who are figured as the objects of his discourse—shy farm girls, librarians, poets, painters, crystal gazers, cancer-ward nurses, maids—want to jump his bones. He gently frustrates their desires by sitting on the edge of their beds in his unwashed blue jeans and reading them song lyrics from his notebooks.

I am just a dreamer
But you are just a dream

That's it right there: the contemplation of the object, whether a girl, a field, or the moon, is the male role. His solos are even more exclusionary, as he throws up a wall of feedback to protect his emotions. Once he finds his way through, note by note, he forms a circle with the Axl Rose guy and the bass player. They jump around together like boys doing their version of a tomahawk dance in someone's backyard.

From the stage, Neil is tossing bags of seeds to the crowd while inveighing against California's seed law, which seeks to standardize seed production and distribution under the control of the state. "Good organic seeds for everyone," says Neil. "California seed law—it's a piece of shit. Just saying." Neil is sorry that the real world is such a mess. "Let's make Earth great again," he urges, with a bare minimum of conviction.

Thankfully, I've found a way of breathing in and out through a wet bandana that traps enough desert dust to put a stop to my hacking cough, but I am starting to feel claustrophobic. I take off my bandana and immediately start to choke. "Got that Coachella cough," my seat-mate says sympathetically. He grew up in San Bernardino, where he saw the Rolling Stones play in 1964. The band played "Little Red Rooster" by Willie Dixon, which is interesting to think about. For all the temptation to assign the Stones to a different era from the Chicago electric-blues artists they worshipfully imitated, the truth is that Howlin' Wolf recorded his famous version of the song in 1961—a scant three years before the Stones' version. Still, it was music of a kind that no one in San Bernadino had ever heard before. "They were out there," he recalls.

On "Rockin' in the Free World," the Axl Rose–looking kid launches into an incredible Southern-fried guitar solo worthy of Buckethead. The crowd takes the song straight, as a celebration of their own belonging. The shittiness of Reagan-era America looks in retrospect like paradise. His toad face aglow, Neil presses his big belly against his younger band-mates in a loving barnyard embrace. Now the whole crowd is in on the secret. You get old and then you die. Those moments of loneliness and longing and anger are dogged by the inevitable all-encompassing dark-ness, which is what makes them so precious. In the end, the darkness always wins. As death draws near, there are songs that he doesn't play. "Rock and roll will never die" is the most perfect lyric that any rock star wrote. But not here.

PAUL MCCARTNEY IS A GENIUS. Happy, bouncy, funny, wistful, bril-liant. He wrote dozens of great songs. Even the thought of singing lead while playing bass is enough to give me a migraine. The Beatles were Paul McCartney's band in the same way the Rolling Stones were Keith Richards's band, even conceding that the true sophisticate of the

There's a bustle onstage and out comes the Empress of Pop, Queen Rihanna of Barbados, pulling at her open shirt and strutting her stuff. Paul McCartney grins, delighted. "I finally found someone under 50," he tells the crowd. He flaps his arms then crows like a rooster at the dirty orange moon.

By the third note of "Eleanor Rigby," I decide again to leave, except this time, Neil Young comes onstage to play guitar with McCartney on bass. When Neil takes the solo on "A Day in the Life," he looks like he's died and gone to heaven. At the end, he throws his arm around McCartney.

"This is the Charlie Chaplin of rock and roll right here," he announces. It's a great line, capturing both the specificity of McCartney's stretchy-faced charm and his centrality to 20th-century pop. Mutually delighted, they jam together, turning "Why Don't We Do It in the Road?" into a randy septuagenarian workout that would make a good backing track for a Viagra or Cialis commercial: Your Seventies Sex Idols Talk Sex in Your Seventies.

Paul doesn't care that his voice sounds like crap. Right now, he's having a great evening in the middle of an orange desert dust-tornado with his wife and his daughters and Rihanna and Neil Young and 80,000 people of varying ages who love his music. Fuck death. He howls at the moon. Then he gets the crowd to howl along with him.

"Helter Skelter" is my cue to exit. In the darkness of the parking lot, lit by the passing, elongated glare of headlights, I find myself humming "Julia," a song John Lennon wrote for his dead mother that matches the shape of my own secret trauma. Mothers are important. The "Mother Mary" who comes to Paul in times of trouble and tells him to "let it be" is probably Mary McCartney. Everyone has their sorrows, but in the end, the sources of art are unknowable, and don't really matter. Paul McCartney is happy. Now that Linda is dead, I imagine he is no longer a vegetarian, out of respect to his current wife. Or maybe it's the other way around. Truly, you can imagine it any way you want, which is why his songs are played at both weddings and funerals.

I N THE DESERT SUN YOU CAN SEE THEM all plain, shorn of the veneer of sexy youth. For Richards, death is the source of wisdom. For Jagger, death is a campy drag performer. For Dylan, death is the female principle, which is unknowable, and holds guys back. For Neil Young, death is another word for loneliness, which is universal. For McCartney, the answer is love.

In the run-up to tonight's final event, the bar is serving Avión Silver tequila and shots of Jameson along with Hess Select Sauvignon Blanc and Silver Oak Cab to wash down the *bánh mì* and the sliders and the spicy pizza. There are dumplings and street tacos, margaritas and Paradise Mules. Back near the Ferris wheel are handcrafted sodas and kettle corn. I am jonesing to ride the monster, though truthfully speaking, I am also scared shitless of being suspended 250 feet in the air on a slowly rotating neon-lit wheel that probably spins faster than it looks from the ground.

"All you young people have come to watch the old people dance," announces Pete Townshend, Grand Guignol guitarist of the Who. He looks down into the mosh pit, where, surprisingly enough, a decent number of young people are in evidence. Desert Trip is the last stop on the Who's fiftieth-anniversary tour, which has lasted a full two years, with a break in the middle for lead singer Roger Daltrey to recover from a heart operation.

> I asked Bobby Dylan
> I asked the Beatles
> I asked Timothy Leary
> But he couldn't help me, either

Daltrey reveals, voicing the Seeker, a character who compelled high levels of identification in the alienated children of the early to mid-'70s. Today's children record the elder Daltrey on the screens of their iPhones.

Daltrey is less of a creative element in the Who than he is a flesh-puppet in the hands of Townshend, the band's songwriter and most underrated of the great rock guitarists. Clearly, the man has demons, I think, as he lurks around the amps. He left rock and roll for a decade to write poems and edit books, which is not something Bob Dylan ever did. There was also the bisexuality and the child-porn bust, which drove Townshend even further into his cocoon. His explanation for the pictures on his computer, which was seized by zealous local policemen, was that he was researching sexual abuse, a subject that horrified and preoccupied him—an answer that seems plausible enough to anyone who ever listened to *Tommy*.

Unlike *Sgt. Pepper's* and *Exile on Main Street* and other classic rock "concept albums" whose progressions are more like song cycles that resist linear narrative form, *Tommy*, Townshend's rock opera, is a single coherent story that can be staged in a conventional way. The uninhibited violence of Townshend's playing tonight has led to a bloody gash over the guitarist's right eye, near the bridge of his nose, which suggests that whatever he is trying to communicate is worth some real level of physical pain. Traditional narrative structure plus emotive zeal is a formula kids can still relate to. As the camera pans up Daltrey's body, starting slightly below the waist, it's possible to make out the singer's love handles, which I can also relate to. I also dig his gold wire aviators with the blue lenses, grandpa style. As Daltrey growls and eats his words, chewing his way out of the early-video-game-music intro to "Baba O'Riley," Townshend grimaces a touch before forcing his arm through one of his signature windmills, probably adding a torn rotator cuff to the gash that continues to seep blood down into his eye. "I really hope you had a good time," he announces sincerely before taking a brief moment to remember his bass player, "who died of rock and roll in Las Vegas," and "our drummer, who also died of rock and roll." His mordant humor is directed at the gods. What else can you do but laugh, and play "My Generation"? Everyone dies.

Y OUNG PEOPLE, THE ONES who can afford tickets to a festival rock concert these days, look clean. They know the meaning of clean clothes, which is that somebody loves you enough to add bleach. Maybe it's your mother or grandmother, or an older sister or brother, who may be working two jobs and going to school but still drags their tired ass to the laundry room to wash and fold your Hanes. During daylight hours, the laundry room is also a place where you can avoid kids who are bigger and meaner. A crisp, clean white T-shirt with that fresh detergent-and-bleach smell means love, which also but not always means safety. The sound is just as good in the back as it is closer to the stage, and the grass is real, which helps to keep down the dust. With the palm trees all lit up, it's actually kind of beautiful.

From this distance the stage disappears. There are only the three screens above the stage, which have merged into one big screen, flanked by two more screens implanted in the middle distance to re-create the triptych minus the actual performers. It's an icon minus the saints. The lit-up green trees, with the bright stars hanging in the desert sky, remind me of a Magritte painting, the kind that Paul McCartney might hang in his living room. As laser light pulses over the crowd, the darkened room, which is what it feels like, fills with the sound of isolation and abandonment, Nick Drake style, but without the promise of solace in friendship or any other shared emotion besides misery.

Pink Floyd is a bummer. Roger Waters makes music for bored stoners who are down on life, which is a luxury only rich kids from the suburbs can afford. Emotionally speaking, he makes Bob Dylan seem super connected. He is vain, so vain that he has replaced his old Pink Floyd bandmate David Gilmour onscreen with a pair of hands shown in close-up and intercut with close-ups of Waters's face, as if to suggest Waters is playing the guitar solos as well as the bass hanging around his neck. The voice is the voice of Jacob, but the hands are the hands of the guy imitating David Gilmour.

The thundering light-and-video mother ship can run without Roger Waters, too. It's bigger than music. It's a highbrow rock-orchestral spectacle of doom and gloom for the masses, who are doomed anyway. I have sucked up most of the remainder of Sean Penn's mushrooms. The Ferris wheel beckons.

Lit up in carnival red, white, and blue, the wheel goes around and around against the mountains, whose lives are measured in geologic time. In line with me are young Latino lovers, and a cool, long-haired hippie dad with his wife and daughter who in another time might have all been lovers in some cool Seventies Swedish porno. Two muscle guys in tank tops are standing with their arms neatly intertwined around each other's thirty-inch waists, which seems uncontroversial here, too, as long as they don't talk too much about How They Do It; Freddy Mercury and David Bowie aside, classic rock belongs to the heteronormative dinosaurs. I find three companions who seem nice enough to ride with, and together we buy tickets and board a car, which clanks and swings back and forth in what I imagine to be an ominous fashion.

As the machine wheels us up into the sky, a cold wind is blowing in from the desert. The wheel speeds up, and I see Bugs Bunny down there in the dust. Magilla Gorilla is there too, in a clean white T-shirt, looking shit-faced. I am close to heaven, with three perfect strangers, going bug-eyed. The guy at the tiller has left us hanging up here on purpose. Or maybe he has generously determined that I should enjoy the view on a night where the wind is actually blowing a little bit harder than I thought. I wonder whether anyone will hear me if I scream. The car falls forward with a sickening lurch, and then we go around at least three more times without further incident, but with the same sinking feeling in my stomach.

Sitting up front was a mistake. My people are in the cattle pens. I disembark, shaky and bow-legged, and make a beeline for Tiffany Tiger, who is dancing in her costume, which reminds me of the Saturday-morning dance shows I used to watch when I was by myself. I give her the rest of Sean Penn's mushroom crumbs in a ziplocked baggie. Who cares how depressing the music is? Beneath his sci-fi Heydrich-Himmler exterior, I can see that Roger Waters is sad. "Wish You Were Here" is the late 20th century's answer to Whitman's "Song of Myself," a message to a friend who is no longer there, because he lost his mind.

Slowly but surely, the crowd is drifting toward the exits, which are manned by kids whose youth has a different sound track. "God bless you," one of them says. I stop and try my best to communicate soulful brotherhood to the kid in the white T-shirt standing right in front of me. He's clearly religious, from the Assemblies of God or one of the local Mexican Jesus outfits. He smiles back, gazing deep into my pinwheeling eyes, delighted to have used the power of his faith to help catch someone who is falling. He feels bad for the souls who are trapped inside the polo grounds, listening to Roger's lonely drone.

Observing that I am not averse to eye contact, his coworker, a black girl in her late teens or early twenties, approaches me and begins to recite a mantra. "If you listen, it is no dream," she says, enunciating each word with great care. The dotted line of her slantwise glance ends at my T-shirt, where the words are written. Delighted by this discovery, we laugh and clasp hands. The kids are alright.

Meanwhile, the dreams of transcendence that the old people once shared have turned to shit. Soon they will die, the noise will stop, and the desert will be quiet once more. In another generation or two, we will all be replaced by machines that dream of the sands from which silicon microchips are forged. Some of the machines may write songs about their feelings.

Here's to hoping. +

ASA NISI MASA

ACE HOTEL
New Orleans Pittsburgh Los Angeles London
Palm Springs New York Portland Seattle

NEW FROM PAPER MONUMENT

SOCIAL MEDIUM: ARTISTS WRITING, 2000–2015

Paper Monument's new anthology gathers seventy-five
texts—essays, criticism, manifestos, fiction, diaries, scripts,
blog posts, and tweets—that chart a complex era in the art
world and the world at large, weighing in on the exigencies
of our times in unexpected and inventive ways.

PAPERMONUMENT.COM/BUY

REVIEWS

A. S. HAMRAH
One Word: Authenticity!

HOLLYWOOD IS A MESS. THE DEBACLE AT THE Oscar ceremony in February was clumsy and revealing. At the end of a long, dull evening, Warren Beatty and Faye Dunaway announced *La La Land* the winner for Best Picture instead of the actual winner, *Moonlight*. Neither Beatty nor Dunaway had bothered to read the front of the envelope they were holding. When it became obvious to Beatty that something was wrong, he didn't reverse course. Instead, the great ladies' man gave Dunaway the card to read. Confused by Beatty's jokey demeanor, Dunaway read it even though it reannounced the Best Actress award, which had been handed out minutes before.

The mistake made all actors look bad, like automatons who read whatever's put in front of them. The show must go on, even if the script doesn't make sense, and professionalism means never having to admit you're an idiot. The revelation of Beatty as a doddering, self-impressed, and unfunny old man was at least a contrast to his sister Shirley MacLaine's fortitude, earlier in the evening, when she received a tribute from Charlize Theron as an alleged inspiration to the younger woman's career. This makes sense in Hollywood, because Theron is the contemporary actress most unlike MacLaine. This dual celebration of Beatty and MacLaine portends at least thirty more years of fawning over the Affleck brothers.

Jimmy Kimmel, the evening's host and an official representative of ABC, the Oscar network and broadcaster of his late-night show, did all he could to pre-dumb the proceedings, apologizing for his inadequacy throughout. As he struggled with the syllables *Isabelle Huppert*, he joked that no one watches foreign films. Later he asked, "What does a production designer do, anyway?" He belabored his phony TV rivalry with Matt Damon, but at least his segment mocking the Damon-starring clunker *We Bought a Zoo* was funny. It was funny because it was mean.

When Kimmel brought a bunch of regular people off the street and allowed them to kiss the hands of the celebrity actors seated in the front row, especially royal Meryl Streep, I heard tumbrels in the distance. Parading these goggle-eyed tourists across the stage probably wasn't what the Academy intended when it decided to be more inclusive. During the confusion at the end of the show, a dazzled white man onstage leaned into the microphone and brought up his "blue-eyed wife." That didn't help either.

Almost pushed to the side, Barry Jenkins, the director of *Moonlight*, remained

A NOVEL

FRANCESCO PACIFICO

"In *Class*, Pacifico turns his attention to Italy's other major religion: 'Cool.' On the trail of Italian hipsters from Rome to Williamsburg, *Class* is both savage and tender, like Antonioni's camera..."

—MARCO ROTH

AUTHOR OF *THE SCIENTISTS*

Available 5/23 wherever good books are sold.

◆ MELVILLE HOUSE

composed as things disintegrated around him. When he finally got to give his speech for his Best Picture Oscar, he extended love to everybody, but not before he said, "to hell with dreams"—a strange but fitting end to the dream factory's annual celebration of itself.

I wrote about *Moonlight, Manchester by the Sea, Toni Erdmann, Fire at Sea, 13th, 20th Century Women*, and probably some other films that were nominated for an Oscar in Issue 27 of *n+1*, and *The Lobster* in Issue 26.

—A.S.H.

La La Land

DAMIEN CHAZELLE'S RESUSCITATION OF THE movie musical sets out to demonstrate a basic tenet of cinema: love fades, but lives on in music. Ryan Gosling's struggling jazz pianist Sebastian, therefore, is privileged over Emma Stone's Mia, who just wants to be a movie star. The scene in which Sebastian jazzsplains music to Mia is inadvertently the most realistic in the movie. Llewyn Davis got his ass kicked for that kind of behavior, but in *La La Land* only hearts get broken.

Chazelle makes sure we can see Gosling and Stone in full when they dance, right away proving he's a better director of musicals than Baz Luhrmann or Rob Marshall. But when Sebastian complains about the dumbness of a tapas restaurant that's also a samba club, Chazelle sets up a problem for his film that lesser directors spare themselves. He raises the question of why people love crap, then answers it by making the kind of crap people love.

Never does the film allow that maybe people can like both a-ha and Thelonious Monk, or that there's a time and a place for everything. That is a hard-won sentiment, but it's in great supply in American musicals of the 1950s, where frivolity and maturity play on a soundstage more level than this one. Here, the director is happy, but his characters are not. The post-classic French musicals that do away with singers and dancers (*A Woman Is a Woman*) or emphasize melancholy and failed romance against a backdrop of societal drabness (*The Umbrellas of Cherbourg*) serve as models for *La La Land*. Their use here seems academic, befitting a director running for Student Council President of the Movies.

Florence Foster Jenkins

SEVERAL OF THE FILMS NOMINATED FOR Oscars in 2017 are already earnest relics of the Obama era. Not *Florence Foster Jenkins*, which takes on unexpected resonance now that Donald Trump is President. Florence (Meryl Streep) is a talentless rich lady and syphilitic weirdo who wants to be an opera diva. The obvious truth of her condition must be ignored by her various courtiers, whose careers depend on her largesse. Her fans, a curious mix of soldiers and snobs, embrace her because her terrible singing provides lulz, while establishment luminaries, like the conductor Arturo Toscanini, humor her while lining up for checks. How does she keep this act going? "One word: authenticity!"

Or, as her cheating husband (Hugh Grant) explains to a reporter he tries to bribe, "Isn't it the truth that a lot of hurt people are having some fun?" It is unclear if the film's director, Stephen Frears, saw *Florence Foster Jenkins*'s aristocratic farce as a lighter, uptown version of *A Face in the Crowd*'s native fascism, or why anyone thought that was needed. After her exposure in the press, Florence's angelic deathbed redemption furthers her self-deception into the cardboard

heaven she sought in reality. Her dementia ends in the music of the spheres, hurting no one. It's a cheesy, gentle apotheosis with no repercussions outside her little world.

Arrival

THE ALIEN-INVASION TALE IN *ARRIVAL* IS A calming parable of breakthrough to opaque beings we can befriend so they won't destroy us—an allegory for dealing with men. It's a reverie dreamed by a wake-and-bake mommy-blogger as she contemplates the rings made by her coffee cup on the morning paper and thinks about the spider sculptures of Louise Bourgeois. Fantasies about her husband leaving her and her child dying bubble to the surface as the day slips by, visions of freedom and solitude.

As in several films made last year, the protagonist is a woman who works as a translator: Amy Adams, named Louise, maybe after the sculptor whose *Maman* resembles the movie's aliens. As a sci-fi drama about international cooperation and defusing violence, *Arrival* values thinking over ray guns, renegotiating the terms of battle between sensitive eggheads and macho soldiers typical of alien-invasion films. Adams's super-translator shouts in Mandarin to convince the Chinese military she can see through time now that the aliens have revealed its secrets to her, an outburst and a plot twist that make sense if you're high and caffeinated.

Lion

GOOGLE EARTH HAS FINALLY MADE A MOVIE, which seems surprising only at first, because while it's hard to believe this story actually happened, it's easy to believe this film was made. Helicopter shots and god's-eye views define this true story of a boy in India who gets lost in a train station, is adopted by Nicole Kidman, and grows up to be Dev Patel. Watching him search Google Earth for his hometown is boring, but it posits the West as a place where people look into computers all day, while in the developing world people carry rocks for a living. This stark distinction would not pass muster in a film made by UNICEF. The contrast is introduced when little Saroo meets his new Australian mother in his new home. Kidman, playing someone in the 1980s, looks like a porcelain doll and waves her non-rock-carrying fingers at a television set in the living room. "Television . . . pictures," she explains to Saroo, enticing him into the world of screens that will one day allow his story to be told in a movie. A final scene could have shown pirated DVDs of *Lion* for sale in the streets of his long-lost village.

Loving

RICHARD AND MILDRED LOVING WERE THE couple in the 1967 Supreme Court case *Loving v. Virginia*, which finally overturned state laws against interracial marriage. They are portrayed in this film with kindness and dignity by Joel Edgerton and Ruth Negga, who continue the recent trend of imported actors portraying Southerners in American films. Jeff Nichols, who wrote and directed *Loving*, saturates the film with longing for a rural America where a couple can build their own house and don't need a phone, where the state won't nose around and interfere, and where there is no racism and no politics—where the only law is natural. In this pastoral idyll, Richard and Mildred are Adam and Eve, until they are expelled from their garden by racist sheriffs and county judges.

The couple's last name plays into the film's metaphoric significance as a story about genuine commitment beset by injustice. Exiled to Washington DC after they are asked to choose between the State of Virginia or divorce, Richard and Mildred long to return to their rural paradise. Under Nichols's direction, the film achieves the simplicity and perfection of certain silent films that pitted city life against country life as lovers were separated and reunited.

Edgerton's Richard barely speaks under his blond crew cut, changing expression as little as possible. Negga, who has eyes that convey so much thought and meaning, gazes with the intensity of Lillian Gish. As this couple seem to reinhabit a cinema that doesn't need dialogue, one in which the racism of Griffith is vanquished by love, so does Nichols's film seem to reinhabit the rural America of the late 1950s and '60s, an analog America the movies inhabit like a shell.

Hidden Figures

HIDDEN FIGURES HAS A SEXY TITLE THAT THE film downplays in favor of pure math and basic domesticity, so maybe it's fitting to point out that the IBM 7090 was first turned on by a black woman. The progression from analog to digital provides an important subtext in *Hidden Figures*, also set in Virginia in the same period as *Loving*. As Octavia Spencer's Dorothy Vaughan teaches herself Fortran in the back of the bus, she has to confront automation and figure out how to make it work for her and the other women on her staff of math geniuses, the "colored computers" who do calculations for NASA as it gears up to put John Glenn into space.

Theodore Melfi's film takes the opposite tack from Nichols's. This is an all-star feel-good movie about American ingenuity, in love with the future, stocked with hit music on the sound track and titles on-screen that tell us where we are. The film makes room for everyone in its cast. Taraji P. Henson, Mahershala Ali, Jim Parsons, Kirsten Dunst, and Janelle Monáe each get plenty to do, whether they are pure and good or shifty professionalized racists. Old pro Kevin Costner chips in, desegregating the restrooms at NASA, a smaller triumph than John Glenn's space flight but one that sped the US in the race to the moon.

Hidden Figures lacks the self-seriousness and concern with special effects of recent space arias like *Gravity* and *The Martian*, proving that history and human society are more entertaining than the lives of lonely astronauts divorced from social context, who talk to themselves on another planet or float alone in space. The future in *Hidden Figures* is in our past, but it unrolls a blueprint to get back there.

Hacksaw Ridge

A THIRD MOVIE SET IN VIRGINIA (AND Okinawa), Mel Gibson's *Hacksaw Ridge* concerns itself with justice only to show how ideals and beliefs can be used to transform people into killing machines. In Gibson's worldview, that combination is the pinnacle of human achievement. Andrew Garfield plays Desmond Doss, a real hero, a conscientious objector who enlists in World War II and finds himself in a rifle unit. Doss signed up to be a medic, refusing to carry a gun, and after enduring several rounds of bullying by Vince Vaughn (his sergeant) and a court-martial trial, which he wins, he's shipped to Japan with his brigade. There he rescues dozens of his wounded comrades, hefting them one at a time across gory terrain and lowering them down a cliffside by

rope, under fire by the Japanese infantry the whole time.

Gibson bathes this spectacular battle in viscera, concentrating on literal blood and soil, with a lot of literal guts strewn everywhere. Rats chew dead bodies in tunnels, a human eye looks out from the mud, half of another corpse shields a soldier from enemy fire as he charges. The actors are plastic army men come to life, here to mouth the clichés of 1940s World War II movies—this is Gibson's *La La Land*. Vaughn, while climbing the cliff at Okinawa as blood rains down on his men, points out to them that "we're not in Kansas anymore, Dorothy," a phrase I somehow doubt drill sergeants shouted in battle in 1945. After Garfield's Jesus figure spends half the movie telling the higher-ups he's not crazy and that he really does believe killing is wrong, he announces, "I never claimed to be sane." That must be how Mel Gibson gets things done, too.

Hell or High Water

THIS BANK-ROBBERY MOVIE OPENS WITH signs dotting the West Texas landscape that say things like 3 TOURS IN IRAQ BUT NO BAILOUT FOR PEOPLE LIKE US, establishing *Hell or High Water* as the only Oscar-nominated film that grappled with Trump's America as the train wreck approached. Right up to the unsatisfying, to-be-continued ending, the film's lugubrious quality marks *Hell or High Water* as an example of grievance cinema, art-directed for a new era of violent self-pity, economic decline, and racial appropriation.

The film indulges its white characters on both sides of the law in fantasies that their pain is the same as that of the minor characters who are Native American. One of the bank-robber brothers (Ben Foster) confronts a Comanche gambler (Gregory Cruz) at an Indian casino, getting in his face to inform him they are the same, and Jeff Bridges's Texas Ranger confronts a sunrise wrapped in a blanket, the film's big chief. When Foster kills Bridges's Native American deputy (Gil Birmingham), it's up to viewers to decide whether the film means to indict this kind of posturing or not. The bank robbers and Bridges face different kinds of disenfranchisement, but the film's analysis of American history favors deadly confrontation as the best way to save the farm, or buy it.

Fences

DENZEL WASHINGTON DIRECTS AND STARS IN this film adaptation of August Wilson's play, opening it up to real locations in Pittsburgh without marring its essential qualities as a stage drama. His performance and direction are generous and sensitive, allowing plenty of room for the actors in smaller parts (Mykelti Williamson, Russell Hornsby) to dig into their characters. Washington's portrayal of Troy does not shy away from the character's bitterness or his unfairness to his son and wife (Jovan Adepo and Viola Davis), and he doesn't make himself look bad in a false, movie-star way. He looks bad because he has embraced Troy's decline. The film unfolds in the limited spaces of the Maxsons' backyard and house, crowding Troy, who is lonely and death-haunted despite the love of his family and his best friend, Bono (Stephen Henderson).

Wilson's evocation of the limitations imposed on the black working class offers a remedy to too much *La La Land*. If Washington holds his thumb down on the scale, it's to emphasize the downer aspects of serious American theater against the relentless optimism of fake unhappy endings.

Captain Fantastic

VIGGO MORTENSEN, IN ALL HIS INDIE GLORY but also somehow bordering on Jeff Daniels, plays a survivalist family man and amateur Maoist in *Captain Fantastic*. Living off the grid in an Oregon forest with his many children, he has taught his kids to hunt with bows and arrows and knives, to revere science and Nabokov, and to speak proper English. If they break into Esperanto to talk behind his back, he scolds them for it. He wants them to "contribute to making a better world" away from the horror of malls, McMansions, and video games, but after their mother commits suicide, this modern Swiss Family Robinson has to reenter modern life in all its bland stupidity. Here is a film not afraid to point out that many of the people you encounter after leaving the woods are fat.

Mortensen's wife (Trin Miller), who has been away from the family, hospitalized for bipolar disorder, is seen only in dreams, flashbacks, and photos. It's enjoyable the way Matthew Ross's screenplay and direction try to denaturalize ordinary American life as it's lived in the suburbs, but nothing everyone hasn't thought a million times before. To provide mainstream balance, Ross tempers Mortensen's nobility by presenting him as a danger to his family, a radical who hasn't really thought things through.

What becomes the most interesting thing about *Captain Fantastic* by the end is the absence of Mrs. Fantastic, his wife and the mother of all these kids. She gets two funerals in the film, one traditional, at the insistence of her wealthy parents, and one presided over by Mortensen after he and the kids dig her up and cremate her. They flush her ashes down a toilet (her idea), then hold an oceanside ceremony at which they group-sing her favorite song, "Sweet Child

O' Mine," a music choice that constitutes a shock ending if ever there was one. In the film's coda, a newly responsible Mortensen has become both mother and father to his brood, emancipated into domesticity on a chicken farm.

Nocturnal Animals

THE FIRST TRULY TRUMPIST FILM OF ITS ERA, this disgusting and absurd neo-noir, by the fashion designer Tom Ford, flaunts its malice and misogyny, presenting them as criticisms of the art world and its hangers-on. Ford cribs from the films of David Lynch, Stanley Kubrick, and Sam Peckinpah as if no one has ever seen them before and he's doing the audience a favor. A notorious recovering Botox addict, he inserts a meaningless close-up of a society lady's surgically altered face into a conversation, just to drive home how much better he is than the people who have made him rich. The obese nude women presented as Jenny Saville–style art objects in the film's opening gallery scenes are used as props and dismissed, a bunch of performers duped into freak-show self-empowerment.

Since most of the film is concerned with brutal rape and murder, Ford's animosity to Amy Adams's character in *Nocturnal Animals* is all the more repellent when the film flirts with exposing her as a rape victim in the story within the story. Instead, we learn she just broke Jake Gyllenhaal's heart when she aborted their child while having an affair with another man. The tables have turned, however, and now Adams's new husband is cheating on her. This handsome, empty-souled dimwit (Armie Hammer) gets off the hook pretty easy here compared with everyone else. Gyllenhaal, a sad-sack novelist, needles Adams by sending her galleys of his new book, a spiteful tome Ford

seems to think redeems him as an artist and a man. "Who are the real animals?" Ford asks, which is a stupid question that probably occurred to him at a dinner party like the one in the film. The lengthy sub-Antonioni ending makes Adams pathetic and unattractive despite the rich trappings of her wardrobe and makeup (more irony), while Aaron Taylor-Johnson, as the main hillbilly rapist, has a perfect haircut throughout the film. The difference exposes Ford's sympathies, if you can call them that. +

TIM BARKER
The Bleak Left

Endnotes 1: Preliminary Materials for a Balance Sheet of the 20th Century, 2008.
Endnotes 2: Misery and the Value Form, 2010.
Endnotes 3: Gender, Race, Class and Other Misfortunes, 2013.
Endnotes 4: Unity in Separation, 2015.

IT'S NO SECRET THAT THE COLLAPSE OF international communism from 1989 to 1991 forced many Marxists into defensive positions. What's less well understood is why so many others took the opportunity to abjure some of Marxism's most hallowed principles. Perry Anderson, in a surprisingly admiring review-essay on Francis Fukuyama from 1992, concluded by soberly assessing what remained of socialism. At the center of socialist politics, he wrote, had always been the idea that a new order of things would be created by a militant working class, "whose self-organization prefigured the principles of the society to come." But in the real world, this group had "declined in size and cohesion." It wasn't that it had simply moved from the developed West to the East; even at a global level, he noted, "its relative size as

IN THE MID-1980S, when we created The Brooklyn Brewery, many people questioned naming the beer Brooklyn. They were wrong. Brooklyn has been an incredible calling card for our company, in the USA and abroad. Over the years, I have been involved in several efforts to develop a slogan for Brooklyn. Some were for the brewery and one was for the Brooklyn Tourism Board. All failed. Fughetaboutit. Brooklyn is simply too vast and too diverse to be described by a single slogan. I am reminded of a line in the Brooklyn poet Walt Whitman's poem, *Song of Myself:*

> I contradict myself?
> Very well then, I contradict myself.
> I contain multitudes.

Brooklyn too contains multitudes. With 2.6 million inhabitants, it would be the country's fourth biggest city if it were an independent municipality and not a borough of New York City. In its 75 square miles there are thriving communities from all corners of the planet. Instead of a slogan, Brooklyn Brewery has relied on the brilliant logo developed thirty years ago by our designer, Milton Glaser, to express our Brooklyn heritage. It was Milton who gave me the confidence to name the company Brooklyn. The elegant script B in the logo has become an iconic symbol of Brooklyn in much the same way Milton's I LOVE NY tagged New York City.

Steve Hindy
CO-FOUNDER

BROOKLYNBREWERY.COM
@BROOKLYNBREWERY

a proportion of humanity is steadily shrinking." The upshot was that one of the fundamental tenets of Marxism was wrong. The future offered an increasingly smaller, disorganized working class, incapable of carrying out its historic role.

In 1992, calling oneself a "socialist" was an anachronism. Today it is a label with which millions of Americans identify. A self-described "democratic socialist" came agonizingly close to winning the Democratic Party primaries in 2016. And the premise that Anderson felt we should abandon has been nonchalantly reassumed. Articles in *Jacobin*, the most popular socialist publication to appear in the United States in decades, routinely conclude with a reaffirmation of the place of the working class at the center of socialist politics.

But lost in the heady rush of leftist revival is the still-nagging problem of agency. The fortunes of the organized working class have never been more dire. In the advanced capitalist core, unions have recovered some prestige but not even a fraction of their mid-century power, while the historical European parties of the Socialist International continue their slow collapse. In the Global South, the Brazilian Workers' Party (PT) and South Africa's ANC–Communist–trade union alliance, rare bright spots after 1989, are losing credibility after decades of accommodation to private economic prerogatives. There are, in absolute terms, more industrial workers than ever, and probably as much industrial conflict. But there is no sense that as the working class becomes larger, it is becoming more unified. The end of the end of history has not seen the resumption of the forward march of labor.

In fact, Marxists have been worried about workers for a long time. After 1917, workers tried to take power in Germany, Italy, Hungary, and Spain; their defeat led to fascism. Beginning with Antonio Gramsci, Marxists outside the Soviet Union tried to understand what went wrong. As fascism and armed resistance gave way to social democracy and a moderated capitalism, some radicals consigned the working class to history altogether. It was harder, though, to discard the idea that *someone*, somehow, would bring socialism to the world. Peasants, national-liberation movements, students, and the incarcerated all provided substitutes. With the emergence of movements like environmentalism and gay liberation after the 1960s, many decided that the whole idea of a revolutionary subject was misguided. Why not recognize a plurality of movements, emerging unpredictably and united not by objective interest but by creative alliances? Today, even as discussions of economic inequality abound, this pluralism remains common sense in activist circles.

But this solution has not satisfied everyone. In 2008, a slim journal published by an anonymous collective began to circulate within the thinning ranks of the revolutionary left. Its cover was solid green except for the journal's name, *Endnotes*, in white, and a subtitle, "Preliminary Materials for a Balance Sheet of the Twentieth Century," in black. The text was produced by a discussion group formed in Brighton, UK, in 2005 with origins in long-running debates in the German and French ultraleft. (Over time the group broadened to include participants in California.) Authorship wasn't really secret; you could find bylined references scattered across CVs and footnotes. But collective authorship was key to the distinctive voice, something like the crossfire of an unusually well-prepared reading group recollected in tranquility. The essays run on, sometimes more than ten thousand words, to simulate the modulations of conversation. Disciplinary specializations sit side by side, with notes on Kant and Schelling following graphs of employment patterns in UK manufacturing. The style is by turns earnest ("The communisation of social relations among seven billion people will take time"), bleak ("There is always someone more abject than you"), and droll ("Proletarians do not have to see anyone they do not like, except at work"). It is a journal whose scope, rigor, and utter lack of piety make it one of the consistently challenging left-wing periodicals of our time. In 2014, Anderson himself called it one of the "most impressive publications to emerge in the Bush-Obama era."

Endnotes emerged from narrow Marxist debates, but in the aftermath of the 2008 crash, the journal supplemented theory with exhaustive analysis of social movements. For the editors, our current age of riots and occupations demands that we confront again the unfashionable question of the revolutionary subject. The editorial collective describes itself as "communist"; its members want the abolition of capitalism, which because of its powerful self-reinforcing tendencies can only be overcome by a coherent social force. But what group of people has enough in common to imagine itself as a social force and also has the strategic leverage to change the world? Unlike many socialists, the editors of *Endnotes* do not reflexively answer, "The working class." They ask the question in order to show that this cannot possibly be the answer.

THE FIRST ISSUE OF *Endnotes* contained a translation, with commentary, of a debate between the militant Gilles Dauvé and the French editorial collective Théorie Communiste. Dauvé and TC began publishing in the 1970s, lonely inheritors of the tradition of anti-Bolshevik (or ultraleftist) communism that ran from Karl Korsch to the Situationist International. They argued that the

European left—whether social democratic, Leninist, or anarcho-syndicalist—aspired to "take over the *same* world and manage it in a new way," whether through government ownership, the dictatorship of the proletariat, or workers' councils. Real communism (the abolition of "exchange, money, commodities, the existence of separate enterprises, the state and—most fundamentally—wage labour and the working class itself") was imagined, if at all, as something waiting far in the future.

Dauvé and TC reject the idea that communism could be instated "after the revolution." Instead, the revolution itself would take place through the establishment of communist social relations—a process they called "communization." Communization is an elusive concept, but it seems to define a politics in which the tactics themselves establish alternatives to capitalism. Think of the difference between a socialist party winning an election in a capitalist country and a crowd of rioters passing out food they looted from a warehouse. In the first case, the socialists cannot help but assume responsibility for running the economy they inherit while they assemble an alternative economy piecemeal. In the second, the riot itself embodies an alternative form of distributing wealth. The communizing current, always tiny, enjoyed a moment of prominence when its slogans ("Occupy everything, demand nothing") were emblazoned on public universities in California during protests against a rise in tuition in 2009. They reappeared during Occupy Wall Street in 2011.

Radicals always accuse one another of being insufficiently radical. But there is a deeper argument between Dauvé and Théorie Communiste. For Dauvé, associated with a journal called *Invariance*, communism is an eternal idea, "an ever-present (if at times

submerged) possibility," latent in all workers' movements. As the left surged in 1917, 1936, and 1968, the promised land came into view, but because of betrayals, hesitation, and tactical errors, no one ever got there. In TC's view, endorsed by *Endnotes*, these failures were unavoidable. Different historical situations call for different kinds of struggle. There is no point in criticizing earlier movements for being bad communists, because the idea of communization could only emerge from the most recent stage of capitalism.

Endnotes/TC elaborate this position by dividing workers' struggles into stages. The century stretching from Marx to the 1970s was the age of "programmatism" (named for the ambitious political platforms—the Gotha Program, the Erfurt Program, the Godesberg Program—routinely issued by socialist parties during this period). Workers focused on capturing industrial production by organizing labor parties, going on strike, or occupying factories. They acted as though they were central to industry and to society as a whole. For a time, no strategy seemed more sensible. The number of industrial wage workers was growing rapidly, and many of them shared experiences and interests. Together, they discovered power: a strike in steel or coal made the entire economy scream. Many shared Marx's confidence in "a class always increasing in numbers, and disciplined, united, organized by the very mechanism of the process of capitalist production itself."

History was not kind to these premises. After May 1968, ultraleftists watched for the reemergence of insurrectionary workers' councils. But absenteeism, sabotage, theft, and walkouts were more common than calls for self-management. Rather than reorganizing work to their liking, workers preferred not to work at all. Drawing on the work of Robert Brenner, *Endnotes* attributes this negative orientation to transformations within capitalism. The percentage of manufacturing employment had peaked by the late '60s and was on the decline. In the '70s, industry reached overcapacity, resulting in cratering profits. Capitalists responded by breaking unions, shuttering plants, and moving production to places where labor was cheaper and regulations more lax. But even where wages were low, automation displaced human labor at dizzying rates. Workers weren't being brought together. They were losing their jobs, their shifts, and everything they once held in common. If politics was possible at all for "a working class in transition, a working class tending to become a class excluded from work," it would not resemble the "programmatist" era.

THE IDEA THAT "the working class as such cannot be the focus of revolutionary theory" was an awkward starting point for a Marxist journal. The second issue of *Endnotes* (2010) dwelled in this discomfort. Marx himself clearly valued parties, programs, and demands. He held that communism required a transition period, during which workers would be paid with coupons according to hours worked. And money wasn't the worst thing that would outlive capitalism. Even the immediate abolition of child labor, Marx thought, was "incompatible with the existence of large-scale industry and hence an empty, pious wish."

Endnotes conceded that Marx, as a participant in the workers' movement, held positions that were once plausible and politically useful, though in retrospect inadequate. But they also believed that Marx had anticipated their own postworker perspective—a reading they derived from a mostly German current known as "value-form theory." In the orthodox reading of Marx, workers produce wealth, but part of their product is taken away from them by their employers; under socialism, workers will produce wealth in much the same way but receive the full value of their labor. This analysis suggests a vision of socialism in which, as Lenin wrote, "the whole of society will have become a single office and a single factory, with equality of labor and pay." The value-form theorists reject this view. On their reading, the problem with capitalism is not how the products of labor are distributed but the fact that society is organized around labor in the first place.

People have always worked to produce useful things. But under capitalism, labor becomes the basis of all social relationships. Marx tried to describe this novelty with his distinction between abstract and concrete labor. In every kind of society, people perform concrete labor—for example, turning a piece of leather into a shoe. In a capitalist economy, people also work in order to acquire the products of *other* people's labor. The shoemaker makes shoes so that he can buy a car, produced by autoworkers he will never meet. This form of social organization—in which workers essentially trade their labor—requires that every form of concrete labor be measurable according to a common metric, as if all were products of "abstract labor," or labor as such. For Marx, this metric is labor time. Workers receive an hourly wage, which they use to buy products whose prices reflect labor costs. Firms compete over the relative cost of their products, forcing them to minimize labor costs and maximize productivity. Society as a whole comes to be organized around the production of value generally, not specific use-values to satisfy specific human needs, and the labor process is constantly reshaped and degraded by the imperative to produce efficiently. Given this reading, socialism would be not a giant factory, but a world where wealth and value no longer took the form of congealed labor time. (The positive form it *would* take has never been clear.) Here, *Endnotes* found a German rhyme for the French ultraleft position that workers need to leave the workplace, not seize it.

A crucial part of *Endnotes*'s reading of Marx was empirical. It was always assumed, by Marxists and bourgeois theorists alike, that the dynamics of capitalism would swell the ranks of wage laborers in industrial employment. And for a while this was true: industry did grow, up to a point, in the capitalist core, and over time this model spread to "developing" countries. But as *Endnotes* pointed out, industrial wage workers never became even a simple majority anywhere (except, briefly, Belgium).

Marx himself had noted that capitalism "presses to reduce labor time to a minimum" as it destroys the once-ubiquitous arrangements through which people directly produced the things they needed. The result he anticipated was a growing number of people who needed to find work at the very moment their human labor was no longer needed—"a surplus population," in Marx's phrase. What he failed to anticipate was the emergence of industries like automobiles that, despite being mostly capital intensive, also required large numbers of laborers. But according to *Endnotes*, the new industries and the state managers who facilitated their rise could only delay the inevitable. Marxists have waited long enough that Marx is right again: we have a surplus population.

Not only communists believe this time may be different. As a more famous unbylined English magazine, the *Economist*, put it in 2014: "Previous technological innovation has always delivered more long-run employment, not less. But things can change."

Around the world, more than a billion people can only dream of selling their labor power. From the point of view of employers, they are unneeded for production, even at the lowest wages. Even in China, the new workshop of the world, there were no net industrial jobs created between 1993 and 2006. The size of China's industrial workforce—around 110 million people—is vast in absolute terms. But relative to the population of China, the number suggests the limited demand for industrial labor, not just in Detroit but around the world.

In the United States, with unemployment below 5 percent, it seems fanciful to talk about the end of wage labor. Seen globally, the exceptional character of the American economy is stark. So is the challenge of imagining a strategy that would benefit or even make sense to proletarians scattered across a planet of slums. *Endnotes*'s pessimism resonates with mainstream economics, especially Dani Rodrik's conclusions in a series of papers on "premature deindustrialization." Rodrik finds that developing countries "are running out of industrialization opportunities sooner and at much lower levels of income compared to the experience of early industrializers," but maintains that while this "premature deindustrialization" closes off familiar development strategies, there may be alternative routes to growth. *Endnotes* takes the darker view that these billions are "pure surplus" whom the system will never find an interest in exploiting. "It exists now only to be managed: segregated into prisons, marginalized in ghettos and camps, disciplined by the police, and annihilated by war." Even in the US, the low official unemployment numbers conceal millions of prisoners literally locked out of the formal economy.

The displacement of human labor from industrial production has not been ignored in recent left-wing thought. In fact, technological change has generated widespread enthusiasm for "postwork" or "antiwork" strains of Marxism, a tendency captured in slogans like "accelerationism" and "fully automated luxury communism." For these thinkers, the crisis of industrial employment can be solved by letting robots do work while the former working class, now sustained by a guaranteed minimum income, devotes itself to noneconomic pursuits. It is an attractive idea, both because of the elegance of the solution (No jobs? Abolish work!) and because it is more pleasant to imagine a future in which upper-middle-class fecklessness, rather than favela desperation, is the future for the entire planet.

Endnotes would likely object, perhaps by invoking one of their favorite lines (slightly restated, in their version) from Marx: "Communism is not an idea or a slogan. It is the real movement of history, the movement which—in the rupture—gropes its way out of history." We can sit around all day talking about the future we want, but we don't get to choose how capitalism ends. In a memorable essay about logistics, Jasper Bernes takes aim at the techno-optimists who believe we can seize "the globally distributed factory" system and do with it what we wish.* Bernes argues instead that many forms of economic organization wouldn't make sense under socialism. He takes logistics—rearranging supply chains and transport costs—as his example. The complex logistical innovations that keep Walmart's shelves stocked are designed not to maximize productivity but to leverage the competition between different low-wage national economies. "Without those differentials"—presumably abolished under socialism—"most supply-chains

would become both wasteful and unnecessary." Revolutionaries cannot simply take over and "reconfigure" the supply chains; they can only obstruct them—blockading ports, blowing up warehouses, sabotaging trucks. This may sound like anarchist fantasy, but for Bernes and *Endnotes* these tactics follow from the strictest realism. The questions they ask are not easily dismissed. In the heroic age of 20th-century revolutions, for example, people could expect that

> some large percentage of the means of production for consumer goods were ready to hand, and one could locate, in one's own region, shoe factories and textile mills and steel refineries. A brief assessment of the workplaces in one's immediate environs should convince most of us—in the US at least, and I suspect most of Europe—of the utter unworkability of the reconfiguration thesis.... Most of these jobs pertain to use-values that would be rendered non-uses by revolution. To meet their own needs and the needs of others, these proletarians would have to engage in the production of food and other necessaries, the capacity for which does not exist in most countries.

This antinormative stance is part of what makes *Endnotes* so fascinating: surely there has never been such a sober magazine of the ultraleft. Its pages are completely empty of exhortations, special pleading, and wishful thinking. The contrast with most political writing is clear, and reading the journal makes one aware of how much left-wing writing traffics in vague optimism. But in the very success of their criticism, the editors place themselves in a rigor trap, where it is hard to see how their own politics could survive the same kind of withering analysis

---

Endnotes occasionally publishes essays with individual bylines, like Bernes's, which they call "intakes." The most remarkable thing about these pieces is how closely, in tone and in politics, they resemble the official, unbylined essays.

they apply to others. Bernes writes quite reasonably, for example, that it is "politically non-workable" to expect that "15 percent or so of workers whose activities would still be useful [after the revolution] would work on behalf of others." But he believes, with the *Endnotes* collective, that communism is somehow workable. It is as if someone has given you a dazzling lecture on the dangers of drinking coffee before offering you a line of coke.

BETWEEN ISSUES TWO (2010) and three (2013), the Arab world revolted. Huge crowds took over squares in Spain and Greece, while somewhat smaller crowds did the same across the US. Riots raged across England for almost a week, and the murder of Trayvon Martin in Florida sparked the Black Lives Matter movement in the US. *Endnotes* deployed the concept of surplus populations to explore how this "intensification of struggle" could occur without "the return of a workers' identity." The crisis of class was evident in the masses of unemployed young people in the squares. It was also clear in the icons of the movements: Mohamed Bouazizi and Eric Garner weren't striking workers but street vendors harassed by the police. Instead of prescribing a dose of Marxism to the protesters, the editors asked Marxists to take a lesson from the absence of workers' rhetoric in the new movements.

According to *Endnotes*, the shape of the new struggles was determined by the ongoing decomposition of the working class into heterogeneous fractions. None of these fractions could plausibly present itself as representative of the common interest, as industrial workers had done. Rather, stagnant growth rates and regimes of austerity had *sharpened* the conflict between different kinds of proletarians. Pensioners and unemployed youth, "native" citizens and immigrants, public employees and non-unionized workers, all found themselves competing for shares in a shrinking pie. What they had in common—the need to earn a living—made them rivals, even enemies.

Endnotes called this predicament "the riddle of composition": which class fractions might add up to a political threat? The movement of the squares answered the riddle by repressing differences under the sign of "the people" (as evidenced in slogans ranging from Occupy's "Bail out the people" to the Arab Spring's "The people demand the fall of the regime"). The populist rhetoric, as well as the characteristic refusal of programmatic demands, eschewed specificity in order to make room for as many groups as possible. Since the "people" ranged from downwardly mobile professionals to the destitute, they could not come together in "neighborhoods, schools, job centers, workplaces." Their common identity existed only in the squares, where exacting democratic procedures supposedly heralded a new society. With physical presence as their only leverage, the movements evaporated when the squares were cleared.

Elsewhere in issue three, *Endnotes* addressed the rioting that swept England after the police shooting of Mark Duggan in Tottenham, London, in August 2011. "It would take quite an optimist to find in all this any literal harbingers of revolution or of building class struggle," they concluded. But riots and looting provided a glimpse of a future where repression by the police was more important than fights with the boss, and the fiercest struggles raged at sites of consumption rather than production. For *Endnotes*, this was not exploitation but "abjection"—the condition of being excluded from prevailing social forms of wealth and dignity but unable to exit the system. The abject is the opposite of the "affirmable" identity of the classical labor movement. Workers used to sing "without our brain and muscle, not a single wheel could turn," or "we have been naught; we shall be all." Today, the casualties of capital are better characterized by the title of Marc Lamont Hill's recent book on Ferguson, Flint, and beyond: *Nobody*.

Abjection is bound up with racism—consider the exclusion marked in older phrases like "ghetto" and "the underclass." In issue four (2015), *Endnotes* analyzed Black Lives Matter as an inheritor of the failures of Occupy Wall Street. "Black" described a group smaller than "the 99 percent," but it reflected a more concrete social reality, and perhaps a more subversive potential. No one but the homeless had an existential stake in Occupy—something that could not be said of the movement for black lives. Despite the existence of class distinctions among black Americans, there was less distance between the black upper class and the black proletariat than there was between rich and poor whites. But as the movement grew, the distinctions would become harder to ignore. The authors pointed to a cleavage between those from the nationally prominent activist layer (who, whatever their origins, were likely to have attended college) and the lower-profile, more victimized, and possibly more active residents of places like Ferguson and Sandtown-Winchester, who first took the streets when their neighbors were killed.

Black Lives Matter did remarkable work suturing these divisions. For instance, DeRay McKesson, who went from Teach for America to Ferguson to a six-figure job as chief human-capital officer in the Baltimore public schools, has consistently refused to condemn rioting. In the terms of *Endnotes*'s Marxism, the class elasticity of blackness (a category stretching from Freddie Gray to Barack Obama) could not be dismissed if it was still able to "induce such large-scale dynamic mobilizations in the American population." But the cleavage was real nonetheless, confirmed by the unsolved murder in September 2016 of Ferguson activist Darren Seals. After his death, national news outlets reported that Seals, who had been beside Michael Brown's mother, Lezley McSpadden, on the night of Darren Wilson's nonindictment, had become a fierce, even violent critic of national BLM leaders like McKesson, whom Seals had accused in social-media posts of "making millions on top of millions because of the work we put in, in FERGUSON."

Understanding the *Endnotes* position on race and gender requires grappling with the particular meaning they assign to the words *capital* and *capitalism*. For most Marxists, the working class is the protagonist of history. For *Endnotes*, the subject of recent history is capital. This is somewhat strange, since capital is not a person or a group of people with intentions or goals. Rather, *capital* here is a shorthand for the whole web of social relations among people living in capitalist societies. These social relations, viewed across historical time, have a distinct pattern of motion, whose course no individual could consciously choose or hope to master. The result of this motion has been the displacement of labor from production and the emergence of surplus populations. Class relations, such as those between workers and their employers, play a role in these developments. For example, when unions raise the cost of hiring workers, capitalists may choose to automate production; or when socialists seize power in an underdeveloped country, they may institute a five-year plan for industrialization. This makes class conflict a constituent part of capital, not a force capable of transcending it.

The workers' movement imagined the development of capitalism would undermine nonclass identities by drawing more and more people into increasingly uniform factories. According to *Endnotes*, this assumption was always misguided. The number of people dependent on the market has always included many who never enter into a wage contract, such as housewives and slaves, to name two indispensable examples. With the onset of deindustrialization, the inadequacy of class as a unifying concept has become clearer than ever. Accordingly, *Endnotes* accords "gender, race, class and other misfortunes" equal importance.* But this is not because they see different forms of oppression as plural and incommensurable. Capitalism is still a single integrated whole, but it depends on and generates many forms of social conflict.

In some cases, it is easy to see what this means: gender and race exist in historically specific forms, and today these forms are shaped by the unfolding of capitalist value production. To take just one example, *Endnotes* thinks capitalism could not exist without a separate, domestic sphere where human life is created and sustained without the direct mediation of the market. Without this separation, capitalists would be responsible for the upkeep of the working class, a contradiction in a system premised on the employer's ability to free himself of workers by firing them. It works the other way, too: before capitalism there was no "domestic" sphere, as most production took place in households, with men commanding (rather than hiring) the labor of their wives and children.

So far, so good: two forms—class and gender—depend on each other for their existence. What is trickier to understand in *Endnotes*'s theory is how the forms of gender and race that exist under capitalism relate to the forms of gender and race that existed before it, or might exist after it. Since capitalism is treated as a systematic whole, the revolution must not only destroy class society but also—and simultaneously—destroy gender, race, et cetera. It's easy to sympathize with *Endnotes*'s desire to resist a hierarchy of oppressions, but trying to imagine an instantaneous revolution in which every division between people is overcome at once strains both the historical and the utopian imagination. It seems far more plausible that forms such as race and gender develop unevenly, retaining aspects that predate capitalism even as they are constantly reshaped by new conditions. Likewise, it is easier to imagine a revolution that would dismantle interlocking social forms piece by piece, just as they were assembled.

Everything is about capitalism, but class is nothing special. This is the distinctive *Endnotes* position on the perennial conflict between identity politics and Marxism. Another way of putting it is that capitalism is a real universal, but only in the negative sense. What can billions of people, different from one another in every way, have in common besides the fact that they all need to work for a living? The upshot, for *Endnotes*, is that we should no longer speak about class consciousness but "consciousness of capital"—an awareness that all our fates are shaped by a single system, even though its pressures, rather than crystallizing resistance, push to break things apart.

CONTINUING THIS LINE of argument, *Endnotes* devoted the bulk of its fourth, most

---

* An interesting effect of the collective authorship is that a reader never knows which sentences have been written by white men. The *Endnotes* member most publicly associated with gender theory is Maya Gonzalez.

recent, issue to a history of the workers' movement as a form of identity politics. From the first issue, the journal had aimed "to undermine the illusion that [the workers' movement] is somehow 'our' past, something to be protected or preserved." Here, in nearly forty thousand words, they performed their most merciless demystification yet. As they had argued before, the workers' movement was based on the premise that the development of capitalism would forge a "collective worker" in "a compact mass," a future already visible in the factories inhabited by semiskilled male workers. When the collective did not arrive at the appointed hour, activists responded by constructing a moral community dedicated to the collective affirmation of a workers' identity. In socialist parties and mutual-aid societies, at picnics and in union halls, "proletarians were made to forget they were Corsican or Lyonnais" and became bound to one another as workers.

The identity was fashioned in response to pressing material problems confronting the urban proletariat. Collective action such as striking was difficult among people who did not trust one another; the propagation of an ethic of mutuality was required to get people to take risks for strangers. Furthermore, the goals of the labor movement were constrained by the exclusion from political power of the popular classes, who (outside the United States) were denied the franchise well into the late 19th century. The culture of working-class organization was partly a tool in the fight for political power: by emphasizing the dignity of labor and promoting moral causes such as temperance, the leaders of the labor movement tried to demonstrate that they represented a class worthy of inclusion in the social order. Inevitably, this involved targeting deviants within—including the lumpenproletariat scorned by Rosa

Luxemburg as a counterrevolutionary "school of sharks." In opposing bourgeois contempt for the supposedly degenerate proletariat, the proponents of workers' identity absorbed many of the values of the dominant society, stressing the respectability and propriety of working men as well as the ability of union leaders to maintain orderly production. Workers built a movement "only insofar as they believed, and convinced others to believe, in a shared identity: the collective worker."

In other hands, this account of class formation would be a success story, proving that the willful construction of identities can be a way to achieve power. Antonio Gramsci, breaking in his own way with orthodox Marxism, understood that the working class would not mechanically come to dominate politics in the advanced capitalist countries, and so communists would need to articulate working-class politics in a coalition with other class fractions and reinforce straightforward economic arguments with an edifice of moral and cultural authority. The political indeterminacy of class politics was a project that socialists could overcome: by exploiting the ambiguity, they could construct a winning working-class bloc in any given historical moment. The base did not determine the superstructure: canny superstructural intervention could potentially transform the economy and society overall.

By contrast, *Endnotes* denies that the cultural construction of class identity can ever cut sharply enough to alter the long-term course of history. The figure of "the worker," though constructed by activists, was powerful because the reality of factory production came close enough to the myth to make it plausible. All of it was undone when the factories closed. In fact, the workers' movement, by promoting economic "growth" and becoming a partner in production, actually helped hasten the maturity of capitalist production and, with it, its own irrelevance. Class, in the final instance, is a dependent variable dragged behind the independent motion of capital. Even the most adept organic intellectuals could never bend history in a new direction; they could only mark time until objective necessity entered a new phase, one that no longer required workers or their identities.

In a brief coda to issue four, *Endnotes* finds a blunt illustration of their thesis in the former Yugoslavia.* Global capital may be largely uninterested in exploiting labor in the Balkans, but the theology of the workers' state remains in living memory, so that "regardless of it standing idle for years, the local factory remained a place of identification and pride." Without power over production—and facing indifferent investors—employees lose access to the conventional forms of labor conflict. When the "workers" occupy factories, to demand back wages or the resumption of production, they resort to tactics reminiscent of prison rebellions: "hunger strikes, self-mutilations and suicide threats," including laying their bodies on train tracks. They are not bringing to birth a new world but desperately seeking a way out.

Endnotes is reluctant to suggest what might replace the workers' movement, and constantly protests—perhaps too much—the assumption that the surplus population might be the new subject of history. But the editors strongly suggest that the basis for new forms of solidarity and struggle

will be a general tendency for things to get worse. There were many college students occupying plazas, but they did so knowing they no longer represent an elite in waiting. Michael Brown and Trayvon Martin were killed in "suburb[s] in transition," hollowed out by the housing crisis. Economic decline was reflected within the movements, which frequently saw "the worse-off entering and transforming protests initiated by the better-off"—occupations and demonstrations giving way to homeless camps and lumpen riots. The entrance of poorer people often revealed that the new participatory structures were not an alternative model of meeting basic necessities. In the past, or at least this stylized rendering of the past, the involvement of more groups of people meant a revolution was growing in strength, swelling until it seemed to represent a universal cause. Today, in the absence of unifying institutions and ideas, the diversification of the protest movement only poses problems.

Endnotes's stress on "descending modulations" leads to a pessimism that strangely converges on conservative conventional wisdom. For example, it dismisses the hope "that the state can be convinced to act rationally, to undertake a more radical Keynesian stimulus." Even before the crisis, sovereign-debt levels had soared (reaching levels much higher than they had been in 1929, before the Great Depression). Governments, in this story, had borrowed money during bad times, intending to pay it back during the recovery. But falling growth rates meant that even when recessions ended, states had trouble finding revenue to settle their debts.

---

* An important source for the history of the workers' movement in the issue is an essay titled "Telling the Truth About Class" by Hungarian philosopher Gáspár Miklós Tamás, who had been a dissident in socialist Hungary. *Endnotes*, like Tamás, sees little difference between capitalist development and Eastern Bloc revolutions that empowered "technocratic communists to focus on the developmental tasks at hand—namely, breaking up peasant communities and displacing peasants to the cities, where they could be put to work in gigantic mills."

These high levels of debt, carried over into the crisis, limited states' ability to borrow more. Keynes (and his followers today, like Yanis Varoufakis) thought they could save capitalism from itself by demonstrating the folly of austerity. But for *Endnotes*, there is no alternative, at least until the revolution—a position disconcertingly close to right-wing dogma.

Just as they scorn antiausterity hopes, *Endnotes* rejects activists who think "communities would do just fine if the police stopped interfering." The editors emphasize "a very real crime wave beginning in the late 1960s" and insist that police bring "a semblance of order to lives that no longer matter to capital." Their account of the Ferguson experience emphasizes, to a degree uncommon outside far-right news sources, chaos and violence: the "small but significant number of guns on the streets, often fired into the air," the nights of "shooting at police, looting, and a journalist . . . robbed," the fact that many victims of police violence may not have been "innocent" in the straightforward sense demanded by moralizing liberals. The point is not to defend police—banished along with the rest of the state in the *Endnotes* ideal—but to point out the ugly realities of a decaying capitalism. Unmanageable chaos, on this reading, is one of the causes of division among supporters of BLM, drawing out some of the class contradictions already latent in it.

If the techno-utopian, accelerationist Marxism can resemble Silicon Valley dreams of pure automation, *Endnotes*'s Marxism bears traces of survivalist pessimism. As the laws of capitalist development take their course, we're told, more and more people will own nothing but their labor, and find that their labor is worth nothing. Having no alternative, some of them will discover ways to "destroy the link between

finding work and surviving." Jacques Camatte, a founder of communization theory and inspiration to *Endnotes*, eventually became a leading anarcho-primitivist. *Endnotes* disavows this later Camatte, but given their insistence that communism dispense with markets and states (not to mention other capitalist mediations such as "nation [and] species"), it's unclear what the editors think would prevent a collapse in living standards. They concede that it is "entirely possible to imagine that hating one another, and ensuring that no one gets slightly better than anyone else, will take precedence over making the revolution." This is a staggering understatement. It's hard to imagine global economic decline unchecked by large-scale political institutions leading to anything *but* Hobbesian disaster. What needs justification is the hope that *Endnotes* retains: that the revolution is still possible, even if "the actual means of reconnecting individuals to their capacities, outside the market and the state, are impossible to foresee."

ENDNOTES, TOGETHER WITH similar collectives in other countries, publishes *Sic: international journal of communization*. Around spring 2014, Manos Manousakis, a Greek communizer who wrote for *Sic* about riots, began complaining to his reading group that "everything is over" and "nothing matters any more since this cycle of struggles leads nowhere." The depth of his disillusion became clear in early 2015, when he joined the new Syriza government as Minister of Economy, Infrastructure, Shipping, and Tourism. His tenure lasted until July of that year, when along with much of Syriza's left he resigned in protest of the government's acceptance of humiliating terms imposed by the European Union.

Manousakis's journey, which scandalized the international ultraleft, encapsulates the dilemma leftists face today. Rejecting the abstract antistatism of communist reading groups, he joined the parliamentary left in taking state power, only to discover the hard limits the system placed on even modest reform. Are there any other choices? It might be worth considering the central *Endnotes* metaphor of the "horizon"—a vision that frames all motion but that can never be reached, something that despite its omnipresence does not objectively exist. In the *Endnotes* critique of the workers'-movement horizon, real trends were extrapolated too far: the temporary explosion in industrial employment in Western Europe was taken to augur the transformation of global society into one big factory. The classical socialists were right that wage labor and industrial organization were reshaping society, and the strength of their analysis allowed them to achieve concrete victories:

"Basharat Peer's new book is impeccably timed. Amid all this loose talk of an authoritarian wave, an in-depth comparison of two oft-cited cases is welcome." — *Bookforum*

A QUESTION OF ORDER

BASHARAT PEER

INDIA, TURKEY, AND THE RETURN OF STRONGMEN

COLUMBIA GLOBAL REPORTS

Available now from COLUMBIA GLOBAL REPORTS
globalreports.columbia.edu @ColumbiaGR

the enfranchisement of the working class across Europe, the establishment of national health services, the erosion of deference on the streets and in the workplace. But the final industrial triumph did not occur, and we face a new horizon.

But what if this new horizon, leading to class decomposition and immediate communization, is accurate in some respects but exaggerated in others? The future according to *Endnotes* draws attention to central trends of our time: the breakdown of capitalism's link between work and survival, the displacement of human labor from production. A move away from the factory can be seen already in movements and discussions around the environment, guaranteed minimum income, mass incarceration, and women's unwaged labor. But perhaps *Endnotes* has overcorrected. Just as the dream of the unified working class has always been haunted by its actual incoherence, the new picture of an insuperably fractured proletariat ignores the ways in which the working class is still unified and meaningful.

Many socialists share much of *Endnotes*'s understanding of capitalist reality without accepting their millenarian conclusions about strategy. Robert Brenner's 2006 analysis of intercapitalist competition, *The Economics of Global Turbulence*, underwrites *Endnotes*'s claim that the global economy has been stuck in a long downturn since the 1970s. If you take their word for it, Brenner's graphs of steadily declining manufacturing profits point a straight line to communization. But his own political comments suggest that he continues to hew to the post-Trotskyist labor radicalism he first embraced in the late 1960s: radical potential remains in the hands of the working class, provided the rank and file can shake off union bureaucrats and the Democratic Party. Workers in the global supply chain (longshoremen, warehouse workers, truck drivers) may still have the leverage once enjoyed by workers in basic industry.

Fredric Jameson, another *NLR* stalwart, was moved by *Endnotes* to proclaim that "*Capital* is a book about unemployment"—endorsing their central claim about surplus populations. But his recent book, *An American Utopia*, returns to Leninist basics to imagine how capitalism could be transcended through the transformation of existing institutions. His conclusion, that the road to revolution runs through universal military service, is self-consciously provocative and less important than the broader message:

> I prefer the word socialism to communism in discussions today, because it is more practical than the latter and actually raises questions of party formation as well as transitions, privatizations, nationalizations, finances, and the like, which the loftier regions of communism allow us to avoid.

Words to make an *Endnotes* editor reach for the revolver: *socialism, party, finance, nation*, and, above all, *transition*. It is difficult to give up on the idea that there might be intermediate measures connecting the world we live in to the world we would prefer. The notion that the increasing complexity and interdependence of the economy points toward "the abolition of capital as private property within the boundaries of capitalist production itself" (*Capital* III) has always been the most exciting part of Marxism, the quality setting it apart from religious chiliasm or existential rebellion. Another world is not only possible, it is already taking form—unevenly, incompletely—around us all the time.

If nothing else, this philosophy allows for the possibility that current struggles could be successful, something *Endnotes* has trouble imagining. At one point, they concede that protest could "renegotiate the terms on which the crisis is being managed" through redistributive political reforms like a financial-transactions tax or a new wave of worker militancy. These are the things that most people on the left, including most Marxists, hope for and are working toward, and *Endnotes* does not claim they are strictly impossible. But the journal still dismisses those possibilities as akin to creating "a workers' council on the deck of the Titanic." Here *Endnotes*'s pessimism persists beyond what rigor and logic call for. If we can force a change in the terms of the crisis, why can't we imagine those proximate victories linking up with longer-term goals, through which things like the state, markets, and money (all of which existed before capitalism did—something *Endnotes* acknowledges) could be made to do things besides immiserate and exclude?

Endnotes unapologetically narrates the fortunes of the working class as the rise and fall of the industrial worker. Back then, labor was "engaged in building a modern world." Today's workers, however, are "employed in dead-end service jobs" and "see no purpose in their work." But "service" is a broad category. Growing numbers of health-care workers, largely women and nonwhite, suffer from exploitation and may hate their jobs with good reason. But the purpose of care work is easier to identify with, and harder for society to dispense with, than working retail. However communism turns out, people will continue to be born, get sick, and die; if for no other reason than this, many existing kinds of work will continue to be socially necessary. Why couldn't this kind of labor be affirmed the way industrial development once was? Couldn't it ground a program that demanded universal guarantees of health and human services alongside the abolition of differential racial and gendered responsibility for the care of others?

Endnotes benefits from the undeniable lack of success leftists have had in achieving either reform or revolution anywhere in the world recently. The experience of Greece's Syriza should trouble everyone who entertains hopes about taking state power and imposing a program. Most left-wing writing tries to cover these deep uncertainties with optimism of the will; it is proper, or at least inevitable, that radical politics involve some suspension of disbelief. Even the rigorous hopelessness of *Endnotes* gives way to a certain dreamlike quality when it imagines our long-run prospects. "Struggle can be endlessly generative," the editors rhapsodize, potentially generating even "the unification of humanity" and the end of "gender, race, class, nation, species."

Every political writer must balance groundless hope against deflating realism. *Endnotes* excels at the latter because it transfers all hope to a distant future. They write with the undisenchanted energy of someone who believes deeply in radical possibility, while refusing to take any unwarranted consolation from the way things are now. They offer the rest of us, who I believe are correct to place our hopes in programs and transitions, challenges that will not be answered easily. Perhaps, despite its cunning and erudition, the politics of *Endnotes* is no more serious than glib forms of anarchism. But on what grounds are our "realistic" politics any less fanciful? +

ALYSSA BATTISTONI
Monstrous, Duplicated, Potent

Donna Haraway. *Staying with the Trouble: Making Kin in the Chthulucene.* Duke, 2016.

THE FIRST TIME I ENCOUNTERED DONNA Haraway, in 2010, I was a graduate student in England doing a one-year master's in geography. The program—a cash cow for the university, I eventually realized—was an odd mix of critical theory and environmental-management advice. Readings alternated between Bruno Latour and lectures from BP executives about their sustainability program. As a form of counterprogramming, one of my classmates organized a reading group on Haraway's Cyborg Manifesto.

On first read, I was dazzled and bewildered. Desperate to impress the organizer, who I thought brilliant, I strained over it line by line in hopes of insight. In the end, I mumbled through our meeting. I didn't understand the Manifesto until I'd read it three more times. In truth, I probably still don't. But for a young woman struggling to understand the world after Hurricane Katrina and a global financial crisis, Haraway beckoned. She offered a way to make sense of the things that seemed absent from politics as I knew it: science, nature, feminism.

The Manifesto proclaims itself to be against origin stories, but its own is hard to resist. In 1982, the Marxist journal *Socialist Review*—a bicoastal publication originally titled *Socialist Revolution*, whose insurrectionary name was moderated in the late 1970s as politics soured—asked Haraway to write five pages on the priorities of socialist feminism in the Reagan era. Haraway responded with thirty. It was the first piece, she claimed, she had ever written on a computer (a Hewlett-Packard-86). The submission caused controversy at the journal, with disagreement breaking down along geographic lines. As Haraway later recalled in an interview, "The East Coast Collective truly disapproved of it politically and did not want it published." The more catholic West Coast won out, and the Manifesto was published in 1985 as "A Manifesto for Cyborgs: Science, Technology, and Socialist-Feminism in the 1980s," though it has been known colloquially as the Cyborg Manifesto ever since.

In one sense, Haraway did what she was asked: she outlined the contemporary state of political economy from a socialist-feminist perspective. Her reading of the shift to post-Fordism was loose but lucid. The rise of communications technologies made it possible to disperse labor globally while still controlling it, she noted, scattering once-unionized factory jobs across the continents. The gender of industrial work was changing too: there were more women assembling computer chips in East Asia than men slapping together cars in the American Midwest. Automation was lighter and brighter: in place of hulking industrial machinery, our "machines are made of sunshine"—but this light, invisible power nevertheless caused "immense human pain in Detroit and Singapore." Family structures were changing: mothers increasingly worked outside the home and headed up the household. The result was what Haraway, drawing on Richard Gordon, called the homework economy—a pointed term for what's euphemistically and blandly called the service economy.

The Manifesto offered a new politics for this new economy. Prescient about the need to organize the feminized, if not always female, sectors, Haraway explicitly called leftists to support SEIU District 925,

a prominent campaign to unionize office workers. She also criticized the idea of a universal subject, whether held up by Marxists (the proletarian) or radical feminists (the woman). A new politics had to be constructed not around a singular agent but on the basis of a patchwork of identities and affinities. How, then, to find unity across difference, make political subjects in a postmodern era, and build power without presuming consensus? "One is too few, but two are too many," she wrote cryptically. "One is too few, and two is only one possibility." Acting as isolated individuals leads nowhere, but the effort to act collectively cannot leave difference aside. Women of color, Haraway suggested, following Chela Sandoval, could not rely on the stability of either category; they might lead the way in forging a new, nonessentialist unity based on affinity rather than identity.

This is where the metaphor of the cyborg comes in. For Haraway, the cyborg is a hybrid figure that crosses boundaries: between human and machine, human and animal, organism and machine, reality and fiction. As a political subject, it is expansive enough to encompass the range of human experience in all its permutations. A hybrid, it is more than one, but less than two.

In place of old political formations, Haraway imagined new cyborgian ones. She hoped that "the unnatural cyborg women making chips in Asia and spiral dancing in Santa Rita Jail" would together "guide effective oppositional strategies." Her paradigmatic "cyborg society" was the Livermore Action Group, an antinuclear activist group targeting the Lawrence Livermore National Laboratory, a nuclear-weapons-research facility in Northern California. The group, she thought, was "committed to building a political form that actually manages to hold together witches, engineers, elders, perverts, Christians, mothers, and Leninists long enough to disarm the state."

What set the Manifesto apart from other reconceptions of feminism was its embrace of science. The cyborg was a figure that only a feminist biologist—herself an unlikely figure—could imagine. While by the 1980s many feminists were wary of biological claims about sexual difference, evading charges of essentialism by separating sex from gender (biology might give you a certain body, but society conditioned how you lived in it), Haraway argued that failing to take a position on biology was to "lose too much"—to surrender the notion of the body itself as anything more than a "blank page for social inscriptions." Distinguishing her attachment to the body from the usual Earth Mother connotations was its famous closing line: "I would rather be a cyborg than a goddess."

Who wouldn't? The cyborg's popularity was no doubt fueled in part by the vision of a bionic babe it suggested—a Furiosa or the Terminator—though it couldn't be further from her meaning. Asked what she considered a true moment of cyborgness in 1999, Haraway responded, "the sense of the intricacy, interest, and pleasure—as well as the intensity—of how I have imagined how like a leaf I am." The point was not that she shared some biological commonality with a leaf, or that she felt leaves to be kindred spirits (though she very well might have). What made her giddy was the thought of all the work that had gone into producing the knowledge that she was like a leaf—how incredible it was to be able to know such a thing—and the kinds of relationship to a leaf that such knowledge made possible.

Despite her frequent reminders that it was written as a "mostly sober" intervention into socialist-feminist politics rather than "the ramblings of a blissed-out,

techno-bunny fembot," many still read it as the latter. *Wired* profiled her enthusiastically in 1997. "To boho twentysomethings," they wrote, "her name has the kind of cachet usually reserved for techno acts or new phenethylamines." (More recently, the entrepreneurial synthetic biologist Drew Endy deployed the Manifesto in support of his bid to label synthetic biological products as "natural" under federal guidelines to increase their appeal to cautious consumers.)

Its Reagan-era coordinates may have changed, but the Manifesto remains Haraway's most widely read work. The cyborg became a celebrity, as did Haraway herself, both serving as signifiers of a queer, savvy, self-aware feminism. Yet she has grown weary of its success, admonishing readers that "cyborgs are critters in a queer litter, not the Chief Figure of Our Times."

Somewhat counterintuitively, it's Haraway herself who sometimes seems the Chief Figure. There's no Harawavian school, though she has many acolytes. She does not belong to any particular school herself, though many have attempted to place her. You can't really do a Harawavian analysis of the economy or the laboratory; other than the cyborg, she's produced few portable concepts or frameworks. Her own individual prominence runs counter to her view of intellectual work as collectively produced. Yet for thirty years she's been ahead of intellectual trends, not by virtue of building foundational frameworks but by inspiring others to spawn and spur entire fields, from feminist science studies to multispecies ethics. Her work tends to emerge from problems she sees in the world rather than from engagement with literatures, thinkers, or trends, yet it manages to transcend mere timeliness.

Her new book, *Staying with the Trouble*, is a commentary on the most pressing threat of our era: catastrophic climate change. It's hard to think of someone better suited to the task. Climate change requires ways of thinking capable of confronting the closely bound future of countless humans and non-humans, the basis for certainty in scientific findings, the political consequences of such knowledge, and the kinds of political action that such consequences call for. If Haraway has long practiced such hybrid thinking, that also means the problem best suited to challenging her thought—to testing its mettle, and its usefulness to our political future—has decisively arrived.

AFTER GRADUATING COLLEGE with a triple major in zoology, philosophy, and literature in 1966, Haraway went to Yale for a doctorate in biology. Her colleagues there were involved in political activism on "their issues," working against chemical warfare and biological racism. But Haraway was miserable in the lab. She argued with fellow students about the nature of cells: where her classmates saw them as discrete objects existing across the eons, Haraway thought of them as the way that broader biological processes had been bounded and defined at a particular point in time. Frustrated, she considered dropping out, but found a mentor and champion in G. Evelyn Hutchinson, known (ironically, given Haraway's disregard for patriarchs) as "the father of American ecology." Hutchinson's lab group read philosophy and literary theory: Alfred North Whitehead, Martin Heidegger, Charles Sanders Peirce.

Under Hutchinson's supervision, she wrote a dissertation heavily influenced by Thomas Kuhn's 1962 landmark *The Structure of Scientific Revolutions.* Kuhn had caused an uproar with his argument that rather than steadily progressing toward truth, the production of scientific knowledge was marked by conflict and upheaval. What scientists had once been certain was true would eventually be considered wrong. Each emerging framework was often incommensurable with what had come before. Kuhn called this phenomenon a "paradigm shift." A classic example was the transition from Newtonian physics to Einsteinian relativity.

Haraway's dissertation, "Crystals, Fabrics, and Fields: Metaphors of Organicism in Twentieth-Century Developmental Biology," drew on Kuhn's idea of interpretive frameworks in describing the rise of the organicist paradigm to replace the previous dueling frameworks of vitalism and mechanism. It's rarely read and now out of print, not to mention style. But it remains an important text for understanding Haraway's view of biology as a "way of knowing the world" shaped by both human language and non-human matter. Where others focused on one pole or the other, Haraway held the two together: the raw stuff of the world and how people made meaning from it. Her commitment to both, she tended to think, was the product of her Catholic upbringing. "If you grew up Catholic," she said in an interview, "your semiotics from the get-go had to do with the *implosion* of sign and flesh, not the separation."

In New Haven, Haraway lived in a commune with a mix of grad students and local residents. One was a member of the Black Panther Party at the time of the trial of Bobby Seale and the "New Haven Nine"; another was Jaye Miller, a PhD student in history who became Haraway's lover and, eventually, first husband. That he was gay posed no obstacle to either: Haraway tends to describe their relationship, fondly and with gleeful provocation, as akin to "brother-sister incest." Together they moved to the University of Hawaii, where Miller taught intellectual and world history and

Haraway taught biology and the history of science to "non-science majors" ("a wonderful ontological category," as she later put it) destined for hospitality jobs.

When they eventually decided amicably to split up, Haraway left Hawaii for a job in the history of science at Johns Hopkins. There she met her eventual second husband, Rusten Hogness, a PhD student in the department who audited her classes ("I was sure he was gay, which is why I liked him"), and Nancy Hartsock, a Marxist-feminist political theorist and editor of the radical feminist journal *Quest*. Together she and Hartsock started a women's studies program, joined a Marxist-feminist group addressing violence against women in Baltimore, and read feminist science fiction. Haraway sought to integrate her politics into her academic work, writing a number of essays examining the history of biology from Marxist-feminist perspectives and attempting to develop a radical epistemology.

In a 1980 letter to the *Radical Science Journal*, a short-lived publication espousing a Marxist critique of science edited by leftist scientists and historians of science, Haraway outlined her views of "radical science" and its direction. "I believe many radicals have been drawn to a critique of science from a betrayal of initial deep pleasure in science," she wrote. "Our pleasure has become impossible and blocked by the consciousness of the multiple levels at which we have been constrained to learn domination." To reappropriate scientific knowledge was revolutionary, and to find satisfaction in science a "major political need." In particular, Marxist-feminist scientists had to build knowledge that could undo domination, but they could not simply critique science as a form of domination or adopt a position of skepticism. Nor could they stand aside and critique knowledge-making practices from

within the academy: they had to involve themselves in active social struggle.

Hopkins disapproved of Haraway's political writing, asking her to erase with correction fluid the more embarrassing publications on her CV. The request was well intended, in the spirit of advice for her tenure file; she complied but was denied a promotion anyway. Years later, she recalled wondering, "How do I keep my job, work on what I really want to, keep doing the political work that really matters to me and write about animals?" In 1979, Hartsock and Haraway applied jointly for an opening in feminist theory—the first such position in the country—in the History of Consciousness Department at the University of California at Santa Cruz ("which made everybody think we were lovers"). When the school declined to consider the joint application, Hartsock withdrew from consideration and Haraway alone was hired.

Established as a loose agglomeration of interdisciplinary courses and affiliated faculty in 1965, the year UCSC began operation, History of Consciousness had no full-time faculty or required coursework for years. Instead, it was organized by a number of student affinity groups: feminisms (lesbian and straight), praxis (Gramscians), mind and world (acolytes of the systems theorist Gregory Bateson). However much the name suggests drug-enabled mind expansion—certainly much in evidence at Santa Cruz—it was intended to allude to the likes of Hegel and Freud. By 1980, the department was undergoing a serious remaking at the hands of the historian Hayden White and the anthropologist James Clifford, who hired the department's first full faculty and transformed it into a bastion of radical and unconventional thought.

The year Haraway arrived, Huey P. Newton was awarded—somewhat controversially—a PhD for a dissertation he'd partly written in prison. The feminist scholar Teresa de Lauretis arrived shortly after Haraway. Fredric Jameson taught briefly. Angela Davis lectured there during the 1980s and became a full professor in 1991. At Santa Cruz, the California mythology was distilled into two thousand acres where the redwoods met the Pacific, and nowhere was the intellectual freedom of the landscape more evident than in HistCon. HistCon and California were liberating for Haraway, decisively shaping her thinking and outlook.

Simians, Cyborgs, and Women, published in 1991 but consisting of essays written between 1978 and 1989, is a document of this transition. The early essays, written at Hopkins, are more Marxist and straightforward than anything Haraway has written since. They address the economy of sex and reproduction in primates, how and why humans acquire "culture," and how the history of biology has contributed to systems of domination. Many of the essays deal with language and storytelling, deepening the attention to metaphor and language that defined her dissertation; "grammar is politics by other means," she declares in one essay. As the book proceeds, you can sense the move to Santa Cruz: her writing, to that point radical in content but legible as academic work, becomes more unorthodox, more experimental.

Besides the Cyborg Manifesto, the major piece in the collection is the 1988 essay "Situated Knowledges," a response to "feminist standpoint theory," a field developed in part by Hartsock. Drawing on Marxist epistemology, standpoint theory held that so-called objective knowledge—representing the view from nowhere—was inevitably partial. Where the capitalist saw equal exchange, the laborer saw exploitation; where the (male) laborer saw home life, the wife saw unwaged labor. That did not mean all views were equivalent, though, or that there was no reality to be seen.

Haraway rejected the "god trick" played by both relativism and objectivity. Denying the possibility of truth altogether was as unsatisfactory as accepting it uncritically. It avoided grappling with the stubborn matter of the world—about which Haraway the biologist still felt passionately—and let feminists dismiss entire areas as subjects for men, giving them "one more excuse for not learning any post-Newtonian physics and one more reason to drop the old feminist self-help practices of repairing our own cars." How, she wondered, could we have a simultaneous account "of radical historical contingency for all knowledge claims and knowing subjects, a critical practice for recognizing our own 'semiotic technologies' for making meanings, and a no-nonsense commitment to faithful accounts of a 'real' world, one that can be partially shared and friendly to earth-wide projects of finite freedom, adequate material abundance, modest meaning in suffering, and limited happiness"?

Her solution was in the title. "Situated knowledge" consisted of "partial, locatable, critical knowledges" that sustained "the possibility of webs of connections called solidarity in politics and shared conversations in epistemology." Situated knowledge did not insist there was no reality, only that it was necessary to look from many perspectives in order to see the whole. Politics worked similarly: true solidarity required recognizing the ways that others' positions differed from, and converged with, one's own.

HARAWAY'S NEXT BOOK was a major work on primatology published in 1989, the result of nearly fifteen years of research. *Primate*

Visions: Gender, Race, and Nature in the World of Modern Science was a five-hundred-page sui generis work of empiricism and theory, inimitable and impossible to summarize. If it is about any one thing, it is about human nature, the ways that science has claimed to understand it, and the projects toward which such understanding has been put.

Primatology made claims about society grounded in science. Deriving human nature from observing apes and monkeys, many primatologists argued that hierarchy, aggression, and domination were natural and therefore unavoidable. The study of primates had served to naturalize human history, and in so doing, to depoliticize it. But primatology was also a historical, and therefore narrative, field. It told stories about the natural world: not necessarily false stories, but stories nonetheless.

Haraway didn't only argue that the world "outside" science had affected it. The pioneering taxidermist Carl Akeley had, to a degree, projected the views of white hunters in Africa onto gorillas; subsequent generations of female primatologists had imported feminist analyses of gender relations into their research. But this wasn't because they were politically retrograde or naive; it was because the boundary between science and society was porous. To read "primatology as science fiction" and "science fiction as primatology," as Haraway proposed in a chapter on Octavia Butler's novel *Dawn*, was to see biology as a site "where possible worlds are constantly reinvented in the contest for very real, present worlds."

The genius of *Primate Visions* lies in the richness and density of its cases and references. As Haraway once explained, "my examples *are* the theories." The deliriously titled chapter "Teddy Bear Patriarchy: Taxidermy in the Garden of Eden, New York City, 1908–1936" examines the dioramas of the Akeley Hall of African Mammals in the American Museum of Natural History via a multiperspectival reading of Akeley's life and work, tracing his movement from colonial safaris to the reconstruction of the jungle in Gilded Age New York. To take a sample passage:

> Frankenstein and his monster had Mont Blanc for their encounter; Akeley and the gorilla first saw each other on the lush volcanoes of central Africa. The glance proved deadly for them both, just as the exchange between Victor Frankenstein and his creature froze each of them into a dialectic of immolation. But Frankenstein tasted the bitter failure of his fatherhood in his own and his creature's death; Akeley resurrected his creature and his authorship in both the sanctuary of Parc Albert and the African Hall of the American Museum of Natural History. Mary Shelley's story may be read as a dissection of the deadly logic of birthing in patriarchy at the dawn of the age of biology; her tale is a nightmare about the crushing failure of the project of man. But the taxidermist labored to restore manhood at the interface of the Age of Mammals and the Age of Man. Akeley achieved the fulfillment of a sportsman in Teddy Bear Patriarchy—he died a father to the game, and their sepulcher is named after him, the Akeley African Hall.

The taxidermied apes in the Akeley African Hall told a story of sexual divisions of labor, family structures, physiological hierarchy. The arrangement of the dioramas themselves told a story of evolutionary progress. Both reflected and justified human social relations in keeping with the theories of eugenics and social order that were popular among progressives in the early years of the 20th century.

If five hundred pages of such prose is too daunting, watch Haraway perform chapter seven, "Apes in Eden, Apes in Space: Mothering as a Scientist for *National Geographic*" on YouTube. The video zooms from Jane Goodall's visits to the "wilds of Tanzania" to HAM, a chimpanzee shot into space in 1961, to Koko, the gorilla who learned American Sign Language in the San Francisco Zoo and adopted a kitten in lieu of having a baby. With her hands full of yarn, Haraway gleefully proposes to "take culture apart," to "pull on a thread and begin to untangle the ball of meanings, and begin to trace through one thread and then another, what gets to count as nature, for whom and when, and how much it costs to produce nature at a particular moment in history for a particular group of people." A minute later, she cuts into a Pepperidge Farm cake (formerly boycotted, she notes, because of a Nestlé bottle-feeding scandal) as if it were history—to reveal the layers of meaning, she proclaims, as she licks frosting off her fingers. She talks about Koko while wearing a T-shirt screenprinted with gorillas in rainbow colors; she describes what it means to be a cyborg while wearing a shirt printed with the ecofeminist slogan LOVE YOUR MOTHER above a view of Earth from space—a view that, she points out, was made possible by the cold war space race, but had since been reappropriated for antinuclear protests on Shoshone land.

Historians of science recognized the book as a tour de force, and it quickly became a classic. Primatologists hated it. Haraway seemed to be accusing them of racism, sexism, ignorance. One review in the *Journal of Primatology* described it as a "jeremiad against science." Haraway was dismayed: she had attempted to take seriously the work of primatology as understood by its practitioners, to whom she felt responsible. The subtleties in her argument were often lost on outside observers, for whom all critiques of scientific objectivity and studies of scientific practice were lumped together as hopelessly po-mo—by then a term of academic abuse. As the field known as science studies grew, so too did the reaction against it. But detachment from or distrust of science was not what led Haraway to repeatedly interrogate how we come to understand it. Rather, it was her genuine curiosity about the world—and her genuine desire to change it.

CALIFORNIA WAS A GOOD PLACE to write about science, technology, and money in the 1980s and '90s. As US federal funding for scientific research declined, a growing number of universities entered into funding arrangements with private companies. They were further encouraged by the 1980 Bayh-Dole Act, which gave scientists an incentive to patent publicly funded research and prompted a surge in partnerships between academic and commercial institutions, particularly pharmaceutical corporations. That same year, the landmark Supreme Court case *Diamond v. Chakrabarty* held that living organisms could be patented, giving rise to a wave of biotech companies headquartered in the Bay Area. Computers, which in the 1960s had seemed part of a dreary bureaucratic order, now hummed with the promise of liberation.

Meanwhile, a new political coalition was forming, if not the one Haraway had imagined. Biotechnology seemed poised to remake life itself at the most fundamental level. Technofuturists imagined a time when humans could upload their brains to immortal machines. The cyber-counterculture was an early adopter of the rising conservative movement, and *Wired* put Newt Gingrich on its cover in 1995, two years before it profiled Haraway, describing him as "Friend and Foe." "Cyberspace and the American Dream: A Magna Carta for the Knowledge

Age," a technocapitalists' manifesto published in 1994 by the Progress and Freedom Foundation, declared that "the central event of the 20th century is the overthrow of matter." It went on to argue that private property would be the future of cyberspace. The Christians, engineers, perverts, mothers, and others were there—but less often the Leninists.

Haraway was well positioned to see and understand this shift. Her 1997 book on biotechnology, *Modest_Witness@Second_Millennium.FemaleMan©_Meets_OncoMouse™*, at first sounds cringingly topical, an academic's embarrassing attempt to be "with it." On closer inspection, the title is sort of brilliant. FemaleMan© was a branded version of the main character of Joanna Russ's 1975 novel, OncoMouse™ a lab rat genetically modified and patented for use in Harvard breast-cancer experiments. Dated web orthography aside, its analysis of genetic technology is searingly perceptive and holds up. Genetically modified food was then being heralded as a way to provide abundance, while genetically engineered designer babies were simultaneously warned to be the new face of eugenics. The race to sequence the human genome pitted an international scientific effort undertaken in the most idealistic tradition of science for humanity against the nakedly commercial ethos of the venture capitalist J. Craig Venter, who had launched his own privatized project.

Haraway navigated a position between left-wing squeamishness about genetic technologies and tech-industry speculation on organisms and bodies. She was enamored of boundary-defying tomato-flounder hybrids, just not of patents on them. It was crucial to distinguish between the two rather than allow the debate to be about the promise and dangers of "science" per se. "Genes for profit are not equal to science itself," she

declared, "or to economic health." The focus on the gene was a form of reification; genes, like cells, were not discrete objects but historically specific ways of understanding ongoing biological processes. The rise of the gene as the key to disease, personality, and "life itself" had to be understood in relation to the rise of biotechnology as an academic field in the late 20th century, and its near-simultaneous commercialization.

Haraway wasn't the only one writing on such developments. A slew of books analyzed the racial politics of the universal genome, critiqued the biological determinism of DNA diagnoses, and considered the implications of genetic technologies for reproductive relationships. But no one else had her range. Only Haraway was able to move from intellectual property in cells and genes to the vampire as a figure troubling biological notions of race and species to readings of paintings that the artist Lynn Randolph had produced in correspondence with her.

In some ways her scope was a drawback, leading some to classify her as primarily a cultural critic. Yet the first figure named in the title—the modest witness—was an explicit engagement with contemporary work in science studies. Bruno Latour's *Science in Action* had argued that scientific knowledge production was a trial of strength characterized by naked power struggles; Steven Shapin and Simon Schaffer's *Leviathan and the Air Pump* compared Thomas Hobbes's and Robert Boyle's views of experimental science in producing truth. In contrast to these projects, which were interested in how exactly science is made, Haraway's concern was to understand how science made its way in the world. The modest witness showed how race and gender operated in the lab, as well as how they were made there. But she wasn't simply critical:

like the cyborg, the modest witness was an immanent, implicated figure, oppositional to its origins in colonialist Enlightenment projects but never only that. "I also remember the dreams and achievements of contingent freedoms, situated knowledges, and relief of suffering that are inextricable from this contaminated triple historical heritage," Haraway insisted. "I remain a child of the Scientific Revolution, the Enlightenment, and technoscience."

In the early 2000s, Haraway turned her attention to a new figure in her menagerie: the companion species, to which she devoted a manifesto and eventually a book. *When Species Meet* explained the new subject as a political choice. Cyborgs had been appropriate for the Reagan years, but their time had passed. Dogs, she thought, might prove a better guide to ethics and politics in a time of ecological crisis, helping humans move beyond narrow anthropocentrism. Yet this manifesto had more to say about kin-making and agility competitions than political coalitions and oppositional strategies. Ethics was its true terrain—what was the good life for a nonhuman and how could we know?—explored via competing theories of dog training.

Haraway had always figured in her own work as a matter of both principle and methodology. But here she focused more than ever on her own life: the feminist praxis of situated perspective inched toward memoir in sections like "Notes of a Sportswriter's Daughter," which explained how her love of language had been instilled by her father, a writer for the *Denver Post*, and extensive notes on her adventures in agility training with her Australian shepherd Cayenne Pepper. Reading a chapter composed almost entirely of email exchanges detailing everything from Cayenne's progress in pole-weaving to an enthusiastic bout of oral sex with a friend's dog ("she is one turned on little bitch with Willem, and he is INTERESTED"), it's hard not to cringe—which, one suspects, is the author's intent. (Haraway seems constitutionally incapable of embarrassment and delights in making others squirm.) Still, in an era of pet spas on every corner and kombucha in every bodega, it seemed worrisomely easy to assimilate Haraway's multispecies bent to bourgeois lifestyle trends without a sharper political thrust.

The politics wasn't entirely gone, though. Nor was the Marxism. In a chapter discussing dogs as both commodities and consumers of commodities, Haraway argues that being a pet was a "demanding job" requiring emotional intelligence and control. And dogs needed jobs where they could be useful, ones that wouldn't leave them "victims of human consumerist whims," trendy tastes, and fickle affections: better to be a sheepdog than a Dalmatian. Dogs with jobs! I think about it every time I see a poster in the library advertising therapy-dog sessions for overworked grad students or pass a service dog at a crosswalk—and also when I watch police dogs snarl at water protectors at Standing Rock or attack black children in footage from Birmingham.

LIKE MOST OF Haraway's books, *Staying with the Trouble: Making Kin in the Chthulucene*, published in 2016, is a compilation of essays, albeit more loosely linked than usual. The most topical entries represent Haraway's intervention into the Anthropocene versus Capitalocene debate that has captured the academic imagination over the past few years. The Anthropocene names the geologic era in which humans have been the predominant force shaping the planet, though its periodization and existence are much debated. The idea of the Anthropocene implodes familiar categories: there is no separating human social activity from biological activity, nor from geologic activity. Critics of the concept have suggested that the geologic era should be known as the Capitalocene, to recognize that a specific economic system, rather than all of humanity, has been responsible for the most profound reshaping of nature.

It's easy to dismiss the "-cene debate" as an academic fad, but at its heart are fundamental questions: the place of humans in the natural world, the relationship of capitalism to modernity, the role of a scientific discipline in declaring a new era of human existence. These are, of course, the kinds of questions that Haraway has been asking for years; it is a debate made not so much *for* her as *by* her.

Haraway prefers the Capitalocene to the Anthropocene, the Latin-Greek hybrid notwithstanding—but preferable to both is something she calls the Chthulucene. This is not, she insists, a reference to H. P. Lovecraft's sea monster Cthulhu (a "misogynist racial-nightmare monster") but—note the additional *h*—to the Greek *chthonios*, meaning "of, in, or under the earth and the seas." The chthonic are bound to Earth, and to staying with the trouble of the world.

Wordplay as argument runs rampant throughout the book, ranging from the humanities to posthuman to compost to humus. Her favored phrases—*bumptious, critters, exuberant*—when repeated across essays, come to feel more like tics. Her favored thinkers, too, often seem like crutches: Ursula Le Guin and Octavia Butler continue to inspire her, as they have for the past three decades, and personalities from HistCon past and present figure heavily. (The Marxists, though, are mostly gone, replaced by multispecies feminists and pragmatist philosophers.) This remains a rich and ecumenical array of texts for understanding the state of our planet, but Haraway's own world feels surprisingly small.

The most relentlessly recurring phrase in *Staying with the Trouble* is an acronym: *SF*. In *Primate Visions*, Haraway cited SF as a reference to the set of literatures known as science/speculative fiction and fantasy, but it has since accumulated new terms, permutations, and meanings: *speculative feminism, science fact, string figures, speculative fabulation, so far*. SF here is both literary genre and "practice and process; it is becoming with each other in surprising relays: it is a figure for ongoingness in the Chthulucene." Becoming-with is crucial. More forcefully than ever, Haraway insists that none of us are individual selves, but are instead hopelessly entwined with other humans, species, critters, worlds—and that this, she argues, constitutes grounds for hope.

One of the benefits of seeing wordplay as politics is that it makes for good slogans. Previous Harawavian slogans were attached explicitly to presidential terms: the Cyborg Manifesto's "Cyborgs for Earthly Survival" is explicitly a response to the Reagan era's restarting the arms race; the slogans of the Companion Species Manifesto, simultaneously more mystifying and more militant ("Run Fast, Bite Hard!" and "Shut Up and Train!") are posed as a response to the "terrifying times of George H.W. Bush and the secondary Bushes." The new book has two slogans, and neither is linked to any particular political figure: "Stay with the Trouble" and "Make Kin, Not Babies." The latter is an obvious reference to the Sixties classic "Make Love, Not War," and Haraway's attempt to recuperate population politics—long verboten on the left—for feminist praxis.

"Make Kin, Not Babies" is most explicitly explored in the final chapter, the only section not previously published and the most significant departure from Haraway's previous work. In it, she tries her own hand at SF (speculative fiction/science fiction/science fact/speculative feminism), or at least describes her attempt to do so, summarizing a story concocted in a writing workshop run by the philosopher of science Isabelle Stengers. Assigned the task of imagining a child and its progress through five generations, Haraway's group—comprising herself, the animal philosopher Vinciane Despret, and the filmmaker Fabrizio Terranova—writes about a child called Camille. The Camille Stories aim to suggest "near futures, possible futures, and implausible but real nows." As they will inevitably err politically and ecologically, it is up to readers to correct them with fan fiction.

All the Camilles belongs to an "intentional, migratory community" composed of a few hundred humans diverse across class, race, gender, and so on (already the makings of a utopian fantasy). Known as the Children of Compost, they move to "ruined places" and aim to heal them. Within these Communities of Compost, decisions about reproduction are made collectively. Children are understood to be "rare and precious" and expected to have at least three parents of any gender—though no one is ever forced to bear a child or prevented from having one if they so choose. Children born by community agreement, however, are born as symbionts with nonhumans chosen by their parents.

To be a symbiont means to be committed to a specific companion species in a deep way: to learn about, care for, and take on the very genetic material of one's animal other. Camille's symbiont is a monarch butterfly; others are paired with kestrels, eels, crayfish, and salamanders. So Camille gets genes that let per (Camille's gender pronoun of choice) sense the chemical signals of flowering plants, eat toxic milkweed, and take on the distinctive orange-and-black patterning of an adult monarch butterfly. Later generations of Camilles become more deeply entangled with the monarchs, as technology and sensibilities permit.

The first Camille is born in 2025, when the world's population numbers eight billion; the last dies in 2425, when the population has declined to a "stable" three billion. Haraway implies heavily that this is in part because the unconventional reproductive practices of the Communities of Compost are so "successful and infectious"; we get no further details, though we could surely use them. The world is gradually remade in other ways, too, via "profound economic restructuring, reconfiguration of political control, demilitarization," but there is little said on these either. It is a strangely immaterial account for a self-professed Marxist; where Haraway once wrote about reproduction as an economic phenomenon, it now appears simply a matter of social norm bordering on lifestyle choice. Nor does she argue that remaking the family will remake capitalism, as Marxist feminists often have. She is interested in making kin primarily in order to avoid making babies.

Death, meanwhile, occurs on a catastrophic scale but is mentioned only in passing; mass-extinction events are a backdrop to the Camilles' lives. The most significant recognition of these catastrophes comes when the fifth-generation Camille becomes a Speaker for the Dead—a designated mourner and rememberer, and a reference to another work of SF, this one Orson Scott Card's. (Card is also infamous for his homophobia; his deployment in service of queering the species is presumably one of Haraway's blasphemous jokes.) This is a troublesome place to end up. Although Haraway claims to be developing a politics for a damaged world, what we get feels more like an elegy.

Thinking is a crucial practice for staying with the trouble, and Hannah Arendt and Virginia Woolf are her guides to it. Haraway is fond of Arendt's comment that thinking is a process of going visiting, of stretching one's imagination toward others in a way that Eichmann famously could not. She resolutely counterposes this practice to something smacking more overtly of politics, insisting that "visiting is not a heroic practice; making a fuss is not the Revolution; thinking with each other is not Thought." Meanwhile Woolf's injunction in *Three Guineas*—"Think we must"—functions essentially as a third slogan for *Staying with the Trouble*, and a refrain throughout.

But Woolf's mandate was paired with an analysis of material conditions. Thinking is necessary—but for that, one needs guineas. (Now, there's a companion-species manifesto for you!) Woolf's thought, moreover, led her to rage: *Three Guineas* is a searing antiwar polemic, one in which Woolf calls to spend a guinea not on rebuilding a woman's college (or, perhaps, a women's studies program) but on the rags, petrol, and matches with which the "daughters of educated men" could set light to the hypocrisies of jingoistic universities once and for all. Would that Haraway had followed suit! She teeters on the cusp—"Revolt!" she cries, "Think we must; we must think." But, she notes, "the devil is in the details—how to revolt? How to matter and not just want to matter?" And then, like a monarch butterfly, she flits off to something else.

By the end of the book, we've learned all manner of detail about the *Acacia* tree genus, made up of fifteen hundred species, living in climates ranging from desert to tropics and found in ice cream, beer, and postage stamps. We learn about the *Pimoa*

chthulu spider, Haraway's neighbor in the North Central California redwoods and another inspiration for the Chthulucene. We learn about the history of Premarin estrogen tablets, made out of horse urine, and their effects on both midcentury reproductive politics and Cayenne Pepper's bladder. Haraway remains a keenly curious, sharp observer of her world, and for her, such stories are not merely tales of surprising connections, but important ethical lessons. "The details matter," she insists: it is in the details that we move beyond general principles toward the actual beings with which we are connected. "It is the details that force us to stay with the trouble, that help us recognize the trouble when we see it, and that make us think about how we should act in response." Details of how to revolt, though, are notably absent. This is intentional. Studying past revolutionary projects, members of the Communities of Compost are disappointed in what they understand as the "foreclosures of utopias." They turn instead to SF, which, in staying with the trouble, "kept politics alive."

"Staying with the trouble" is a stance derived from the process philosophies that have guided Haraway's thinking since her days reading Peirce and Whitehead in the Hutchinson ecology lab. Rejecting the artificial boundaries of beginnings and endings, process philosophies are a necessary rebuke to escapist fantasies of starting over, whether on Mars or in California, and a useful reminder that we are always remaking ourselves with others, human and otherwise. Process comes paired with a pragmatist orientation toward practices over ideals. People congregate around shared problems—water shortages in California, for example—and try to solve them, even if they don't agree on the underlying cause—say, climate change. (This approach bears resemblance to the unlikely coalitions of most actually existing climate politics; in particular, the Communities of Compost bring to mind Blockadia, Naomi Klein's constellation of local movements against fossil-fuel development.) The combination usefully directs attention to the ongoing and oft-overlooked work of doing politics: "Stay with the Trouble" is a slogan apt less for the work of thinking than that of organizing.

But Haraway's suspicion of a teleological and ideologically dogmatic Marxism leads her to abdicate the question of political ends almost completely. There is little sense of how a group might transcend the conditions that originally brought them together, or organize a collective toward a long-term political goal. How might struggle itself transform our situated selves and partially shared purposes such that they might become more fully shared over time?

Twenty years ago, Haraway had declared in the postscript to *Modest_Witness*, "I am sick to death of bonding through kinship and 'the family,' and I long for models of solidarity and human unity and difference rooted in friendship, work, partially shared purposes, intractable collective pain, inescapable mortality, and persistent hope." But here, kinship is the only model of solidarity on offer. It's no wonder we're left generating empathy for other species via genetic modification.

LAST DECEMBER, I went to Santa Cruz with friends. I'd made no attempt to contact Haraway in advance, but went to the building that housed the HistCon Department anyway. It was locked. I walked around the empty campus to soak up the vibes ("research"). Wandering through the redwoods at twilight, watching deer graze as the sun set over the Pacific, it was hard to worry about Donald Trump or the ocean's gradual rise. And yet—though the HistCon utopia had succeeded on its own terms—the

department was dying by attrition: as Clifford, Haraway, Davis, and other faculty luminaries had retired, they hadn't been replaced—budget cuts, of course. The fields it had spawned—Chicano studies, gender studies, queer studies—were being killed off, too, and embattled or cloistered where they survived. Back East, my friends and I were involved with our rich private universities' unionization campaigns; how to organize the production of knowledge seemed less pressing than how to organize our colleagues so that we might assert some collective power over our work and our uncertain futures. The life Haraway had lived, and the conditions that made it possible for someone like her to emerge, felt like a speculative fiction of what intellectual life could be that had, for a brief moment in time, been spectacular fact.

I still think about Haraway all the time. In the past few months, the new category of "alternative facts" emerged, and postmodern academics were blamed. Human strangers on the internet continued to ironically mourn the death of a captive gorilla. The left returned yet again to disputes over the significance of race, gender, and class in building power. The tech entrepreneur Elon Musk proposed to leave the troubled Earth behind for a colony on Mars, provided one could afford the trip. Hundreds of thousands of people converged on capitals around the country wearing hand-knit hats intended to signify sexual anatomy in the image of a domesticated animal. Though the world seems to be getting more Harawavian by the day, it's been that way all along

But if Haraway remains invaluable for understanding that primates, science fiction, and sex are central to politics, she's proved less helpful in figuring out what to do about it. This, too, has been the case all along: for all the Manifesto's lasting political acuity, its cyborg societies, focused as they are on their own never-ending formation, appear ill suited to addressing climate change or capitalism. Those problems require building not only unwieldy new coalitions but *power*, to be used in service of ambitious goals on terrain more expansive than the space of the commune—to win over the state, perhaps, rather than merely disarm it.

Haraway never claimed to have all the answers. Pointing out the limits to her project feels more like intellectual matricide than the fan fiction she requested. Then again, Haraway never wanted to be a mother. She imagined in the Manifesto that "a world without genesis" could also be "a world without end." Critique doesn't have to kill: it can simply lop off a limb, letting what remains regenerate, salamander-like, into something "monstrous, duplicated, potent."

Haraway wants to stay grounded in the mundane, the mud, the humus, the compost. But the trouble that she refuses to stay with is, in fact, that of politics. What could be more mundane than that old bore, more down in the mud than that dirty game? But this is the trouble that we most need to stay with—not because it is generative or exuberant in the manner of a dazzling essay, but because it is unavoidable, monstrous, repetitive, and, most of all, potent.

Might politics itself be utopia? In the science-fiction author Kim Stanley Robinson's *Pacific Edge*, the final novel of his Three Californias trilogy, utopia is not a final destination but "struggle forever." An ongoing process, yes—but one that fights for a better world. Struggle forever—now there's an SF I can believe in. +

LETTERS

No Human Is Illegal

Dear Editors,

Joshua Cohen ("The Last Last Summer," Issue 27) writes that Connecticut and New York legalized tribal casinos. But the states did no such thing. Tribal nations governed here before the United States was even a theory in the white imagination. As such, these nations hold tribal sovereignty, a legal framework the US federal government uses to recognize that tribal nations are immune to state law, among other things. Tribal sovereignty is the same concept by which the Supreme Court has ruled that states lack the authority to regulate tribal casinos. That's why tribal nations enter into *compacts* with states; those compacts are agreements between governments.

I understand that Cohen is lamenting a peculiar kind of loss of Atlantic City, which he uses as a proxy for the rest of the United States. But there's an irony in failing to identify colonization as the premise by which the sea change Cohen describes is taking place. Absecon Island was much more than, as Cohen snidely writes, the "desolate sandspit that had been fishing-and-hunting grounds to the Lenni Lenape." Before Absegami territory was essentially stolen, what is now known as Atlantic City was the site of annual summer ceremonies for indigenous people (who also spent one last last summer there). Tribal dispossession in the past facilitated Atlantic City's reality today. Public traces of the indigenous names that dot the region reveal how profoundly this is misunderstood—perhaps most notably at Absegami High School, which uses a woefully racist mascot with an equally offensive motto: "Home of the Braves." But I digress.

Later in the essay, Cohen chooses to describe some people as "illegal immigrants." It was that word choice that persuaded me to stop reading. That term, another residue of colonization, is based in a dangerous idea that some human beings can be illegal. It might be easier for other readers to endorse or ignore the term. But I couldn't seem to spend my free time reading past that mark.

I know that this precise moment demands that we ask different questions, and that we come up with different answers. Yet here we are in 2017, asking the same questions we've asked for a long time: the ones about the way we understand and misunderstand history, and the ones about the way we use language to further dehumanize the most vulnerable among us. We're still here 525 years later, waiting for different answers.

—*Aura Bogado*

Ada, No Ardor

Dear Editors,

Presidential campaigns name their data instruments colorfully: Houdini in 2008, Golden and Narwhal in 2012, and Ada in 2016. David Auerbach's criticism of the Clinton campaign's use of Ada ("Confirmation Bias," nplusonemag.com)—particularly

**THE
POINT**

A magazine founded
on the suspicion
that modern life is
worth examining.

n+1 readers subscribe
at a **30%** discount.

Use code **NPLUSONE**
when you sign up at
thepointmag.com/subscribe.

IN ISSUE 13 | WINTER 2017
Midwestworld
A Country Is a Country
OkCupid Vitae
Blackness American
Don't Ask, Don't Tell
I Love Dick
+ *what is america for?*

THEPOINTMAG.COM

the campaign's preference for expected outcomes—is in many respects harrowingly correct. But his final admonishment, against analytics, would be better aimed at the puzzle of learning from failure. In 2008, Houdini, an Election Day reporting tool, was dismantled at launch, but it didn't impede millions of door knocks or the organizing that preceded them. Narwhal, a 2012 dashboard for online organizing, fell short of expectations, but exposed a generation of campaign staff to software design, sprints, gaffes, and all.

The lessons we see chart our ability to change, and his skepticism of an algorithm seems too slight, too quick. Auerbach chided the Clinton campaign for falling for Ada, an electoral-forecasting tool, as if he were criticizing a match, leveling imprecations against "her" family and character. His descriptions of Ada as "starved," with its undertones of anorexia, made me wince as a woman and alumna of presidential campaigns (though not Hers). Throughout his rendering, Ada lacks a sense of scale, drops necessary variables, and hurtles toward hysteria. He closes with "Democrats should be careful that Ada does not pull her con again," alleging the final feminine deception: trickery. In literature, we hew to a long history of mad women, but it's unnecessary to read that onto our mathematical ciphers. There is no mad woman behind this loss, only the need for more ways of seeing.

In 2012, my team in Obama Analytics deployed a simulator, Golden, now remembered fondly for winning, but also remembered as "it." I wonder how Ada's loss would be written if she had been anything larger than a girl.

—Caroline Grey

The Secret Lives of Dentists

Dear Editors,

Reading about Tama Janowitz's Peyton Amberg—who, according to Naomi Fry ("The Age of Insolvency," Issue 27), "manages to achieve a middle-class marriage to a milquetoast Jewish dentist" only to find herself in "a swamp of boredom and dissatisfaction"—brought a smile to my face. Until my insurance changed a few years ago I had a milquetoast Jewish dentist in my life, too. I am sure Peyton Amberg would have hated him as a husband, but I liked him. I think his wife, who manned the reception desk of their small office, did too, and even if she didn't, it was clear she took pleasure in running the business. He, for his part, liked to complain to me about having to clean her father's teeth for free.

Comparing the two of them to Peyton Amberg and her dentist made me think of a passage near the end of Ford Madox Ford's *The Good Soldier*:

> Conventions and traditions, I suppose, work blindly but surely for the preservation of the normal type; for the extinction of proud, resolute and unusual individuals.
>
> Edward was the normal man, but there was too much of the sentimentalist about him; and society does not need too many sentimentalists. Nancy was a splendid creature, but she had about her a touch of madness. Society does not need individuals with touches of madness about them. So Edward and Nancy found themselves steamrolled out and Leonora survives, the perfectly normal type, married to a man who is rather like a rabbit. For Rodney Bayham is rather like a rabbit, and I hear that Leonora is expected to have a baby in three months' time.

Janowitz's heroines (I'm taking Fry's word for it here; I've never read her) get steamrolled out, just like Edward and Nancy do in *The Good Soldier*. But isn't life always going to be easiest for the perfectly normal? For he or she who can find happiness in a milquetoast dentist? What evolution (or revolution) could change that?

The consequences of being steamrolled out, however, vary. Where are they least severe? I don't know. But wherever that is is probably a good place to live.

—*Thomas Brown*

In the Name of Reality

Dear Editors,

Hi. I just saw a bit of a current *n+1* Nikil Saval story ("Turf-Guarding," nplusonemag.com) saying the Democratic Party is against the left.

First, I'm further left than you are.

The American left includes the continuum from just left of center to the far left edge of democratic socialism. This includes most of the Democratic Party.

You cannot help the 99 percent if you do not include the whole continuum from just left of center to the far left edge of democratic socialism.

We cannot help anyone if we do not win a majority.

Nikil Saval does not have an accurate view of the Democratic Party, not that changes shouldn't be made.

—*Monty Johnston*

SUPPORTERS

SUPPORTERS

The Baskin Family
Ronald Barusch and Cynthia Dahlin
AJ Brown
Maria Campbell
Christopher Cox and Georgia Cool
Jeremy and Rebecca Glick
Jeff Gramm and Susie Heimbach
Eddie Joyce and Martine Beamon
Courtney Hodell

Megan Lynch
Richard Parrino
Chris and Whitney Parris-Lamb
Susie Simonson
Susan and Peter Tortorici
Mark White
Sarah Whitman-Salkin
Scott Wood-Prince

ADVISORY BOARD

Carla Blumenkranz
Kate Bolick
AJ Brown
Georgia Cool
Christopher Cox

Eddie Joyce
Katy Lederer
Allison Lorentzen
Chris Parris-Lamb
Whitney Parris-Lamb

Henry Rich
Sarah Whitman-Salkin
Ben Wizner

INSTITUTIONAL SUPPORTERS

Audible
Elyse Cheney Literary Associates
Farrar, Straus and Giroux
The Gernert Company
Grove/Atlantic
Harper Perennial
HBO

ICM
Knopf Doubleday Publishing Group
Lippincott Massie McQuilkin
Penguin Random House
Purslane Catering
W. W. Norton

Special thanks to
Orenna Brand   Emily Clancy   Bailey Miller

n+1 is published with the support of the New York City Department of Cultural Affairs and the New York State Council on the Arts.

OUR CONTRIBUTORS

Tim Barker studies the history of political economy at Harvard.

Alyssa Battistoni is a PhD student in political science at Yale University and an editor at *Jacobin*.

A. S. Hamrah is *n+1*'s film critic. His last column, "All That Counts Is Getting to a Normal World," appeared in Issue 27.

Arvind Krishna Mehrotra's most recent book, *Collected Poems*, was published by Giramondo in 2016. He lives in Dehradun.

Meghan O'Gieblyn is a writer living in Wisconsin.

Sara Rai is an Allahabad-based writer and translator. Her most recent work of translation is *Kazaki and Other Marvellous Tales* by Munshi Premchand.

Thea Riofrancos is a professor of political science at Providence College.

David Samuels is a writer living in Brooklyn. His last piece for *n+1* was "Weirdos" in Issue 24.

Elizabeth Schambelan is a writer and editor living in New York.

Trevor Shikaze is a writer living in Vancouver.

Vinod Kumar Shukla lives in Raipur, Chhattisgarh. He has published several collections of poetry, a volume of short fiction, and five novels.

Jenny Zhang's "Why Were They Throwing Bricks?" is excerpted from *Sour Heart*, her debut collection of short fiction. It will be published this August by Lenny.

"Victoria Lomasko's gritty, street-level view of the great Russian people masterfully intertwines quiet desperation with open defiance. Her drawings have an on-the-spot immediacy that I envy. She is one of the brave ones."

—Joe Sacco

"Powerful . . . Though Lomasko's figures are rendered in broad, black-and-white strokes, her depictions of God-fearing old ladies, young skinheads, and striking truckers never fall into the traps of parody, contempt, or stereotype."

—Sophie Pinkham, NewYorker.com

NEW FROM N+1 BOOKS

OTHER RUSSIAS

BY VICTORIA LOMASKO
TRANSLATED BY THOMAS CAMPBELL

WWW.NPLUSONEMAG.COM/OTHERRUSSIAS/